The Marketing Power of Emotion

THE

MARKETING

POWER

of

EMOTION

John O'Shaughnessy
Nicholas Jackson O'Shaughnessy

OXFORD
UNIVERSITY PRESS

2003

OXFORD
UNIVERSITY PRESS

Oxford   New York

Auckland   Bangkok   Buenos Aires   Cape Town   Chennai
Dar es Salaam   Delhi   Hong Kong   Istanbul   Karachi   Kolkata
Kuala Lumpur   Madrid   Melbourne   Mexico City   Mumbai   Nairobi
São Paulo   Shanghai   Taipei   Tokyo   Toronto

Copyright © 2003 by Oxford University Press, Inc.

Published by Oxford University Press, Inc.
198 Madison Avenue, New York, New York, 10016
www.oup.com

Library of Congress Cataloging-in-Publication Data

O'Shaughnessy, John.
  The marketing power of emotion / by John O'Shaughnessy and Nicholas Jackson
O'Shaughnessy.
    p.   cm.
  Includes index.
  ISBN 0-19-515056-2
  1. Consumer behavior.   2. Consumers—Psychology.   3. Marketing—Psychological
aspects.   4. Advertising—Psychological aspects.   5. Decision making—Psychological
aspects.   6. Emotions—Economic aspects.   I. O'Shaughnessy, Nicholas J., 1954–   II. Title.

  HF5415.32 .O743 2002
  658.8'342—dc21   2002070905

9 8 7 6 5 4 3 2 1
Printed in the United States of America
on acid-free paper

Preface

We all acknowledge the pervasiveness of emotion in our lives, and shopping is no exception. What has been missing is a systematic exposition of the role played by emotion in consumer behavior. Where there have been books on the subject, the concept of emotion has been regarded as unproblematic, with no model proposed that explains how and in what ways emotion operates. This book aims to fill the gap. This is helped by the recent increased interest in the subject in psychology, neuroscience, and philosophy. In fact, it can be said that emotion is now a hot topic. The renaissance of interest in emotion has endured beyond the usual quarantine period for academic fads and fashions. In marketing, there is a large and growing body of academics who are anxious to move away from the view of the highly rational consumer that saturates the marketing literature and to formally concede that the calculating-machine model of the consumer is a myth.

In the *practice* of marketing (as opposed, in general, to academic texts on marketing) there seems to be a roughly equal split between those who perceive consumers as mainly emotional and those whose perspective of the consumer is based on something approximating the rational choice model of the economist. Perhaps this distinction is commonly used in thinking about other peoples and nations. Plato and his fellow Athenians regarded Ionians as emotional, only concerned with the appearance of things. In contrast, the Athenians had an image of themselves as highly rational, which automatically proclaimed their superiority! There is a danger in treating consumers as purely rational, focused solely on technical and economic criteria, and so perceiving them as bundles of fixed wants that marketing sets out to identity, filter, map, and satisfy. The consumer's motivational capacities are made up not only of a set of wants and needs but also the capacity to imagine, a general yearning for novelty as well as stability, and a disposition to be moved by the emotional resonance of events. Consumers have an underlying appetite for an infinite number of products to meet latent wants. The purely rational model presupposes that consumers are not influenced by either the way products are presented or the emotional context of buying.

The argument of this book is that emotion is always a factor in decision-making and that rationality will always be invaded by emotional influences. This book is about the significance of emotion in marketing and consumer experience. It sees consumer experience as emotion-drenched; no experience is completely empty of emotion, and no pure rationality is ever at work. Emotion is never a semidetached adjunct to consumer processes.

There are two audiences for this book, the managerial and the academic, and we have sought an exposition that is intelligible and meaningful to both. For professionals in consumer marketing, this work offers something fresh in delineating the power of emotion in marketing, enabling practitioners to better interpret the perplexing surfaces of consumer behavior by understanding emotional influences. Academics in marketing are all too aware of the absence of any systematic account of the role played by emotion in consumer behavior, an absence partly accounted for by the neglect of emotion in the mainstream approach to consumer psychology, namely, the information-processing approach of cognitive psychology. This is not surprising, given an approach that is intent on exploiting the metaphor of the mind as a computer; to place emotion onto such a metaphor would always be an illicit graft.

We thank various colleagues and former colleagues who have contributed to improving versions of this book: Morris Holbrook, Gordon Foxall, Roger Dickinson, John Whitney, and others who offered encouragement after reading the manuscript. We would also like to thank the *Journal of Macromarketing*, which published the substance of our section in chapter 7 on the nation as a brand in a previous article.[1]

Contents

The Marketing Power of Emotion

1

The Scope of
Emotion in Marketing

Marketing's Interest in Emotion

Marketing folklore suggests that emotion can stimulate buying interest, guide choices, arouse buying intentions, and influence future buying decisions. All these popular beliefs about the power of emotion have received research support.[1] Thoughts about buying are not listless mental acts. They can be exciting and can involve strong likes and dislikes, anxieties, and aspirations. Just think about the emotional component of buying a new car. Emotions intensify wants and desires and intensify motivation. Even ethical behavior can be suppressed because of a failure to generate the emotion needed to motivate moral action.

Emotion is not an aberrant element when making buying decisions but a necessary condition if decisions are not to be continually postponed. The emotional is so paired with making trade-offs in decision-making that it is impossible to identify situations where deliberated decisions do not have an emotional dimension.[2] This is true even in the hard sciences. As

Horgan says: "It has become a truism by now that scientists are not mere knowledge acquisition machines; they are guided by emotion and intuition as well as by cold reason and calculation."[3]

Elster dramatically sums up the importance of emotions as follows:

> Emotions matter because if we did not have them nothing else would matter.
>
> Creatures without emotion would have no reason for living, nor, for that matter, for committing suicide. Emotions are the stuff of life. . . . Emotions are the most important bond or glue that links us to others. . . . Objectively, emotions matter because many forms of human behavior would be unintelligible if we did not see them through the prism of emotion.[4]

Elster points out that the spending of public funds on museums, opera houses, sports facilities, and so on must, in a final analysis, be justified in terms of the emotional experiences they provide to the general public.

Emotions enter into all decision-making when trade-offs are made. Some academics forget this and view the consumer as an emotion-free calculating machine. Such a view has obviously no place in situations where the consumer acts simply on his or her feelings, but it is an impoverished view in any case. Many who do freely acknowledge the ubiquity of emotion can write nonetheless as if emotion were absent when it comes to buying. Writers on marketing seem to divide into supporters of Pascal (1623–1662)—"The heart has reasons that reason does not know"—and Descartes(1596–1650), who used only the method of mathematics and non-contradiction to establish truth. In other words, it is common to find writers in marketing focusing exclusively either on the rational or the emotional, though when it comes to buying, neither can be ignored.

When we make trade-offs in buying, such as car comfort for style, we are implicitly taking account of our *values* (whether aesthetic, hedonistic, moral, or economic). And behind these values lie emotions. When the blind Gloucester exclaims in Shakespeare's *King Lear,* "I see it feelingly," he is describing the experience of being blind but is also saying that his emotions have opened up and he has learned to be sensitive to others. It is our emotional experiences that most determine our system of values. These values reflect what we most seek to preserve or enhance, like freedom, justice, and survival, as well as less elevated concerns like preferring to be rich rather than poor, to be in control of life rather than feel at the mercy of events, to have high self-esteem rather than low self-esteem, and so on. Any gap between what we desire and actual reality has the potential for arousing our emotions. Thus people value having skill in simple mathematics for survival and self-esteem, yet many have suffered emotionally over mathematics when young. One study of mathematics education comments on the consequence: "The extent to which the need to undertake even an apparently straightforward piece of mathematics could induce feelings of anxiety, helplessness, fear and even guilt in some of those interviewed was, perhaps, the most striking feature of the study."[5] Negative emotions like this tie into values, and behind values are past emotional experiences that largely create the system of values in the first place.

The deepest concerns of the consumer arouse emotions, energize motivation, and act as guides to wants, and uphold values. Emotional arousal can arise from anything that deeply concerns us at the time. Thus no American could be other than emotionally aroused by the terrorist atrocity of September 11, 2001. This is because what happened concerned us deeply. And we can be moved by others showing concern for our concerns. Thus few would not be emotionally moved by this simple note attached to a bouquet outside the American Embassy in London: *To our best friends the Yanks. If you need help, just call.* The problem with ensuring ethics in marketing is that unethical conduct by someone may strike no emotional chord within that person because upholding ethical conduct is not part of the person's values. Thus it is seldom the case that managers do not know what constitutes the ethical thing to do. They simply lack the will to do it because of an absence of an emotional commitment: social outrage and the law are merely ways of reinforcing the will to be good. Without emotional commitments, there will be no strong evaluations—or firm ethical leadership. This is not to suggest that people may not act against their emotional commitments when it comes to ethics but that strong emotions constitute a high barrier to surmount. Emotions are the energizers of meaning. It is the emotions that signal the meaning or personal significance of things, whether these things are objects like a sports car, events like a holiday, or the actions, say, of doctors and waiters. To say something is meaningless implies that it is devoid of emotional significance for us.

Emotion is the adhesive that, when mixed with trust, equals loyalty. Trust means we can accept an unequal exchange on occasion because we "know" things will even out over the long term. We may accept the higher price, the delay in service, and so on because we trust the supplier will make amends in the longer term. When consumer trust in a brand is undermined, there is a corresponding loss in market power, as customers have less faith that the company will live up to expectations. Trust is even more unquestioning in the form of loyalty. Some trust is always necessary in any business transaction. However, the basis of that trust may be the legal system that enforces contracts and consumer "rights" and may have nothing to do with the buyer's trust in the supplier. Customer loyalty to a brand or a supplier demands more than this minimum level of trust and, as noted, involves sentiment. And loyalty can start early, as, for example, it does to football teams and often continues regardless of whether the team is on top.

Emotion blinds us to evidence that challenges loyalties. Strong emotions typically explain why we cling to beliefs when faced with evidence to the contrary. Consumers may continue to buy some health product that scientific evidence has shown to be ineffective because faith, with its emotional overtones, can be more persuasive than the evidence of the laboratory. Emotional commitment to a position, a person, a cause, or a place is what we mean when we speak of an *ideé fixe,* which is something that goes beyond intellectual conviction. Buying is tied to feelings as well as beliefs, and this explains why, even in buying a major product like an automobile, there may be little reflection or investigation of options. Much buying is rooted in strongly held feelings of likes and dislikes. We only make sense of buying if we recognize that buying engages people emotionally.

Emotion and Consumer Choice Criteria

We all have reasons for choosing one product rather than another, which implies that we have criteria against which we may compare options (we use the term *product* here to cover goods, services, and associated experiences). Choice criteria can be complex or a single criterion such as which brand has most immediate appeal. Emotion influences the weighting of choice criteria, and this points to the need to give emotional significance to the choice criteria that fit a firm's competitive position. Choice criteria can be grouped into six categories, and it is useful to sketch their emotion potential:[6]

1. Technical criteria. The *core* "technical" function of a product is the primary purpose for which the product is designed. Thus the core function of a watch is to measure time. The very concept of a watch is defined by core function. We use words in advertising like "state-of-the-art technology," "smooth performance," "fast results," "dependable," and so on to excite interest and evoke positive emotional feelings toward the brand.

To call a watch "good" is first and foremost to claim efficacy in its core function. But products have other technical functions besides the core function. There can be ancillary-use functions and convenience-in-use functions. *Ancillary-use* functions are the permanent or optional technical features associated with the core function. An ancillary-use function of a detergent is to soften clothes and of a clock to speak the time. Advertisers use words like "extra features" and "enriched" to excite curiosity in ancillary-use functions. *Convenience-*

in-use functions are the additions, modifications, or packaging of a product that facilitate the performance of its core function, such as the toothpaste tube pump or power-steering on a car. Consumers seek a care-free, turnkey system where little or no learning is involved; anything less is emotionally frustrating. Advertisers promote such functions with words like "fast," "easy access," "easily adjustable," "amazingly simple," "easy to follow," "user-friendly," and "light as a feather" to resonate with the emotions. Typically, competition in a mature market is no longer on the basis of core-use function, since high performance in the core function is often taken for granted. Instead, competition is over other aspects of the offering, such as ancillary-use and convenience-in-use functions, price, distribution, and brand image. Any technical function can arouse emotion because any technical function can be of high concern to the consumer. There is the excitement of anticipating high performance in a computer and the pleasure arising when performance turns out to be even higher than expected—and disappointment if performance is below expectations.

2. Economic/sacrifice criteria. All buying is an approach/avoidance situation in that benefits are set against price paid and effort expended. The effort expended is the effort involved in finding and choosing the product *or* in using the product. Marder thus distinguishes *choice-effort* from *use-effort*.[7] Use-effort is reduced by convenience-in-use features and choice-effort by better distribution. If choice-effort is broadened to include taking the hassle out of buying, like the frustration that comes from waiting at the cash desk, there is considerable scope for choice-effort reduction. Underhill shows how stores can and should make shopping a more pleasurable experience.[8] As Underhill says, no one knows how much a shopper will buy until the shopping experience is made as pleasurable as possible. In other words, no one knows what people might want until the most persuasive case has been put forward.

Price is always a concern. This is not surprising. As Brittan says, "When you purchase any good, your enjoyment is reduced by the psychological cost of paying for it."[9] Consumers and marketers alike benefit if they explicitly seek pricing systems that let people enjoy things without having to think about paying for them and thereby dampen the enjoyment. The possibility of enjoying things immediately is facilitated by installment buying, which in fact could be said to have got the car industry into the mass market.[10] This should not blind us to the fact that there are always those who will pay a high price for the same functional performance if it signals wealth, status, and power to all and sundry.

Emotionally *deal-sensitive* buyers switch among their favored set of brands, depending on current prices, in contrast to those who are *price-sensitive* in an absolute sense. The following factors influence the maximum price that can be obtained by the seller:

1. The centrality of the product for the function for which it is being bought
2. The uniqueness of the product to a particular seller
3. The social perceptions of the wisdom of paying the price being demanded
4. The perceived fairness of the price
5. The purchase location

These are all factors that have emotional resonance. In addition, contrary to the rules of rationality in economics, the framing of price is important—for example, a 3% charge for using a credit card versus a 3% discount for cash. Being charged 3% for using a credit card is a much more emotional issue.

We find it less emotional to spend in a foreign currency as we are less conscious of the sacrifice. Club Med exploits this finding by having its "guests" buy beads to use instead of cash. At least one Florida developer attracts prospects by offering them hotel accommodation at an extremely low cost—and then giving most of it back in "village dollars" that are accepted in all the stores around the development. In this way, those accepting the offer spend time savoring the lifestyle without any sense of its costing them.

Consumers become emotional about "hidden" charges, (e.g., in renting a car) with the "all-inclusive" price having the additional advantage that it reduces the number of payment decisions, which, in turn, reduces the emotional burden of payment. Prepaid cards, like domestic or mobile phone cards, are ways of reducing the emotional burden (what Brittan calls the "moral tax") of payment and the anxiety of uncertainty about the final bill. Emotive words in advertising covering economic criteria include words like "fabulous bargain," "pays for itself," "no frills pricing," "designer quality at affordable prices," and so on. Advertising anticipates emotional reaction to a premium price by stressing enhanced benefits, as in "You won't need to repair" a quality garment, car, or machine for years. This emphasis influences the inner dialogue consumers conduct when they want something emotionally that reason refuses to authorize.

3. Legalistic criteria. Buyers are often guided by what others demand or want; that is, buyers take account of criteria decreed by others. Such buyers can be said to take account of *legalistic* criteria. While some "legalistic" criteria are imposed by legal regulations (seat belts in cars), there are also the requirements of others whose wishes the consumer feels obliged to consider. In supermarket shopping for groceries, the tastes of various family members might, for example, be considered. The paradigm case of legalistic criteria is the husband shopping in the supermarket from a list written by his wife. On the list his wife has written: orange juice, lettuce, fish cakes, and so on, and the husband in his

purchases is governed by that list. Children, too, have quite an influence. One study by the J. Walter Thompson ad agency found that even children under 12 years of age played a decisive role in parental decisions, for example, on 31% of all vacation destinations, 30% of all car models, and 22% of all stereo brands.[11] While parents may be the ones who pay, children may be the key decision-makers.

Legalistic criteria can evoke emotion. Trying to buy something for someone else can be stressful (e.g., a wedding present), and any rules imposed from outside (even edicts on how much to spend) can give rise to frustration at not being completely in control. On the other hand, being successful at meeting the expectations of others—friends, for example—gives rise to a glow of accomplishment. All this is not to deny there can be a conflict of values in gift-giving between the desire to give what is desired and what would be more in tune with the giver's own values.

4. Integrative criteria. Integrative functions refer to the desire for social integration and integration with one's sense of identity. Integrative criteria involve the following considerations.

Social acceptance. How consumers think others might view them as a result of their possessions influences what is bought. Buying what is not socially endorsed by one's social milieu implies nonconformity, and any kind of nonconformity is associated with potential embarrassment that can undermine confidence. Of course, there are consumers who reject conformity or just "couldn't care a damn" what others think! This is their way of signaling individuality. Today's individualism is described as keeping away from the Joneses rather than keeping up with the Joneses, though this usually means rejecting the larger culture for some subculture. Consumers may no longer be conforming to societal norms, but their behavior is still conformative to their subculture. Elites and not just out-groups are involved in nonconformity, as the elite may want to signal hostility to the majority just as much as punks and other out-groups.[12] Those adopting deviant fashions or challenging the prevalent ethic follow the principle that power can come about either from sticking rigidly to the rules or by the creation of new rules.

Self-identity and possessions. It is now orthodoxy to argue that people take their self-identity from their possessions.[13] Dittmar views possessions as *material* symbols of identity, as *expressive* symbols of identity, and as *reflections* of identity in terms of gender and social-material status. But it is a parochial view to equate self-identity with mere possessions. Self-identity comes with a life history.[14] Many other factors enter into self-identity, such as personal history, socioeconomic status, religion, ethnicity, roles in life, job and so on. In fact, as Flanagan argues, the whole narrative of our lives and what concerns us enters into self-identity.[15] Self-identity is something more than the sum of our appetites. As Erving Goffman says, no one's self-identity is limited to a singular "core image," as people have many different sides to their personalities, revealed on different occasions.[16] This is not to deny that consumers use goods as a way to express aspects of their *social* identity and to distinguish themselves from others "in a world in which traditional social bonds and class boundaries are weakening."[17]

Another half-truth is that self-identity is now more a matter of individual choice than social ascription. But self-identity is not developed in a vacuum: it is very much influenced by the way others view us in social interaction. There is a limit to the extent that consumers *can* express a completely distinct self-identity. There is the matter of time and financial resources while, as said earlier, someone who seemingly is nonconforming to societal norms may be conformative to the norms of his or her subcultural group. Subcultural social pressures are likely to produce a strong family resemblance in possessions among the members of the deviant subgroup.

Products bought as *symbolic* possessions link to the emotions. Flanagan suggests such products are

1. those that, like photographs, symbolize the *historical continuity* of self, family etc.
2. those that express artistic or intellectual *interests,* such as a book collection
3. those that signify wealth and symbolize *status,* such as a sailing boat[18]

And we would add

4. products that express a preferred social persona like being youthful, bohemian, establishment, or whatever.

Status, visibility, fashion, or standing within one's social milieu. Although people crave social acceptance, they also aim for status in their group's "pecking order," together with social recognition. It was Simmel who first stressed the opposition between the individual and the wider social group.[19] Humans need other people for emotional, intellectual, and material sustenance but, at the same time, do not want to submerge their individuality and independence.[20] There is a constant tension provoked in trying to get the balance right that continues throughout life.

Consumers, in buying products, seek *status* and *visibility* to rise above the crowd. They do not want to be tokens of each other in their clothing or anything else. Status and social visibility are sources of power, a feeling of being in control of the world around one. Status symbols enhance self-esteem, and anything that adds to self-esteem is emotionally satisfying. Any formal association with a celebrity or an institution of status is a source of such satisfaction and is highly valued, as university fund-raisers know. Emotive words here are "upscale"; "caters to the discriminating few"; "you'll join the ranks of"; "exclusive," and so on. A novelty that becomes widespread ceases to be a novelty, with the result that those seeking visibility and status supplant and replace the old novelty with a "genuine" new one.

Fashion. Fashion satisfies the desire for status and novelty even if it only does so by recycling old styles. Simmel points out that *fashion* enters into all aspects of our lives from clothes, to cars, to investing, to science and the selection of first names. Simmel views fashion as combining novelty of aesthetic charm with the play form of socializing. Consumers adopt fashions to fulfill attempts at image management—to signal social aspirations and identifications. Fashion in clothing helps one to camouflage imagined deficiencies and to savor the emotional fantasy of being like some famous person or part of some lifestyle. Fashion is fed by the insatiable demand for novelty in stylistic innovations. Campbell argues that fashion functions as a substitute for taste, in that fashion fulfills a social role originally played by standards of good taste and can be as socially binding as standards of taste once were.[21]

Fashion has expanded in scope more than ever with the demand for "difference" in social identity. As Gronow says, one characteristic of modern consumer society is that the extension and social influence of fashion has greatly increased.[22] He acknowledges that consumer demands are determined no longer by an "economy of needs" but by an "economy of desire and dreams," or the yearning for something new and unexperienced. Among the affluent of the world, who have everything they need or want in terms of clothing, housing and other durables, wants move to the desire for new and rare experiences, so a Christmas present can become the experience of driving a tank (as has happened in Britain). Gronow reminds us that all conscious experiences reach beyond themselves, with each thought reminding us of other thoughts. This "overflow" of thought leads to fantasies about the pleasures of buying, particularly buying things for personal adornment—and, he might have added, the pleasures of anticipating some experience.

Personal integrity. Kagan rejects the notion of human action being mostly motivated by a desire for sensory pleasure but claims there is a universal motive to regard the self as possessing good qualities.[23] People are inhibited from actions that are likely to bring about guilt, embarrassment, or shame, contributing to what Kagan calls a motive for virtue. People have a sense of being moral agents. Adherence to ethics or moral norms is tied to self-respect, while the violation of social norms gives rise to the emotion of shame. A growing number of consumers take account of the environment in their buying and choose manufacturers who exhibit social responsibility, such as those who are not exploiting child labor, polluting the environment, and so on. It also violates integrity to accept an unfair transaction, so consumers may ask what something is worth in some objective sense rather than just what it is worth to them. A consumer may forgo buying not because the utility of the product to her is less than the price to be paid but because she considers the price a "rip-off." People will not willingly be cheated or seen as willing to be cheated. This seems to be part of our evolutionary inheritance.[24]

5. Adaptive criteria. Adaptive criteria reflect the desire to minimize risk, reduce the anxiety of uncertainty or fear of regret.[25] Risks can entail potential (1) financial cost; (2) physical cost, since products can be harmful or dangerous; (3) social cost, in that significant others may not approve; (4) performance deficiency; or (5) hassle, as in, say, having to return the product; and so on. Many products cannot be completely evaluated prior to purchase. Inspection of the product may give some certainties (that the product has certain features) and may provide some idea about quality, but there are often uncertainties about effectiveness (e.g., equities). A significant purchase with a high risk attached to it (what marketers call a "high-involvement purchase"), arouses anxiety—fear of making a mistake or coming to regret the decision.

Consumers adopt several *heuristics* or rules of thumb for dealing with uncertainty. The easiest is simply to sidestep responsibility by trusting the *advice* of others. Consumers will often pay dearly for some expert to make the decision for them. This commonly happens with financial services and in matters of taste. Older adults are more limited in their information-processing capacity (easily becoming mentally overloaded) and are likely to collect and evaluate less information and so be more inclined to rely on "expert" advice.[26] Consumers, like people in general, are conditioned to some extent to accept the advice of people in authority, whether they are teachers, doctors, policemen, or those regarded as authorities on matters of taste or a line of products. In fact, the advice may come from someone who simply projects a relevant authority persona, as when Robert Young on TV recommends Sanka, a caffeine-free coffee, while wearing the white coat of the doctor he played in a TV series (*Marcus Welby, M.D.*).

Making the habitual buy or letting others decide releases time to come to grips with other problems and relieves the burden of decision. Other heuristics are to *imitate* others assumed to be "in the know"; seeking *guarantees;* buying on *reputation* or buying on *brand image; sampling; diversifying* to spread risks; or buying on the basis of just *liking.* Most of these heuristics or rules of thumb are perceived as indicators of the attributes sought, just as a buyer might view price as an indicator of quality. Emotive ad terms here are "You can't lose"; "We stand behind our claims"; "genuine"; "authentic"; "proven"; "pure"; "nothing artificial"; "We provide training and support services"; and so on. Where consumers are in a state of uncertainty over matters of taste and social appropriateness, an attractive and credible salesperson plays a vital role in establishing credibility. Think of what the salespeople do in a jewelery store.

6. Intrinsic criteria. The criterion that enters into most buying is intrinsic liking: how the product looks, feels, tastes, smells, and sounds. Pleasing the senses is usually crucial. Buying purely on the basis of liking means that the only objective is pleasure/enjoyment and nothing more. Anything that diminishes the prospect of the pleasure inhibits buying. Thus the new wave of "functional foods" add nutritional attributes (like cholesterol-lowering margarine and so on) and so provide consumers with additional reasons to buy. Nonetheless, consumers appear unwilling to trade off taste for nutrition. Intrinsic liking often rests on the images conjured up by emotive words, names, and labels. Emotive ad words that suggest intrinsic criteria are "enchanting," "juicy," "crisp," "sizzling," "gripping," "refreshing," "alluring," "sparkling," "elegant," "relaxing," and so on.

Csikszentmihalyi claims, contrary to current orthodoxy, that pleasure has a function beyond being indulged in purely for its own sake, as it can be a reflex response built into the genes for the preservation of the species.[27] He quotes the French anthropologist Roger Caillois on the pleasure of games:

- With competitive games, pleasure comes from meeting the challenge of an opponent.
- Games of chance give pleasure by creating an illusion of controlling the future.
- Games like riding the merry-go-round provide pleasure by transforming the way we perceive reality.
- Games involving pretense and fantasy create the feeling of being more than we actually are.

Buying on the basis of intrinsic liking does not necessarily mean being driven by a desire for instant gratification. Consumers may postpone instant gratification in order to savor future possibilities of getting what they really want, as in saving for that expensive dress. Intrinsic liking is molded through education. Thus we may look at a work of art without any pleasurable response until told about its associations, who made it, and the criteria by which it should be judged. This is why the perfect counterfeit is not the same as the real thing. Knowing it is the real thing makes all the difference. This is the reason people continue to buy diamonds even though the naked eye cannot distinguish diamonds from zircons.

Consumers are more likely to buy if they like the smell, as smell connects directly with the emotional centers of the brain and immediately influences feelings and emotional memories. Examples in marketing are:[28]

- School books that smell of chocolates
- The smell of freshly mown grass in car ventilation systems
- The smell of lavender in dentists' offices
- The aroma of toast and fresh coffee exuding from an alarm clock
- Travel brochures smelling of suntan lotion
- Cigars that smell of herbaceous borders
- Airplane toilets that spray Chanel No. 5

There are organizations, like International Flavors & Fragrances in New Jersey, who will design and manufacture the smells and tastes of potato chips, grilled hamburger, pet food, toothpaste, or just about any designer fragrance. It is a big business.

The sense of touch is also important. As Sheldon and Arens said in the 1930s, "Every day the average person makes hundreds of judgments in which the sense of touch casts the deciding vote. Acceptance of a towel, hairbrush, underwear, stockings, hinge on how things feel in their hands. . . . Designs should be executed with an appeal to the tactile senses.[29]

Intrinsic criteria include the *curiosity* appeal, as acting to satisfy curiosity can be an end in itself, just as we might seek to know things for the sake of knowing. Curiosity is the tendency to seek novel or complex stimuli. In either case, seeking to satisfy curiosity can be exciting—and sometimes dangerous! A stimulus is novel if it is new or different. Consumers have an appetite for novelty since the familiar, while reassuring, can be a bore. Novelty, though, can be too novel and complexity too complex in terms of the consumer's level of experience, education, and willingness to persist in trying to comprehend. There is an optimal level of novelty and complexity for each individual at which point curiosity and the accompanying emotion is at a maximum. With the advent of the microchip, the provision of more features in, say, watches, has become irresistible, since little is added to cost and seemingly more in immediate appeal. Yet few of these additional features may be used, and they may simply add to complexity, hindering operation.

Gronow (1997) argues that consumers grow tired of continuous change and fall back on the "tried and true," in order to feel "at home" and to counteract "alien social forces" that demand constant change. This is true of those with "old money" who are seen wearing old and unfashionable clothes. But then, they can afford to buck the trend. Gronow argues, like many other fashion commentators, that fashion is a thoroughly aesthetic phenomenon even if some fashion creations are ugly. The opposite of fashion is a uniform, and modern affluent societies reject uniformity, unless it is imposed as in the army or is part of a shared expression of solidarity.

Aesthetic appreciation has emotional overtones. In fact, art has been defined as *the* expression of emotion, though it is more correct to say that art expresses an emotional quality. The aesthetic is all-pervasive in our lives, in products we buy like cars, clothes, furniture, and in the presentation of food, as well as in paintings, music, cinema, the countryside, birdsong, and so on. Human appreciation of the aesthetic influences all the choices consumers make in daily life in designing their environments and choosing what to buy. Fisher claims that *wonder* is the essential emotion of the aesthetic experience.[30] Fisher describes this emotion as the hospitality of the mind or soul to newness; the mind feels rejuvenated. "Wonder" has some of the attributes of "novelty," the key factor in drawing attention to any new product.

Consumers seek to turn their everyday lives into an aesthetic enterprise when trying to achieve a coherent style in what they wear and what they buy for the home. The coordinating principle for much durable goods purchasing is aesthetic liking. What typically gives purchases a coherence and links them together into a unitary whole is that they appeal to us aesthetically. Like all intrinsic liking, aesthetic pleasure is an end in itself. Aesthetic judgments are based on a feeling of pleasure, and perceptions of beauty may account for the unity in all aesthetic experience.

Underhill (1999) claims that almost all unplanned buying is the result of touching, hearing, smelling, or tasting something on the premises of the store, which, he argues, is why merchandising in the store is so important and why the internet, catalogs, and home shopping on TV will complement but never seriously challenge real live stores. He points out that sales in stores like the Gap are enhanced by the company's policy of fostering intimate contact between shopper and goods.

In marketing, Holbrook has been the most prolific scholar and researcher in aesthetics (for a list of his major articles on aesthetics, see the references).[31] In contrast to the six categories of choice criteria discussed earlier, Holbrook talks of eight types of consumer value.[32] The term "value" is used to mean that quality or property of an offering that makes it useful, desired, or esteemed. This is *value in the singular,* to be distinguished (as he makes clear) from *values* in the sense used in this book, that is, the central ideals around which goals become integrated. (Another sense of *value,* the one used by economists, refers to the net worth of a thing as determined by what price it will bring in the market.) Holbrook's eight types of consumer value are transparently tied to the emotions. This is not surprising, since Holbrook views products in terms of their capacity to create need- or want-satisfying *experiences*. On this basis, anticipated experiences are the primary influence in buying. If experiences are key, it is because few experiences can be said to be emotionally neutral. Holbrook's focus is on consumer values *sought,* not on choice criteria per se. Listing his eight values shows how his view of consumer value can be tied to our discussion of choice criteria and emotion. Holbrook's eight values are as follows; in parentheses we show how they can be tied to the six choice criteria already discussed:

1. *Efficiency.* As measured by the ratio of input to output and convenience, the consumer has an emotional investment in minimizing the input for any specific output and maximizing convenience. (Economic/sacrifice choice criteria plus technical performance choice criteria in the convenience-in-use function)
2. *Play.* This is tied to intrinsic pleasure. (Intrinsic choice criteria)
3. *Excellence.* This is tied to optimal performance in quality, the desire for which has an emotional dimension. (Technical performance choice criteria in the core use-function)
4. *Aesthetics. Aesthetic reaction* refers to an appreciation of consumption experience. It is tied to intrinsic pleasure with the pleasure of beauty being its main manifestation. (Intrinsic choice criteria)
5. *Status.* Success and impression management are tied to status, but what the consumer is essentially buying is a set of symbols to construct a certain persona tied to success. (Integrative choice criteria covering status and visibility)
6. *Ethics.* This covers the desire for virtue, justice, and morality. (Integrative choice criteria covering integrity)
7. *Esteem.* Holbrook views esteem as the counterpart to status in that esteem "tends to result from a somewhat passive ownership of *possessions* appreciated as a means to building one's *reputation* with others." (Integrative choice criteria covering self-esteem)
8. *Spirituality.* The reactive side of spirituality is faith (sacred experience) while the active side is works (good deeds). (Intrinsic choice criteria)

What our discussion of choice criteria and Holbrook's eight types of consumer value mean is that explanations of buying lack explanatory depth if the emotions are ignored. If we focus simply on the rational and not also on how people feel, we cannot hope for other than impoverished theories of buying behavior. The exclusive focus on the objectively rational brings with it the danger of our having a "trained incapacity" to recognize the pervasiveness of emotional phenomena. We are sensitive to what we are taught to see and, as a consequence, may lack sensitivity to emotional phenomena in buying. However, there is increasing recognition of the importance of emotion among marketing managers. There are techniques like the *benefit probe,* where respondents are asked to cite two *functional* benefits of each *product* benefit and two *emotional* benefits for each functional benefit. Thus in a benefit probe of a mouthwash the respondent might relate the functional benefit of breath cleaning with the emotional benefits of eliminating worry, fostering confidence, and being less anxious and more relaxed. Another technique tries to "measure" the consumer's *emotional* bonds with a brand. Emotional feelings are first listed and then weighted for relative importance for the product. The brands are next assessed for their perceived delivery of each of the emotions, and a final overall score for each brand is calculated. Current brands are then rated against the emotional ideal to judge if there is an emotional gap to be filled. If beer is linked to camaraderie and friendliness, the associated emotions need to be generated by advertising. While tangible, rational benefits are vulnerable to being copied, emotional bonds are more difficult to break.

Services: Customization and Personalized Execution

Anything that is of acute concern to us can give rise to an emotional reaction, so it can be exciting, say, to find a product that is unique to a certain manufacturer and central for the function we have in mind. Nonetheless, interactions with others are the most common source of positive and negative emotions. We are social animals, and our earliest memories tend to be memories of interactions with other people. Not surprisingly, then, dealing with service providers can be emotional.

Pure service industries are distinguished by the need to *customize* the offering and to *personalize* the carrying-out of the service. Consumers have a need to feel engaged with the service provider. An exemplar of customization and personalized execution is a hairdresser. Hotels, legal services, travel services, realtors, educational services, financial services, advertising, and restaurants must first identify the customer's requirements to determine what service is appropriate. Customization, of course, has its limits, because of costs but also because customization of the details uses up too much consumer energy. As an article on Dell in *The Economist* says, "Consumers want to customize PCs, but within limits: faster or slower processors, more or less memory, but not their own colour or trim. Such a limited customization encourages a build-to-order model."[33]

Once the service need is identified, how it is carried out becomes paramount. If, as is typical, service people are interacting with the customer, there is a need for courtesy, warmth, and a general sense of caring. Personalizing a service or interaction with the customer is not simply a matter of pointing out its importance to all those dealing with customers. It is also a matter of training: a matter of knowing how, not just what. Personalizing lies in the tactics adopted. Thus giving a $10-off coupon for fragrances selling for over $29 to women entering a store was considered more personalized and resulted in more sales than when fragrances at the counter were similarly labeled. In general, the extent of customization achieved will be the performance on which the service provider will be judged, but if customization among rival service providers is generally high, the extent to which the service is *personalized in execution* is what most enhances goodwill and loyalty.

All communications carry an emotional tone, and all interactions with service providers have the potential for being an irritant. Being at ease with someone is feeling relaxed and emotionally in tune with that person. Barlow and Maul point out that staff need to remind themselves when faced with an emotional outburst that something of importance has happened as far as this customer is concerned and accept, as their responsibility, the management of emotions in service exchanges.[34] They point to the need to teach staff to recognize the importance of emotions behind customer behavior.

If service providers are to be emotionally in tune with customers they need to avoid communicating in the following ways:

- *A peremptory way,* whether verbal, in writing, or in nonverbal communication, is perceived as showing a lack of respect, which is likely to arouse anger in the person addressed. Consumers, like people in general, have a strong need for ego gratification and an emotional need to be seen as having status and power and being given respect.
- *A condescending way* implies that the person being addressed is less able and of lesser merit, which is a blow to self-worth. Consumers, like people in general, have a strong emotional need for reassurance about personal worth. No interaction with customers should in any way undermine that sense of personal worth.
- *An obsequious way* suggests that one is being ingratiating for a sale or approval, which inhibits an honest and open exchange of opinions and can be frustrating.

Not just the emotional style of a communication but also the following behaviors can be emotionally frustrating:

- *Discursiveness* in communicating: "long-windedness" frustrates the audience's desire for the communicator to come to the point.

- *Ambiguity:* if what is being communicated can have several very different meanings or can be taken in more than one way, it can be frustrating, since few of us want to acknowledge ambiguity of meaning if the context suggests we should know which meaning is right.
- *Vagueness:* that is, what is being communicated is not detailed enough to be operational for the purposes the audience has in mind.

British Airways' new rules for passengers assert that the company can bar passengers from boarding its aircraft if they are threatening, abusive, insulting, or disorderly in some way (*Financial Times,* July 3, 2001, p.14). The rule, as given, is much too vague and ambiguous to be operational for the purpose; too much is left to discretion and subjective impression. There is a need to explicate the relevant behavior through "thick" description and videos illustrating the banned behavior. But, more important, is this the right approach, since it focuses attention on classifying behavior instead of teaching staff how to manage passengers who are in an emotional state? After all, except for drunks, who can indeed be a serious problem, passengers only get emotional about matters that really concern them, such as service providers not living up to expectations that were built up by promises that were made. People are only disappointed to the extent that their expectations are let down, and empty promises often lie behind disappointment. Emotions are particularly aroused when passengers are "kept in the dark" about reasons for flight delays or whatever, since this is to treat passengers with disdain. What British Airways may be doing is reinforcing tendencies in their staff to make the *attribution error* and the *self-serving error.* These errors relate to *attribution theory,* which reminds us that people attribute causes to explain another's behavior. The *attribution error* is failure to understand the influence of external causes on the actions of others—in this case actions (or lack of actions) by the service provider—but instead to attribute bad behavior purely to the personality of the individual passenger. The *self-serving error* is to attribute all personal success in doing one's job to one's own efforts but attribute any failures in doing one's job to causes that have nothing to do with one, like awkward customers. British Airways' new policy is likely to be popular with staff, as it gives them a greater sense of power and control in their job, but it is not giving priority to the right issues and may only serve to corrode service to their customers.

A useful aid in thinking about emotion and services are the categories developed by Ortony, Clore, and Collins, who point out that emotions relate to:

1. The outcome of events
2. People/actions
3. The attributes of things[35]

All emotions arise from a negative or positive reaction to one of these, that is, a positive or negative reaction to events, to people/actions, or to attributes of things that concern us. Ortony, Clore, and Collins argue that we appraise *events* by reference to our *goals;* appraise *actions* relative to our *standards;* and appraise the attributes of *objects* relative to our *attitudes.* In each case, marketing's attention should focus on the customer's likely reaction if the firm aims to develop good customer relationships. We return to the Ortony, Clore, and Collins categories in the next chapter.

With any service it is not just a matter of getting what is sought, since it is recognized that the process itself is part of the gratification. As a consequence, we often talk about the "goodness" of the overall service, as if we can break down the consumption experience into parts, assign each part a measure of value, and then add up the score. But a good start may not compensate for poor service at the end, since later events alter the emotional significance of what happened early on. The final significance of a service incident is not determined by its impact at the time. The "halo effect" can operate, in that something about the service that is outstandingly good can cast a halo over the dismal parts. On the other hand, service that diminishes the self-esteem or sense of self-worth of the buyer is guaranteed to be remembered, and every opportunity will be taken to get even.

But What Is Emotion?

The Family Resemblance in Emotions

When we speak of humans having "emotions" it means that humans have certain dispositional tendencies that, when activated, give rise to emotional experience. Thus people have a dispositional tendency for the emotion of "excitement," but the emotional experience of excitement has to be aroused if it is to be meaningful in people's lives. Hence there are emotions as (1) latent dispositions to have certain types of experience and emotions as (2) the experiences themselves that affect people's behavior. Emotions as dispositional tendencies are part of a person's makeup, while emotions as experiences are apt to be short-lived. In this book we are not concerned so much with emotions as dispositions; we focus on emotions as experiences.

"Emotion," as an experience, is used to cover a variety of mental states and bodily processes that arise from highly positive or negative appraisals of some real or imagined event, action, or attribute. The word *emotion* is a contraction of two words, *exit* and *motion;* the ancient Greeks believed that an emotion is the soul coming temporarily out of the body! An echo of this idea continues. There is the belief that emotional displays contain the core truth about a person and that to "be emotional" is to reveal one's true self. In a sense this is true, since what people get emotional about reveals what concerns them. Whenever consumers are encouraged to have high expectations about a product, they are concerned when such expectations are not fulfilled—hence the anger accompanying disappointment. If the anger is unexpressed, resentment can fester.

An emotional *mental* state can be pleasant (e.g., joy) or unpleasant (e.g., fear). These alternative states are the *hedonic tone* of emotion. On the other hand, emotional *bodily* processes are states of arousal, from calm to excited. It is the emotional mental states that are described by emotion words like *shame*, *guilt*, or *pride*. We speak of a mobile or expressive face as one that is a strong register of the emotions. Literature is about emotion, and it is impossible to imagine great literature without it, as a literature describing thought processes and the mind's interior in rational terms would be a moribund literature. The reading of novels and literature allows us to savor our emotions vicariously.

If we seek a single definition of emotion that describes the essence of it, the answer will elude us, as any attempt to define emotion will have theoretical implications about which there will be debate. Yet *emotion*, as the term is used in English, describes states and processes that have a *family resemblance*, as follows.

1. Emotions have an *object*. Emotions are *about* something, so we speak of having fear about something, being angry about what someone has done, being embarrassed about something or very proud of something, and so on. This is one way the emotions differ from visceral feelings such as pain. If we are to really understand the consumer's emotional experience, the object of the emotion needs to be identified and analyzed to establish what attribute, characteristic, or property of the object is responsible for the arousal of emotion. That said, the object of the emotion need not exist beyond the imagination, since consumers can get emotional about things they imagine to be true.

2. Emotions arise from highly *negative* or *positive appraisals*. We generally think of appraisals as highly cognitive, that is, as being thought-generated and based on beliefs and wants. But there is a preconscious processing of inputs to the mind that screens for what interests and concerns us. If there is something that concerns us, there is an immediate nonconscious appraisal that gives rise to a "reflex" emotion. The process is perception → emotional experience, with no conscious cognition in between. If nothing in the processing of inputs concerns us, that is, does not relate in any way to what we *value*, there is nothing to activate the emotions.

3. Emotions are associated with *autonomic physiological activity* experienced (if at all) as feelings. It is typically assumed that having highly unpleasant or pleasant feelings involve high arousal. This need not be so, in that boredom, for example, can be very unpleasant when arousal is low. It may be, however, that for an emotion to be motivating there must be high arousal accompanied by high pleasantness or unpleasantness. Although we talk of feeling happy, angry, guilty, embarrassed, frightened, or sad, we can have feelings of pain, nausea, and so on without these things being in any way connected to the emotions. "Feelings" include bodily feelings, like feelings of stress, and "feelings toward," like the warm feelings toward the object of love.[36] The output of a highly positive or negative appraisal always gives rise to "feelings toward" the object of concern. A consumer's highly positive appraisal of a product is accompanied by a positive feeling toward the product. Without feelings toward the object, there would be no emotion. When it is argued that emotions need not involve feelings, the reference is typically to bodily feelings and not "feelings toward" the object of the emotion. Of course, people are not always conscious of either their bodily feelings or "feeling towards." Thus, as Goldie says, we can be afraid without being reflectively conscious at the time of our thoughts or feelings. A traditional view is to treat emotion as *felt* experience. Many writers talk about the need for marketers to create the right customer experience. This can be another way of discussing (emotional) experiences. This has the advantage of being less abstract and more reality-focused than merely talking about emotions and emotional reactions. Barlow and Maul (2000) talk of "experience providers" providing *emotional value* which they define as the monetary worth of feelings when customers experience an organization's product/services positively. However, there is always a need to fall back on emotional concepts and what we know about emotion if explanatory depth is to be achieved.

4. Emotions give rise to a *tendency to action*. The feeling of anger gives rise to a tendency to aggression, though in the case of sadness the behavior may simply be expressive, as in an expression of grief.

5. Emotions express themselves in *involuntary facial displays* and other physiological expressions like body posture. Thus an appraisal giving rise to fear can register on the face before the conscious mind can act to control the reaction. Hence we speak of "reading" someone's face, and if we are political animals we need to acquire considerable expertise in this.

The most significant division in the emotions is that between the universal, biologically driven emotions of fear, anger, surprise, disgust, and sadness and the higher cognitive, culturally molded emotions such as embarrassment, guilt, pride, and envy. There are a number of distinct approaches to conceptualizing and studying the emotions that reflect this basic division, but a discussion of these approaches is not necessary for our purposes; for those interested, Griffiths offers the best overall review.[37] One debate, though, is important for what we discuss later. In psychology and the consumer behavior literature, there is debate about the primacy of affect over cognition versus that of cognition over affect. (The term *affect* is used by psychologists as a synonym for emotion or emotional feelings. More specifically, it is used to denote the subjective aspects—as opposed to the observable signs—of emotion in order to illuminate the feeling side of mental activity.)

Zajonc argues for the *primacy of affect* over cognition.[38] By this he means that we experience emotions before any conscious appraisal of the triggering stimuli has occurred, though beliefs about the triggering stimuli may happen in parallel with, or even as a direct result of, the emotion arising. Emotion on this view can arise through a simple reflex process. The work of neurologists like Damasio[39] and LeDoux[40] demonstrates that the initial appraisal of things that are tied to our values or core concerns is nonconscious and may be at variance with the more reflective (conscious) appraisal that occurs subsequently. Goleman summarizes the Damasio position:

> Damasio's conclusion was that our minds are not designed like a computer, to give us a neat printout of the rational arguments for and against a decision in life based on all the previous times we've faced a similar situation. Instead the mind does something much more elegant: It weighs the emotional bottom line from those previous experiences and delivers the answer to us in a hunch, a gut feeling. We could have no preferences, unless feelings enter into the pros and cons to establish the relative weight of each.[41]

Damasio's claim is that if a person is unable to attach positive or negative emotions to his or her mental representations of proposed courses of action, then there can be no emotional appraisal of the possible courses of action. Without such emotional appraisal, people cannot decide what most concerns them. As a result there is an inability to reach a decision in serious cases. The idea that there is pure rational thought devoid of feeling is a myth. It is in fact commonly an insult to suggest that someone is this rational; one politician called another, to insult him, "a desiccated calculating machine." The political consultant Roger

Ailes dismissed Michael Dukakis as "that little computer heart" who "isn't going to know what hit him." Behind all this rhetoric is the same idea, the stigmatization of the unfeeling rationalist. This is not surprising, as our rational economic models tend to focus on technical and economic criteria, which, when deployed exclusively in the choice of policy, can alienate people.

One argument of those stressing the primacy of affect is that in our evolutionary past, conscious appraisal came too late for appropriate action; better first a nonconscious appraisal to fight or flight. From a marketing point of view, this idea coheres with the old adage that "First impressions count," in that consumers, in the absence of other information in the immediate view, are apt to go along with a first "gut" reaction. What immediately resonates with the consumer emotionally has a big impact on subsequent action. Popular expressions evoke this kind of unexamined visceral response, as in phrases such as "knee-jerk reaction" or "rush of blood." Thus consumers can be strongly swayed by brand image or associated factors.

Moods and Emotional Sentiments

Mood

Every conscious mental state has a qualitative character that we refer to as *mood*. We are always in a mood that is pleasurable or unpleasurable to some degree. It may be that bad moods relate to their being too little positive reinforcement in a person's current life and too many punishments.[42] In any case, moods are distinguished from emotions proper by not being tied to any specific object. But, as Goldie (2000) says, this distinction is not watertight, in that emotions need not be directed at objects that are completely specific (we can be angry just at people generally) while there is always a sense of a mood having a general objective like the state of the world at large. Moods manifest themselves in positive or negative feelings that are tied to health, personality, or perceived quality of life. Moods can also relate to the emotions proper, as in the aftermath of an emotional incident such as the failure to secure a loan. A mood on this basis is the mind's judgment on the recent past. For Goldie, emotion can bubble up and down within a mood, while an emotion can involve characteristics that are non–object specific.

What is important for marketing is that moods color outlooks and bias judgments. Hence the importance of consumer confidence surveys, as consumer confidence typically reflects national mood. There is *mood-congruence* when thoughts and actions fall in line with mood. As Goleman says, there is a "constant stream of feeling" that runs "in perfect parallel to our stream of thought."[43] Mood congruence occurs because a positive mood evokes pleasant associations that lighten subsequent appraisals (thoughts) and actions, while a negative mood arouses pessimistic associations that influence future judgments and behavior. When consumers are in a good mood, they are more optimistic about buying, more confident in buying, and much more willing to tolerate things like waiting in line. On the other hand, being in a bad mood makes buying behavior less predictable. It is not surprising that efforts are made to put buyers in the "right mood" by the use of music and friendly staff or, say, open bakeries in shopping malls that delight the passer-by with the smell of fresh bead.

Thayer views moods as a mixture of biological and psychological influences and, as such, a sort of clinical thermometer, reflecting all the internal and external events that influence us.[44] For Thayer, the key components of mood are *energy* and *tension* in different combinations. A specific mixture of energy and tension, together with the thoughts they influence, produces moods. He discusses four mood states:

- Calm-energy: he regards this as the optimal mood of feeling good
- Calm-tiredness: he regards this as feeling a little tired without any stress, which can be pleasant
- Tense-energy: involves a low level of anxiety suited to a fight-or-flight disposition
- Tense-tiredness: is a mixture of fatigue and anxiety, which underlies the unpleasant feeling of depression

People generally can "feel down" or "feel good" as a result of happenings in the world around them. This represents the national mood. People feel elated when the national soccer team wins an international match or depressed when their team has lost. An elated mood of calm-energy is an optimistic mood, which is good for business. Consumers, as socially involved individuals, are deeply influenced by the prevailing social climate. Marketers recognize the phenomenon and talk about the national mood being, say, for or against conspicuous consumption. Moods do change, though. Writing early in the nineteenth century, Toqueville describes an American elite embarrassed by the ostentation of material display; in the "Gilded Age," sixty years later, many were only too eager to embrace a materialistic vulgarity. The problem lies in anticipating changes in national mood, since a change in mood affects everything from the buying of equities to the buying of houses and washing machines. Thayer would argue that we should be interested in national events that are likely to produce a move toward a tense-tiredness state or toward a calm-energy state, since these are the polar extremes and so are more likely to influence behavior. Artists sensitive to national moods express the long-term changes. An example is the long-term emotional journey from Charles Dickens's depiction of the death of little Nell to Oscar Wilde's cruel flippancy about it ("One would have to have a heart of stone not to laugh at the death of little Nell"), which reflects the mood change from high Victorian sentimentality to the acerbic cynicism of the end of the century, as shown in writers like Thomas Hardy and artists like Aubrey Beardsley.

Whenever the mind is not fully absorbed, consciousness is no longer focused and ordered. Under such conditions the mind falls into dwelling on the unpleasant, with a negative mood developing. Csikszentmihalyi argues that humans have a need to keep consciousness in an ordered state, and this experiential need to keep consciousness fully active is what influences a good deal of consumer behavior.[45] Sometimes it does not matter what we are shopping for—the point is to shop for anything, regardless, as consuming is one way to respond to the void in consciousness when there is nothing else to do.

Emotional Sentiment and Brand Loyalty

To have an *emotional sentiment* toward a brand or product is to have a strong positive feeling of liking for that brand. Strong brand loyalty involves emotional sentiment. Having a choice makes for the expression of loyalty, as it provides an opportunity to be against alternatives disliked. If the product has attributes that are unique and of central importance to the consumer, together with risks attached to buying, the product is termed a "high-involvement product," as being most likely to engage the consumer in deliberations when choosing. This is because high-involvement products are those that generate the most consumer concern.

Trust and sentiment are the ingredients of brand loyalty. In contrast to moods (but in line with emotions), sentiments are not persistent conscious states but are dormant until aroused by the object of the sentiment. Emotional sentiment ties into *emotional memory,* in that memories have sentimental content. Every firm catering to the consumer should seek to develop an emotional sentiment for the firm's brand by fixing it in the consumer's memory as part of a valued way of life. It is the vestiges of emotional sentiment that allow the successful resurrection of old brand names, such as the revival of the name Buggatti. It is ignorance of the emotional sentiment that can attach to eminent brand names that leads to many such brands being dismissed as worthless assets. The emotion still attached to the name *Pan Am* is not simply that arising from the Lockerbie air bomb atrocity.

Loyalty is not just a matter of habitually buying the same brand, since all habitual buys are not grounded in trust and sentiment. Yet this combination of trust and sentiment (loyalty) is the best barrier to brand switching by customers, while it facilitates brand extensions and word-of-mouth recommendations. Of course, there may be no loyalty to any particular brand when the various brands in the market are perceived as mere tokens of each other with differences that are marginal and of no significance to the consumer. This is not to suggest that meaningful differences will always be confined to the product itself, since things like brand image and distribution can be crucial. In any case, being a loyal customer does not imply just buying the one brand. Brands in different segments of the market may be bought simultaneously by the buyer for different use-occasions or for different family members. Thus a woman might want a fresh light perfume during the day and a strong sophisticated scent for the evening.

Functions of Emotion

Emotions serve many useful functions. Only those relevant to marketing will be mentioned here. First, emotions help us *survive* by directing attention to what is important for survival like threats to life and limb. Second, emotions *provide information* to others (e.g., that we are in an angry state), to influence their behavior, and to ourselves, so that we may know our likes, dislikes, values, and concerns. Third, emotions contribute to *social control* in that violation of social norms leads to emotions like guilt, embarrassment, shame, and regret. Fourth, the display of emotion plays a role in persuasion to indicate commitment to a particular position. But it goes without saying that emotions on occasions have dysfunctional consequences, as when they distort judgment and lead to irrational action. Fifth, and most important from the point of view of this book, the function of emotion is to make up for the insufficiency of reason.

Reasoning can proscribe by logically pointing to inconsistencies, clarifying thoughts, and making legitimate inferences. But reason alone cannot determine trade-offs among alternatives without involving values, as values point to the relative importance of the trade-offs. Yet behind these values are not just biologically pressing demands such as the need for survival but past emotional episodes that shape whatever it is that concerns us. Some emotional episodes can be the inherited myths of history that are exploited in emotional advertising by associating brands with great historical figures or events. As de Sousa says, "emotions, by being tied to values, determine what is considered important; what options are considered; the patterns of salience among options; the relative importance of attributes while limiting the inferences actually drawn from a potential infinity of possible inferences."[46] Reasoning tells consumers a great deal about the features of a product, but it is the link between reason and emotion that decides the actual trade-offs that are made.

Damasio, too, shows that the emotions are necessary for serious decision-making. Without emotions, consumers, in making deliberated decisions, are unable to assign values to different options or product attributes. This implies decision paralysis, as consumers would be unable to make up their minds. Damasio uses the expression *somatic markers* in connection with the emotional gut feeling that arises from a highly positive or negative appraisal. It is "somatic" because it relates to bodily feeling, and it is a "marker" because it marks an image, however fleetingly. Somatic markers are analogous to "sentinels" who raise an alarm that helps survival. Negative somatic markers set off alarm bells, while positive somatic markers encourage action in line with any positive (nonconscious) appraisal.

With the recognition that emotional reactions can arise without any conscious cognitive participation, there is the implication that we can form instant attitudes about things that concern us. This rules out the idea that attitudes *always* start with cognitive appraisal. In fact, the very idea that the consumer's *attitude* toward a brand can be best viewed as a tripartite concept, consisting of a fixed temporal sequence of the cognitive (awareness and comprehension of the product), the affective (feeling/assessment of the brand) and the conative (action), has been undermined. There is too much of an interdependence between the cognitive and the affective for such a division to be considered realistic.

What all this means is that the calculating machine model of the decision-maker is a myth. The myth of pure rationality arose from the Enlightenment in eighteenth-century Europe. Kant called this the "Dare to know" period; it was shaped by an optimism about the possibilities of reason in controlling human life, The Enlightenment writers deeply distrusted emotion, which was associated with the backward, the primitive, and the superstitious. There is no such thing as decision-making without an emotional component. Textbook exercises, where we choose via a money metric the alternative that yields maximum profit, are deceptive, in that the superordinate value of profit maximization is laid down and trade-offs can be converted into a common money scale. In practice, goals and values are multiple and competing, and trade-offs are not measurable on a common scale. However, where value priorities are uncertain (and they can be), indecision is the rule, since when values are unclear, trade-offs can be less confidently made.

Illustrative Example: Emotion in Cola Buying by Teenagers Aged 13–14

The following is a record and analysis of the thoughts of 25 youths, aged 13 and 14, attending a parochial school in a blue-collar area of New York City, on the buying of various cola-type soft drinks. It illustrates the emotions that can be involved in such a simple purchase. The record was built up from consumer protocol statements, defined here as a record of what these youths, encouraged to think aloud "off the back of their heads," had to say (1) before buying (the anticipatory account), (2) during buying (the contemporaneous account), and (3) after buying (the retrospective account).

The focus is on what comes to mind at the time, as opposed to what might be recalled at a later date, as is the case with focus groups. The youths were given the money to buy the cola.

Values

Associated with cola drinks for these teenagers is a consumption experience tied to the following preferred life vision or set of values:

1. Being full of life, not miserable and sluggish
2. Being relaxed, not tense and anxious
3. Being part of a social group, not an outsider looking on

Pleasurable Anticipation

There are pleasures in contemplating and anticipating the following.

Location/ambiance/occasion (where the cola will be drunk). An appropriate location or ambiance is implicitly accepted as intensifying the consumption experience as indicated in the following quote:

> I am now going to flick on TV, open the blinds, and make sure the mood is right. I'll put on my Max Headroom sunglasses and think to myself: "Catch the wave, Coke." . . I'm going to drink now in the privacy of my room, sit on the bed, leaning against the wall.

If a cola is not something that can be had on demand (e.g., from the household refrigerator), the child may save the cola for the "right" occasion, location, or ambiance. The right occasion or ambiance might be with friends, since drinking together means participating in a ritual that highlights shared identifications conducive to friendship.

Preparation (how the cola is "prepared" for drinking). Getting the cola ready gives rise to several rewarding experiences associated with:

- *Anticipation* that such preparation will enhance the pleasure of drinking, as in: "I take my favorite glass and some ice and make it nice and cold."
- *Listening* to the "pop" and the "fizzing, bubbling sound" as the can is opened or the cola is poured, as in: "How I enjoy putting it in a glass of ice and hear[ing] a cracking sound."
- *Smelling* the aroma of the contents, as in: "The smell is all relaxing."

Consuming (how the cola is drunk). Consuming the cola involves thoughts about:

- *Manner of drinking,* as in: "I don't guzzle but drink it slowly to admire the flavor."

- *Flavor tasting,* as in: "What a treat my taste buds are having—they thank me with every sip."
- *Actions taken,* as in: "How I love swishing it around the can and letting it fizz again. . . . I chew on the ice and hear a cracking sound as I taste the cola drips in the ice."

Consumption feelings (how it afterward feels). There are emotional feelings before, during, and after the cola is drunk:

- *Activation:* feelings of being alive and full of vitality, as in: "I start feeling energetic."
- *Hedonic* tone: achieving inner harmony (a move away from tension) as in: "After drinking I felt calm and relaxed. . . . I'm thinking about how it feels when I drink other kinds of soda. I remember the Coca-Cola commercial and I think how I'd felt when I drank the last Coke."
- *Relatedness:* feelings of solidarity with one's social milieu (a move away from loneliness and isolation), as in: "I'm going to buy Classic Coke—my friends are all returning to it."
- *Competence:* a feeling of being able to cope (a move away from a sense of not being able to cope), as in: "I felt so revived, I could tackle the whole world with full energy."

Choice Criteria

Certain criteria are involved in choosing which brand of cola drink to buy, as follows.

1. *Intrinsic liking of experiences.* The following comments express these criteria.

This has a delicious cherry flavor that plain Coke and Pepsi do not have. . . . Cherry in Coke really gives it life and zestfulness.

[I like] pouring it over the ice cubes with the Coke climbing every ice cube until it reaches my mouth.

I like a colorful can. . . . the design and color of the bottle itself is important. I would never buy a plain ugly and tacky bottle of soda.

2. *Technical criteria.* It seems the can itself can have ancillary-use functions, as in: "I wipe the can across my forehead and the perspiration disappears."

3. *Integrative criteria.* Perhaps surprisingly, integrative criteria (integration with self and one's social milieu) were important in the buying. In fact, social validation was important as evidence of popularity. For example, one of the students was "discouraged" at finding "the shelf-space devoted to Coca-Cola less than [that] devoted to Pepsi." Further examples:

Peers must approve. I could never buy a soda that wasn't popular with my peers.

The true American should drink Pepsi. Just look at the can, and you can plainly see the colors—red, white and blue. I am certainly a true red, white, and blue American. That's how I like to think of myself after drinking Pepsi.

The soda I am buying has a great commercial to go with it—Max Headroom.

4. *Legalistic criteria* were also a factor in buying, as in: "I think for a while what kind of soda my mother likes best."

5. *Adaptive criteria.* Uncertainty was common, as in: "Buying a [cola] is difficult because I have to decide against other [colas] that I might enjoy more to drink. . . . Which has the power to lift my exhausted spirits? . . . Which has the one-of-a-kind taste?"

6. *Economic criteria.* Although soft drinks were generally around the same price at the time, cost sentiments were nonetheless expressed, as in: "I look at the price and see if it is really worth the money. . . . I'm going to buy something that is worth paying its price for."

Some Key Assertions for Marketing

1. If marketing management is to understand the consumer, then understanding the role of emotion in buying is critical. A major function of emotion is to make up for the insufficiency of reason. Emotions, through their connection to values, identify what is considered important; what options to consider; the pattern of salience among options; and the relative importance of features/attributes/properties of the brand, while limiting and coloring the inferences drawn from a potential infinity of possible inferences.

2. If the marketing manager is to understand the consumer, there is a need to know the significance of the firm's product for the consumer, that is, what it *means* to the consumer to buy the product. It is the consumer's emotions that signal the personal significance or personal meaning of any actual or potential purchase. Reasoning about what to buy involves the emotions, and these can on occasion dominate the buying process. Much buying is rooted in feelings of like and dislike. Emotions in buying are tied to negative or positive appraisals of the firm's offering (product, price, promotion, and distribution) and a tendency to take action, for example, buying or not-buying, complaining or praising, and so on.

3. If the marketing manager wishes to understand the consumer, he or she must understand not only the product attributes/features/properties sought but also what it is that concerns the consumer when buying the product. Are these concerns technical, social, economic, or something else? The notion of what concerns the consumer tells us what will receive his or her attention. Concerns link to emotional experiences in the past, which shape the consumer's system of values, which, in turn, through generating negative or positive appraisals about the product, affects the trade-offs made. Consumers belonging to the same culture are typically subject to many of the same emotional experiences and cultural conditions that affect what emotional feelings are generated by what situations.

4. If the marketing manager is to appeal emotionally to the consumer, he or she should identify the consumer's choice criteria and try to attach emotional significance to criteria most identified with his or her brand. Thus, solidly based claims about high technical performance, less use-effort, less choice effort, easy payment , all-inclusive price, meeting social expectations, offering visibility and status, supporting moral integrity, eliminating risk, and, last but not least, intrinsic appeal can all have emotional resonance with the consumer and swing a sale. Marketing managers should try to make use of the benefit probe, where customers are asked to cite two functional benefits for each product benefit and two emotional benefits for each functional benefit. They might list the feelings that are evoked by the product and seek to weight them for relative importance. They can rate their own and competing brands for their tie to each of the emotions to achieve a final score for each brand.

5. If the manager is to exploit emotional liking, he or she will try to give the product an edge, appealing to the senses or instinctual gut liking, as happens when products have a nostalgic appeal. Often the only coordinating principle in the buying of a whole range of goods (say, for the home) is aesthetic appeal and sense of liking.

6. If the marketing manager is to bring out new products, upgrade existing ones, or develop promotional appeals, *novelty* is basic to generating interest and attention (sustained interest). Novel features and novelty generally have the potential to excite positive emotions, since novelty attracts and, most important, generates emotional *curiosity*. The novelty may reside in the product's complexity. But there is an optimal level of novelty and/or complexity beyond which the effort to comprehend becomes too burdensome, with a consequent loss of interest.

7. If the marketing manager is to improve service, the focus should be on customization and personalized execution. Customers want to feel emotionally relaxed and in tune with the service provider, which means avoiding communications whose tone is peremptory, condescending, obsequious, or emotionally frustrating because of being discursive, ambiguous, or vague.

8. If the marketing manager is to appeal to the consumer, there is the importance of symbols in people's lives. Many products are bought more for what they symbolize than anything to do with technical performance. Thus photographs symbolize historical continuity, books and courses symbolize intellectual interests, other products symbolize wealth and status, and some products, like a tattoo, are bought to signify a certain social persona.

9. If the marketing manager accepts that "mood" plays a part in buying, he or she recognizes that every conscious state has a certain qualitative character that can be referred to as "mood," ranging from pleasurable to unpleasant. A certain mood can be the aftermath of an emotional incident, but in any case mood colors outlooks and biases buying decisions. Those in a good mood are more optimistic about buying and are more likely to buy. The optimal mood for buying is that of "calm-energy," where there is

no anxiety but a feeling of being very much alive and well, so that the buyer buys without reservations.

10. If the marketing manager wants to develop brand loyalty, he or she needs to develop both trust and sentiment for the brand. In contrast to moods, emotional sentiment is not a persistent conscious state but can lie dormant until aroused by the object of the sentiment. Sentiment has allowed many an old brand name to be resurrected. But trust in a brand is earned through meeting expectations. The consumer can trust a brand without liking the product and can have sentiment toward the brand without trust (which is analogous to the brand being a likable rogue). There is a need for both trust and sentiment.

11. If the marketing manager is to aim at a memorable service, he or she should not just think of how the service is overall but should seek to make some part of it outstanding (to generate the halo effect) and to ensure that no part of the service is below par: top service does not transcend the remembrance of bad food.

2

Generating Emotion: Value Systems, Emotive Stimuli, and Appraisal

This chapter and the next two chapters describe the process by which emotions are generated. A process is a sequence of steps that occurs to bring about the outcome of interest, in this case emotion. For every emotional experience, there is a narrative process of antecedents, such as relevant stimuli, wants, and beliefs, that gave rise to the emotional experience. If the process is intended to be explanatory, it must show how the events in the sequence are connected in a way that makes the outcome (an emotional experience) intelligible.

It was an article of faith at one time that the social sciences, like the natural sciences, aimed at discovering explanatory laws as a basis for the prediction, regulation, or control of behavior. Today social scientists are more modest. As Elster says, there are no universal laws when it comes to emotion, either in terms of predicting precisely what conditions will give rise to a specific emotion or to predicting the precise action that will be generated by a specific emotional state.[1] Specific contextual circumstances can undermine any generalizations. But this does not undermine the importance of trying to explain the process of generating emotion. Problems of generating emotion or inhibiting emotion are more likely to be solved by those with the profounder conception of how emotions come about. There are some marketing managers who have a high degree of skill in the business of building emotion into marketing. But without some understanding of the generation of emotion, skill can become mechanical application, no longer effective in changed circumstances. Indifference to explanation results in the cultivation of ad hoc tactics with no overall direction being given by a theory-based strategy. A theory or model of the process of generating emotion sensitizes marketers to relevant concepts so they can know what to look for and how to handle emotion issues.

The Processes Generating Emotion

Any causal or quasi-causal process used to explain behavior involves identifying:

1. The state of mind of the individual. In the case of emotion, the states of mind to be specified are the consumer's values, beliefs/imaginings, and wishes/wants/desires.
2. The relevant stimuli: that is, the emotive stimuli in the world outside or self-generated stimuli emanating from the imagination. These stimuli are appraised or evaluated against the consumer's values, beliefs, and wishes/wants/desires. It is this appraisal that gives rise to "feelings toward" the stimuli. The stimuli are typically the object of the emotion and can be an event, an action, or an attribute of the object.
3. The (emotional) effects or experience. These can be thoughts (cognitive effects), feelings, facial displays, or action.

In what follows, these three components are disaggregated and shown as a quasi-causal chain consisting of five stages in the production of emotion, with the final stage of emotional responses being shown to consist of cognitive effects, arousal of feelings, behavioral expressions/displays, affect-driven consumer action, and the choice processes themselves. Figure 2.1 illustrates:

1. The consumer's *value system* or key concerns, whether of evolutionary origin or cultural
2. The *emotive stimuli* (typically the object of the emotion, whether an event, action, or attribute)

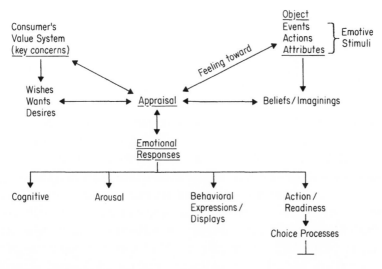

Figure 2.1.   Production of emotion.

3. The *appraisal* of emotive stimuli
4. *Beliefs* or imaginings and *wishes/wants/desires*
5. *Emotional responses* (cognitive effects, arousal of feelings, behavioral expressions/displays, and affect-driven consumer action and the choice processes themselves)

This chapter focuses on the first three, namely, consumer value systems, emotive stimuli, and appraisal. Chapter 3 covers the pervasive role of beliefs and wishes/wants/desires, and chapter 4 deals with emotional responses.

The Consumer's Value System or Key Concerns

Emotions as Responses Tied to Values

As Frijda says, emotions are responses to events and so on that are tied to values or key concerns.[2] The very existence of values implies the existence of humans to whom things matter. Our system of values structures the relative importance of things. Our emotional responses tell us what it is we value, and these emotional responses can reinforce particular values. Whenever the consumer perceives a threat to values, emotions are aroused. For example, one value is to avoid being cheated, so perceived sharp practice by the seller arouses an emotional reaction. Similarly, if the consumer in buying perceives the potential to promote his or her key values, this can be emotionally exhilarating.

The consumer makes trade-offs in line with values, so narrow hedonism may trade a future of good health for the instant nirvana of drugs, overeating, or whatever. But most trade-offs are less dramatic: for example, a larger house versus a lower price or more land versus fewer chores in looking after less land. Emotional reactions track salience in respect to values or key concerns.

The events, actions, or attributes that are checked or appraised against values need not be real. They can be fantasy. But they must be matters of concern. Something is always of concern if it presents an opportunity to enhance what people hold dear or, alternatively, threatens what people hold dear, that is, what people value. Rokeach recommended that social scientists shift their emphasis from studying attitudes to studying values and value structures.[3] He spoke of terminal values as those reflecting what people want out of life or find worth striving for. Examples of terminal values for Rokeach are a comfortable life; an exciting life; inner harmony; an enjoyable life; self-esteem; social recognition; true friendships. He acknowledged people differ in the relative importance they attach to these various values and that values change both generally in the culture and individually.

An individual's system of values is an orientation to an individual's highest-level preferences. A consumer's values tell us what is of significance to him or her. What a person gets emotional about tells us about his or her values, as people (including consumers!) only get emotional over things that concern them, like blows to self-esteem. A system of values may be entirely materialistic, though few people are motivated purely by materialistic concerns. Education is a major influence on value systems, and education increases the likelihood that people adhere to socially desirable goals. Thus Hyman and Wright in their book *Education's Lasting Influence on Values* show the enduring effects of education on values such as racial and religious toleration.[4] But values do change, and with that change come different appraisals of past events. Thus we tend to review past treatments of people and people's behavior in terms of our newly acquired values or value priorities.

Values and the Concept of a Preferred Life Vision

One way to conceptualize a *system* of values is through the concept of a preferred life vision. Levi-Strauss points out that people are sensitive to contrasts in the human condition.[5] Examples are seeking excitement versus being bored, being rich versus being poor, or being healthy versus being ill, and so on. People seek the life that captures the more preferred polar extreme. But, as all aspects of the good life cannot be pursued with equal vigor, the consumer's value system reflects the particular weightings he or she attaches to various components of the preferred life vision. These weightings have some stability but can change with circumstances and cultural drift. Indifference to any contrast is equivalent to giving equal weighting to the polar extremes: a possibility that can be dismissed for all practical purposes. Rokeach spoke of both terminal and instrumental values, though this distinction has not caught on, presumably because values, as the concept is being used here, are usually viewed as terminal by definition. If we were to tie values to consumer buying, they might look like the following for many people:

- Preference for a less-pressured over a fast-paced lifestyle
- Preference for an environment less threatening to health over a more technologically driven way of life
- Preference for a more meaningful, simpler life over a more materialistic one
- Preference for more solidarity, face-to-face communication, and sense of sharing with others over mere luxurious isolation (bowling alone is not pleasurable)
- Preference for more to be preserved from the past than overthrown in the name of progress
- Preference for staying young-looking rather than old-looking

There is no complete homogeneity of values, consumer or otherwise, within a culture—simply a family resemblance. Consumers attach different weights to various values; hence psychographic segmentation, which is based on different values and lifestyles. Values differ among social classes and differ among people of different generations within the same class, depending how refined our categories of values are. Sharp differences in values between generations have led to "generational marketing" and "cohort marketing" in segmentation.[6] While different generations are separated by about 25 years, cohorts are formed by common defining experiences in their history. As a consequence, cohort groups are assumed to be "value-bonded" by similar preferences. Thus the "postwar cohort" came of age between 1946 and 1963, experiencing a time of family togetherness, economic growth, and social tranquility. In spite of the Korean conflict, it was an experience of security and stability. Marketing campaigns to cohort members exploit nostalgia with symbols of the experiences behind the bonding. Such symbols can incite a good deal of nostalgic emotion.

Accepting that early emotional experiences are most involved in molding the consumer's system of values, the question becomes: How influential are common cohort experiences in shaping values? Are they sufficient to direct preferences? Values can be poor predictors of buying *until or unless beliefs are taken into account*. Consumers can have the same set of values but show different buying patterns because they have different sets of beliefs about the appropriate means for promoting their values. Values operate like goals for the individual, but the paths to goal attainment are many. Thus a consumer may place a high value on buying the "best tennis racquet money can buy," but this depends on beliefs about the criteria that reflect "bestness," while other beliefs about personal finances and buying opportunity will also play a role in what tennis racquet is bought.

If No Values Then No Deliberated Choices

Meehan regards values as a *necessary* condition for choosing among alternatives. As a necessary condition for doing something is a sufficient condition for failing to do something, Meehan is saying that without values no decisions would be made: "Values are the tools needed to make choices or to express preferences, to order or scale potential outcomes on some reasoned basis. . . . Without sets of values, all human actions are equally significant or equally meaningless."[7] The role that Meehan attributes to values is the role de Sousa attributes to the emotions that underlie values, namely, to determine the salience of the considerations entering into a decision.[8] There must be some way to judge the utility of various trade-offs if a decision is to be made. This is where values implicitly play the crucial role. There is no such thing as "value-free" education, a value-free social science, or value-free marketing literature. It can never be. Whenever deliberated decisions have to be made, there are trade-offs, and trade-offs reflect values. Values are always at work when the consumer is deciding the make of car to purchase or which house to buy. All trade-offs are made against criteria, and the weighting of the criteria connect to value systems. It is because values are so pervasive that the whole process of striving, choosing, and selecting is value driven. For de Sousa it is the linking of values to the emotions that determines the importance given to various considerations. *Values are emotionally grounded and emotionally developed.*

Values interpenetrate everything we do, and even everyday decisions have a value component. If political campaigns are a case of issue marketing, political debate is over issues that symbolize values. The issues may be insignificant in themselves but highly significant for what they symbolize. Events that highlight division in society's values, like the "marches" led by Martin Luther King in the United States, can turn a society into two hostile camps. Politics is a theater of values, with many trivial issues assuming political significance because they carry value symbolism. In fact, the very "meaning" or significance of a political issue can usually only be interpreted in terms of the value of the sym-

Figure 2.2.   An unambiguous appeal to values. Courtesy Oneida Ltd., N.Y.

bolism to the rival parties. The most powerful issues in politics reflect what has been called "the civil war of values." The abortion debate, for example, is structured around appeals to opposing values, namely, the "right" of the fetus versus the "right" of the woman to choose. Values are the very stuff of political rhetoric.

Values Are Multiple and Conflicting

Values, like goals generally, are multiple and conflicting. One way of reducing the conflict is to control information. Education is rife with controversies over values. Although the classics in literature are not assigned to students just to acquaint them with the values of a previous age, those who criticize the stress on this literature in schools argue that "by forcing these works on the young people of today the schools and universities perpetuate misogynist and anti-egalitarian values still dominant even in present-day western societies."[9]

Values conflict both in respect to the individual consumer and among consumers. In buying breakfast cereal, the consumer may want the cereal both to meet the tastes of his or her children and to have the highest nutritional value. Consumers experience a conflict in values between those that relate to environmental issues and their preference for non–environmentally friendly products, like disposable diapers, that are the most effective for the purpose.

The consumer can be alienated on occasion from his or her core values. This can happen when indulging in conspicuous consumption, where the consumer is driven to spend, spend, spend for some emotional reason yet feels a powerful sense of not acting in accordance with his or her sense of personal morality. The result is a strong approach/avoidance situation, which can be distressing.

Values Expressed as Value Judgments

A doctor is making a value judgment when he or she decides that the relief of pain has a higher priority than prolonging life. The consumer is making a value judgment when he or she chooses a holiday abroad rather than to repaint the house or gives greater priority to paying off the mortgage than spending the money on other things. What is important here is that value judgments can change without necessarily any change in consumer values.

Values Cannot Be Proved but Only Defended

Values cannot be proved; they can only be defended. As MacDonald says, we do not refer to John Stuart Mill's proof but to his "magnificent *defence*" of civil liberty. Because values reflect ultimate concerns, threats to them are emotionally arousing, and direct appeals to values are much more motivating than appeals to technical and economic benefits. This is a lesson that needs to learned and relearned in marketing even though corporate image-makers never cease repeating it. MacDonald says it well:

Value utterances are more like records of decisions than propositions. To assert that "Freedom is better than slavery" or "All men are
of equal worth" is not to state a fact but to choose a side. It an-
nounces *"This is where I stand."* (p. 732)

I mentioned earlier that in the late war propaganda appeals to
defend our comforts and privileges would have been rejected as
uninspiring but that appeals to defend the rights of all men to freedom and equality obtained the required response, at least in all but
the depraved and cynical. I now suggest that they did so because
they accorded with our decision about these ultimate social values.[10]
(p. 732)

Values announce where we stand. This is why declaring values has become
so important in corporate image management. Hitler claimed that no appeal
to altruism per se would ever work, but the appeal to self-sacrifice was something different. Goebbels was quick to copy Churchill's "blood, toil, tears, and
sweat" speech. Later, there was Kennedy's famous exhortation: "Ask not what
your country can do for you but rather what you can do for your country." These
appeals were effective because they resonated emotionally with the country's
values. The declaration of superordinate values induces emotional unity, a
sense of solidarity through bonding and persistence in the achievement of
common goals.

The values entering into buying reflect somewhat the choice criteria discussed in chapter 1:

1. Projecting a certain self-image (e.g., of being practical and efficient) to
   buffer self-esteem. Consumers value feeling good about themselves.
   Anything about a product (goods or services/experiences) that
   promises a boost to self-esteem will have a powerful appeal. High self-
   esteem goes with self-confidence, a more calm-energetic mood, and
   more optimism in buying. Although the desire for high self-esteem is
   only one of many motives, it is a powerful one. Anything that increases
   or decreases self-esteem is highly emotional. For people with low self-
   esteem, the solution may be to associate with successful others rather
   than seek greater personal attainment. The more closely some product
   or brand can symbolize that association, the more its perceived value.
   One may in effect tie oneself to the fortunes of the football team, the
   pop star, and so on, so that when their success fades one also feels the
   loss. One solution is to have associations with different types of success, extending even to the success of a brand of product.

2. Protecting a sense of integrity (e.g., buying "green"). Consumers, like people generally, desire to preserve personal integrity. Acting with integrity allows people to "hold up their head with pride" and to have the satisfaction of being a good citizen. Integrity for some consumers can be enhanced by confining purchases to those suppliers considered to be socially responsible. It is a sense of personal integrity that makes us walk away from any "shady" transaction or sharp practice, even if self-interest would have been served by just going along. Without an emotional commitment to integrity, behavior not in line with narrow materialistic self-interest would make little sense.

3. Enhancing interpersonal relations (e.g., purchases to conform to group norms). Consumers value good interpersonal relationships, as everyone depends on others for emotional, material, and intellectual sustenance. Shame is avoided by going along with community standards. There are many social norms that appear to be almost universal. One is the principle of reciprocity, which dictates that we should repay favors (or injuries) done by others. We may even feel obliged to buy a food product after taking and eating a sample in a supermarket! We feel obliged to reply in kind to any favor or even any concession made in bargaining.

4. Avoiding risk (e.g., by buying well-known brands). Consumers value certainty in their lives and the avoidance of unnecessary risk. While some may take risks for thrills, in general consumers are risk averse and want to avoid making a mistake and having future regret. To make a mistake reflects on self-confidence, while feelings of regret can be painful. An unknown brand, uncertain consequences of buying or of entering a contract, lack of product information, and so on leads to a risk-averse attitude when it comes to buying. If customers are to buy without reservations, attention must be paid to eliminating any sense of risk in making the purchase.

5. Ensuring the achievement of utilitarian functions (e.g., washing the dishes or making a request). Consumers value being able to carry out their plans, and this often depends on having dependable products and knowledgeable service staff. Whenever products fail to live up to expectations there is frustration, as the failure in performance means plans are incomplete—and the inability to complete any plan results in frustration. Consumers are constantly being frustrated in both shopping and consuming. We find frustration rampant in services. In fact, more than at any other time period, the problem today of being even able to reach someone who can deal with the customer's problem is more acute than ever, as one is passed over the phone from

one phone number to another. One consumer in a letter to a newspaper spoke of trying to buy a switch to connect a burglar alarm to a telephone line: "I spent 1 hour [and] 35 minutes on the telephone, gave my telephone number and zip code 18 times, listened to 29 recorded messages, and spoke to 10 real people, six of whom put me back into the recorded message loop." Some of this arises from putting in standard systems when standard conditions don't exist or putting in fixed systems in advance of experience. In any case, what is happening is that companies are confusing efficiency with effectiveness; the system to deal with inquiries is the cheap solution, but it is not effective and simply frustrates any tendency to loyalty.

Appeals to Values; Changing Values versus Changing Value Judgments

Marketing typically focuses on *appeals* to existing consumer values rather than efforts to *change* values. Values are difficult to change, as the rightness of values is not open to factual proof, even though they may on occasion be changed by a dramatic rhetorical defense of alternative values, as shown by Mill's defense of liberty. More generally, marketing seeks to change value *judgments* rather than the underlying values themselves, which change only slowly over time and are difficult for marketing to hurry along.

Why? Changing value judgments is easier, because value judgments are tied to descriptions of the situation and descriptions of anticipated consequences. Marketing is commonly able to redescribe situations and consequences to fit values. The situation itself does not change, but the judgment changes because beliefs have changed by changing perceptions. Marketing influences perceptions by:

- Getting people to focus on one description of the situation rather than another, for example, price described as an investment rather than a cost
- Altering what the consumer attends to, for example, focusing attention on the features of the house rather than its location
- Influencing memory by dramatizing what the seller wants the buyer to remember

The antiabortion movement does not seek to change the values of the prochoice group, but by describing abortion as murder it hopes to link its case to more deepseated human values. As head-on appeals to a change of values rarely work, it is better to think in terms of subsuming values rather than changing them. This is not to suggest that the values within a culture never change. Traditionally, both in the United States and Europe, society has been organized around a set of widely shared values, many of them emphasizing self-discipline and personal responsibility. But more recently the move in values has been toward a more permissive ethos with an emphasis on personal fulfillment and a toleration for a more pluralistic morality.

Propaganda is typically the art of the spin, that is, a redescription in order to alter perceptions, a matter of fitting a perspective into an existing framework of popular values. What considerations consumers take into account depends substantially on how an issue is framed. When put one way, a clear majority of citizens endorse the rights of those with AIDS, but when put another way the majority does not.[11] A great deal hinges on how an issue is framed, as in whether the defense budget is described as a vital issue of national defense or simply the apparatus of a jingoist foreign policy. It is easier to reframe an issue to fit an existing value perspective than undertake a change of perspective. Reframing suggests putting another slant on the matter, that is, not trying to change a whole perspective but reordering value aspects. Different words for the same thing (e.g., *aroma* instead of the word *stench*) evoke different images in the mind as these images are manipulated symbolically in advertising. The tobacco industry frames the banning of smoking as an issue of civil liberties and not health. Values conflict on occasion. Framing, by giving higher visibility to one value rather than another, makes that value more available in memory: the consequence is to prime values differently.

We need to distinguish between arguing *for* a certain point of view and arguing *from* a certain point of view. If an appeal is to be effective in arguing *for* a certain point of view, it needs to also argue *from* the perspective of the audience. This is because an effective argument (including persuasive appeals) assumes the audience is "on the same wavelength," that is, has the same perspective, paradigm, or model. It is no use arguing for a particular religious denomination if the audience does not believe in God; there is a need to start from the atheistic perspective or set of presuppositions. Every argument or persuasive appeal takes some set of beliefs and values for granted. When perspectives differ, things are viewed differently. Thus, if a person's values revolve around individual rights, then any law making everyone carry an identity card is viewed as suppression of individual freedom, while others might simply regard it as a more efficient means of establishing identity for social purposes. It is because perspectives differ that the same argument or persuasive appeal persuades some but not others. As Kleinberg says, doing a rain dance to end the drought only makes sense to those who assume the weather is the gift of the gods; it would not make sense to meteorologists.[12] A perspective acts as a set of beliefs tied to values to which people are emotionally attached so that trade-offs in reaching a decision fall in line with the perspective.

Nozick on Intrinsic Value

Nozick accepts that emotions are a response to things that *involve values* but argues that emotions in particular are a response to things having *intrinsic* value, that is, being valuable in themselves.[13] He conceptualizes the emotions as a psychophysical replica or an analog of values. The psychophysical configuration of an emotion models the structure of the particular value or values to which the emotion is a response. Whatever is emotionally arousing is a guide to values. Nozick's intrinsic value covers anything that is valuable in itself, which he further defines as anything that brings unity into diversity to provide internal coherence. For Nozick, "good" music and "good" paintings have intrinsic value because the diverse elements within each of them form an integrated and united whole. The greater the diversity is unified, the greater the *intrinsic* value of the item within its class and the stronger the emotion of pleasure. This concept of intrinsic value is of interest to marketing, though basic questions remain: How is such intrinsic value measured as opposed to merely described? How does intrinsic value translate into value for the consumer? Intrinsic value will certainly be tied to product design but will also be tied to the whole consumption experience, since all of it can be designed to provide an organic unity.

Whatever gives enjoyment is typically related to cultural values. For example, "self-improvement" is a particular American value, so enjoyment for many Americans is likely to be tied to self-improvement. To demonstrate this point, the bestsellers in America are psychological self-help books. In Britain it is books on gardening. Whatever it is about a product that gives enjoyment has a connection to values. However, things that ostensibly provide enjoyment, like smoking, may yet be rejected because they are in conflict with more important values, like personal health.

Campbell on the Pleasures of Consumption

Campbell, a sociologist of mass culture and religion, claims that when it comes to consumption, the major value lies in *fantasizing in anticipation* of the new or novel, as this gives the most pleasure. The pleasure in consumption arises from the fantasized anticipation of novel new experiences. Campbell distinguishes pleasure (enjoyment)–*seeking* from *satisfaction-seeking*.[14] (Campbell uses the term *pleasure-seeking*, not *enjoyment-seeking*, but the ambiguity of the

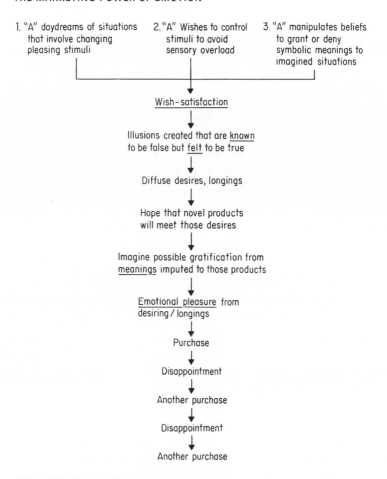

Figure 2.3.   Belief-dependent emotional pleasure.

word "pleasure" makes the latter more preferable). For Campbell, the pleasures of consumption reside in anticipation ripened in imagination. Consumers imaginatively *anticipate* the pleasure that a new product will bring, even though reality never quite lives up to what is anticipated. It is all a saga of continuous hope and continuous disappointment, with perfect pleasure perhaps taking place only in the imagination. Figure 2.3 diagrams Campbell's position.

Campbell views satisfaction-seeking as simply satisfying biological needs—to relieve discomfort arising from deprivation (e.g., hunger). In contrast to satisfaction-seeking, pleasure-seeking seeks *emotional experience*. Satisfaction-seeking is the *push of needs* demanding satisfaction. Pleasure-seeking is the *pull of hope* about experiencing fresh stimulation. Whatever the doubts of consumers, they can still have hope: hope is not inconsistent with having doubts. And to have hope in the face of overwhelming odds is not irrational. Frankl observed, in his concentration camp, that hope was the principal determinate of survival: all the survivors still hoped.[15] A terminally ill person will buy anything purporting to be a cure if there is a chance of success. As the saying goes, "There are no atheists in foxholes" (though perhaps a few agnostics who none-theless have hope!). Consumers may doubt but still hope, as the alternative to hope is despair. Revson, the founder of Revlon cosmetics, is reputed to have said: "We don't sell products, we sell hope." The opposite of belief is not dis-belief (since this is a type of belief itself) but doubt. Marketers often fail to ap-preciate this and are put off launching a product because of doubts expressed by the consumer. The consumer is still open to persuasion when in doubt. A good proportion of new products are sold to consumers who have doubts about the product's efficacy but still want to give it a try (e.g., wrinkle creams).

Marketers who cater to satisfaction-seeking stress the relationship be-tween the inner discomfort (e.g., acid indigestion) and their brand's ability to relieve the situation better than rival brands. But those catering to enjoyment-seeking appeal to the *senses*. Whereas satisfaction-seeking means trying out real products to see which are effective, pleasure-seeking aims at stimulating the senses. While satisfaction-seeking depends on what a product is, a prod-uct's pleasurable significance (perceived potential for pleasure) depends on what it can be taken to be, since illusion and delusion operate to provide plea-sure.

When an emotional state is so intense as to be out of control, the consumer is engulfed by the excess of stimulation, with little likelihood of its being plea-surable: the sensory overload and the pressure to act interfere with pleasure. (If this is true, it may have lessons for Las Vegas!) However, any positive emo-tion that is *willed* and *controllable will* provide pleasure. Hence the pleasure of "experiencing" horror, pity, sorrow, and even fear that arises from reading books, newspapers, or listening to radio or watching television. These "experi-ences" are pleasurable because they are willed and controllable. The more ap-parently "real" the synthetic experience, the better. This explains the enduring popularity of such staples as ghost trains and Madame Tussaud's chamber of horror or the popularity of scenes of Nazi brutality in modern media and the traditional amusement park commonly devoted to such horrors as roller-coast-ers. The pleasure of these experiences is due somewhat to the assurance that they are limited and contained, so that users dive through air and plunge be-neath water knowing that all will be well. The best exemplar, according to Campbell (1987), of using the imagination to stimulate pleasurable emotions is *nostalgia*, since the triggers for this emotion are largely self-referential. Ad-vertising (particularly cohort advertising) exploits nostalgia in its music and its scenery or in whatever in the past experience can be emotionally arousing. The Chrysler PT Cruiser is an example of nostalgia in product design.

Campbell distinguishes between emotions imposed by events (what he calls "event-dependent emotionality") and emotions that are largely willed. The latter arise from manipulating belief or suspending disbelief to grant or deny symbolic meaning to things so as to create illusions and wishful thinking (what he calls "belief-dependent emotionality"). According to Campbell, understanding today's *hedonistic* buyers means understanding how consumers use (and came to use) "daydreaming" (fantasy/imagination) to generate feelings. While no great pleasure can be derived from mere imagined sensations, it is easy to imagine situations (e.g., love-making) and events (e.g., meeting one's lost love) that have the capacity to stimulate an emotional experience. Much advertising is built on fantasy rather than the fantastic. This is because the world of daydreaming or fantasizing is the world not of the absolutely bizarre but of what might conceivably happen. It is not uncommon for consumers to fantasize about the "threats and promises of products."[16] Glasses "threaten" to break if dropped, sugar "promises" to sweeten our tea, a motor car threatens to break away from control but promises to reach the destination, and so on. The fantasized threats and promises of products reflect hopes and fears that influence buying.

For Campbell, modern hedonism is characterized by daydreams giving rise to illusions that are known to be false but felt to be true. This is interesting for marketing, since it undermines consistency theory, which claims there is universal discomfort with inconsistency. What Campbell is saying is that when consumers feel something to be true, that feeling may be all that is needed to determine a preference. Consumers commonly go along with what they simply *feel* to be true. This can amount to self-deception. It is well known that diamonds are not an uncommon rock (as assumed), but the consumer, abetted by advertising and the De Beers diamond cartel and its marketing arm, the Central Selling Organization, continues to defy truth in asserting that "diamonds are a girl's best friend." De Beers spends $200 million a year on advertising to uphold the message that diamonds are precious.

One premise of Campbell's argument is that the consumer suspends belief or manipulates beliefs to get enjoyment because beliefs are seldom firm convictions. This premise is contested. Carroll claims that we cannot just *will* what we believe. In fact, he sees no need to make such an assumption, since a thought alone can generate emotion.[17] Just as we can feel embarrassed merely by reflecting on some embarrassing occasion or feel fear by imagining ourselves leaning over the edge of a cliff, Carroll points out that simply *entertaining a thought* can generate emotion. This is so; imaginings are not beliefs, even if they can play a similar role in behavior (see chapter 3). Imaginings support action based on liking. There is the *likability heuristic* (rule of thumb) in consumer decision-making, where the consumer simply chooses on the basis of liking. Similarly, one may be excited at seeing a "bargain" and imagines one has a use for the product though one will in fact never use it. It is not beliefs that fall in line with emotional demands but that when intense emotions dominate the mind, they prevent or inhibit the retrieval of relevant beliefs.

In line with marketing, Campbell (1987) claims that gratification from the use of a product cannot be divorced from brand image and other associations (e.g., between champagne and the luxurious lifestyle) attached to the product. Images and other symbolic meanings are as much a real part of the product from the consumer's point of view as the real stuff of which it is made. The failure to appreciate this lies behind much nonsense said by critics of marketing who only count as relevant to consumer fulfillment that which is tangible and can be directly observed. This goes with the distorted view of the consumer as a bundle of fixed wants that it is marketing's job to identity and serve instead of the recognition that, within value constraints, consumers have an underlying appetite for an infinite number of products to meet latent wants. Consumers often do not know what they want until a product is on the market and promoted in a way that captures their imagination with what it symbolizes for them. What something symbolizes can come about through association, as association influences perception. Consider a study by Rozin et al.[18] Their experimental subjects were quite happy to eat fudge when it was molded into the shape of a disk but very, very reluctant to eat it when then molded into the shape of animal feces. Similarly, subjects were reluctant to eat sugar labeled "sodium cyanide" in spite of the fact that they had seen the sugar being poured from a sugar box and arbitrarily labeled with the name "sodium cyanide." The image arising from the negative associations generated an emotional reaction which the known facts (true beliefs) did not overcome. Many new fragrances are created just to exploit the symbolism of a name. The name comes first and the design of the fragrance aims to capture the persona and other connotations of the name.

Image over Substance

Stuart Ewen claims that, in the contemporary world, where mass media serve as arbiters of reality, the *primacy of image* over substance "has become the normative consciousness."[19] Though this (wrongly) downplays the importance of substance and exaggerates the dominance of the mass media, it offers a needed corrective to the claims made for substance *always* being ascendant over image. Even in medicine, there was once more image than substance. Porter, in his history of medicine, points out that from the early Greeks to World War I, medicine had little substance;[20] as far as medicine's substance lies in healing, its effectiveness is recent (previously sanitation was the key to the lower death rate). Yet, in spite of its impotence, medicine had a powerfully positive image. As Porter says, medicine was socially, politically, and ideologically powerful, quite apart from its efficacy in curing or even ameliorating diseases. We speak of an imagistic literacy today, which is based on the consumers' familiarity with the vast store of cultural images from which advertising draws. With brands more and more undifferentiated in substance, differentiation in image can become crucial. There can on occasions be a primacy of image over objective facts.

Brand labels have a long history—Wedgwood plates, Chippendale furniture, Bechstein pianos were great labels long ago. Some manufacturers succeed in creating names that resonate down generations with compelling associations between product, brand name, and image. Thus Louis Vuitton was luggage-maker to Napoleon III. What is recent is the speeding up of this process and the recognition that it need not happen haphazardly. Consumers buy designer labels as much because they symbolize status, social acceptance, or a sharing with some celebrity as because they believe these labels offer a guarantee of quality that compensates for the higher price. As Ewen (1988) argues, sellers promote images without the reality that is assumed to go with the image, as when products are associated purely with experiences, like being successful in love, that are not deliverable. But the Campbell thesis suggests that the promotion of such experiences does in itself provide pleasure, as it allows consumers to fantasize as if in anticipation of the experience. In fantasizing the idealized self-image or self-identity takes shape to influence buying. Hope (e.g., for the lottery, "It has to happen to someone") is crucial in fantasizing. The modern hedonist anticipates novel and new products as offering the hope of realizing the idealized pleasures imagined in daydreams; such products symbolize the possibility of new excitements. There is a "hunger" for new images, with new meanings that delight the senses. Fantasy is valued, as it can be a co-conspiracy, a mutual production of meaning between the consumer and the advertisers. The net result is a longing for novelty, because novelty allows the consumer to attribute exciting meanings and images to the product.

Because the whole question of fantasy, imaginings, or daydreaming is so associated with Freud, psychologists who are hostile to Freud are apt to ignore fantasy. Person, a clinical psychiatrist who is not dismissive of Freud, views a fantasy as an imaginative story or internal dialogue that serves some wish-fulfilling function or helps contain anxieties.[21] Fantasizing can be either wish-driven or affect (emotion)–driven. (While a "want" implies some realism about what is possible, a wish does not. Even incompatible wants can be contemplated in wishes.) For Person the vast majority of people have fantasies, in that they have internal dialogues and indulge in reveries or imagined scripts. Fantasy may compensate for what people lack in life. Fantasies or daydreams provide symbolic gratification and so can be highly pleasurable.

Pleasures of Consumption, Possessions, and Subjective Well-being

Robert Frank argues that the pleasures from consumption are both relative and fleeting.[22] The pleasure derived from owning, say, a particular size of house is tied to the status attached to owning such a house relative to those owned by neighbors. Moving to a relatively better house provides pleasure only for a short time, namely, until the new level of luxury seems routine or the neighbor goes one better. Frank uses the metaphor of the arms race to characterize the reasons for conspicuous consumption because it was motivated by a desire to keep up with the Joneses. He concludes by claiming that consumers in affluent societies would be more content if they spent less on luxury goods, resulting in less of a need to work long hours and more time spent with families.

Csikszentmihalyi quotes a number of studies showing that beyond a low threshold, material well-being does not correlate with subjective well-being.[23] He goes on to say that research indicates that excessive concern with financial success and material values is associated with less satisfaction with life. In fact, excessive concern for material goals is a sign of dissatisfaction with life: people report being happier in life when they are actively involved with a challenging task and less happy when they are passively consuming goods or entertainment. On the other hand, there is a minimum level that needs to be provided. Bauman argues that communism failed in the eastern European states because it was incompatible with modern consumer society, as the demand for diversity and novelty could not be met by governments focusing on just satisfying basic needs.[24] This is not to deny the claims made by Frank. While it is undoubtedly true that purchases will not satisfy the deepest configurations of human need, they add zest to life and on occasion can—at least in the short term—live up to a fantasy or dream as the following statement from a protocol statement made by a young boy and recorded by one of the authors illustrates:

> When I play Nintendo I have a big feeling of delight. It is so exciting that it feels like everything is for real and it's really happening. I'm thrilled every time I play. It is a sort of contest to see who is faster, smarter, and more powerful, me or the computer. I love the challenge, having to react faster and better than my opponent, having to

compensate and recompensate [*sic*] for every move the computer makes.

Consumers have vague longings, which they hope will be met by novel new products. On the other hand, with too much novelty, consumers have difficulty in categorizing and comprehending a product, while extreme novelty is associated with complexity and risk. It was for this reason that one marketer in the 1920s used to claim that the success of a novel product always depended on its ability to evoke something of the product being displaced. In the case of the automobile, this was certainly true. The first cars were called horse-less carriages, and it was a long time before the automobile finally realized an identity independent of this idea.

Campbell's daydreaming or fantasizing relates to the strategy of *displaced meaning* in anthropology,[25] which consists of reconciling hopes and ideals with harsh reality by wishful thinking to the effect that the ideal will be a reality in the future (e.g., "after we have socialism," "after marriage," "in heaven") or the ideal is already a reality elsewhere (e.g., in another country). For many intellectuals in the twentieth century, the Soviet Union seemed to promise that utopia. Politics in the twentieth century was replete with defunct utopias and tarnished visions of a perfect world order.

No one in consumer marketing doubts the insatiability and inexhaustibility of wants nor that people have diffuse longings. One social historian, Loren Baritz, sums up the frenzy to accumulate with the bumper-sticker slogan: "Whoever dies with the most toys wins."[26] He goes on to show how the middle classes act as if they are looking for some intangible element missing from their lives while they follow any orgy of spending with an "Is-this-all-there-is" malaise. The traditional French critique of the "bourgeoise" was their materialism as a result of being in the middle—looking above and below and so being reminded of what they have and didn't have and where they could sink if what they have were taken away. But material appetite is limitless and not confined to the middle classes. Imelda Marcos filled an office block with her shoes, and the wife of Haitian dictator "Baby" Doc Duvalier had the largest collection of furs in the world, though Haiti is near the equator.

Self-interest and Action

Campbell (1987) is not suggesting that modern hedonism equals self-indulgence. Not all hedonism is so narrow. The self-illusory pleasure-seeker may be led in the direction of idealistic commitment. Campbell argues that human motivation involves not only self-interest but perceptions of moral obligations, since embarking on any action has to be justified to the consumer's moral self. As a consequence, the distinction between true motivation and simply justification (legitimization) is not as sustainable as it appears, since legitimization may simply be articulations of motives. Morally idealized self-images can be just as much sources of pleasure as can aesthetic experiences.

This debate about self-interest being always the dominant concern is still with us. Classical microeconomics assumes narrow self-interest in human motivation. It assigns no role to generosity, social conscience, goodwill, or fairness yet the evidence shows that people emotionally resist transactions they perceive as unfair and that customers resist price increases that do not seem to be justified by cost increases.[27] Consumers can get emotional about issues that are not directed to boosting self-interest because their set of values goes beyond narrow self-interest. And as Barlow and Maul say, unethical practices create cynical customers, who become increasingly difficult for each subsequent service provider to handle.[28] Customer expectations act as a standard for what is fair, and so equity issues are commonly linked to expectations, as when consumers' expectations are violated on finding that their hotel has made exorbitant charges for phone calls. Expectations always play a role in perceptions of what is fair, and such expectations are intimately connected to social norms and the emotions that support them.

Rawls regards acting purely from self-interest as "unreasonable" behavior, on the ground that willingness to be guided by reasons from an impartial or intersubjective viewpoint defines what is called "reasonable" behavior.[29] Darwall claims that an intimate relationship exists between something being a justificatory reason for taking action and its capacity to motivate even if only under ideal conditions.[30] He argues there are intersubjective values like justice, respect for privacy, seeing meaning to life, and so on that are basic to the idea of community. Such values translate into a set of shared, objective, justificatory reasons for action. They emotionally motivate, in that there is a connection between upholding the values and having a sense of self-worth and self-respect, while their active promotion expresses our identification with others and they with us. As Darwall says, if we were to always act on the strongest desire, then the very notion of settling trade-offs by reasoning would probably make little sense: the strongest desire in practice may not be the desire to which we give greatest priority.

Darwall's fundamental point is that practical reasons are at base impartial rather than entirely self-centered. This is because thinking about justificatory reasons for taking action can lead to new desires. For example, I may have no active desire to support "animal rights," yet seeing a film on cruelty to animals might activate a desire to do something about it. People (including people as consumers) can be moved by new considerations without their being any active antecedent want. As Quine points out, pure self-interest, however enlightened, affords no general rational basis for altruism.[31] Yet altruism exists and stems, partly at least, from the relationship between acting morally and maintaining self-respect: the capacity to care is tied to our emotional nature. Acting morally is tied to emotional reinforcements.

Fantasizing: A Learned or Innate Skill?

Campbell (1987) regards the ability (as opposed to the capacity) to daydream as analogous to the ability to read, that is, as something that requires a particular type of exposure and learning. Csikszentmihalyi[32] seems to agree, quoting Singer's assertion that fantasizing or daydreaming is a skill that some children never learn to use.[33] Csikszentmihalyi regards daydreams as helping to bring emotional order to the mind, allowing both children and adults to rehearse imaginary situations so that the best strategy for confronting a situation can be adopted. Daydreaming performs the psychological function of achieving detachment through its transcendence. Csikszentmihalyi concedes that daydreaming can be enjoyable, but for a different reason from that of Campbell, namely, that daydreaming can help increase the complexity of consciousness. By daydreaming, people cope with the mundane, the ordinary, and the repetitive and with stress. The more appalling the economic conditions, the more movies offer fantasy, like the Busby Berkeley epics in the 1930s, while the "action films" of Stallone and Schwarzeneggar can be viewed as male power fantasy films, allowing the reconciliation of men to feminism and the Vietnam fiasco!

The inevitable question is: Are people really able to get emotional pleasure by fantasizing as they anticipate the novel? A strong case could be made that this is so, but it seems that not everyone has acquired the ability to indulge in imaginative daydreaming. Some people are constantly made miserable by emotional states they are unable to completely control; such people who would love to be able to substitute pleasurable emotions but find that such activity is beyond them.

Carroll on Enjoyment

Carroll, explaining the *enjoyment* of horror films, argues that the source of consumer enjoyment in horror films is *curiosity*.[34] (Curiosity as a motive is very neglected by marketing, yet it explains much buying of magazines, say, on the rich and famous.) The horror story engages its audience by involving them in the processes of disclosure, discovery, proof, explanation, hypothesizing, and confirmation. He shows that the horror film narrative is constructed to stimulate curiosity, the desire to learn about the monsters, and so on, and the desire to know the outcome. Curiosity is aroused by the plot and the objects of horror. Fascination compensates for whatever negative emotions are stimulated: the fascination with impossible beings more than compensates for the distress evoked, since we know the monsters do not actually exist.

Is the positive response to fictional characters based on some sort of identification with them? Do audiences watching a "slice-of-life" advertisement identify with the characters? "Identification" suggests some sort of sharing with the characters of interests, feelings, values, or circumstances. Identifying with some other person is, at the very most, managing to imagine oneself in the other's shoes, but such identification is rejected by Carroll as a basis for evoking positive (emotional) responses. He points out that audiences do not even always identify with (positive) fictional characters. While the responses of characters may cue the emotional responses of the audience, this may not happen. Thus the audience may feel suspense when the characters in a mystery film do not.

Carroll claims we do not so much identify with fictional characters as *assimilate the situation,* coming to see the situation from the point of view of the characters in the film or TV commercial and from the outside as well. In neither case is it necessary to identify with the characters. *Ads should aim to facilitate this assimilation of the situation.* However, all this leaves open the question of the mechanism at work. There are at least two candidates. A positive response could arise through (1) conditioning (e.g., a loving child) or (2) contagion, in that the behavior of others (e.g., laughter) can be infectious. Both mechanisms are commonly adopted.

Gosling's Modern Hedonism

Gosling defines *modern hedonism* as occurring whenever people can throw their heart and soul into buying or other activity without the slightest reservation, that is, without, say, reflecting on the cost.[35] For Gosling, pleasure is a way of *attending,* not a sort of feeling, as most views on hedonism assume. Gosling claims that pleasure lies in the *contemplation* (e.g., of buying) rather than the achievement itself.

Gosling is saying much the same as Campbell, as anticipation, attending, and contemplation are conceptually related. Gosling's idea also links with the importance attached by Holbrook (see chapter 1) to anticipating experiences. Anticipation implies attending and contemplation. We might bring the two views together by saying that the greatest emotional pleasure lies not in possessions but in fantasy involving anticipation, attending, and contemplating.

This means that marketing needs to feed the fantasy, stress curiosity to shape the anticipation, and dramatize the consumption experience to stimulate contemplation. One of the aims of marketing is to induce consumers to (1) anticipate/contemplate buying with pleasure and to (2) buy without reservations, as to buy with reservations is to buy with anxiety, which makes the buyer susceptible to postpurchase dissonance.

Emotive Stimuli: Events, Actions, or Attributes (Real or Imagined) Constituting the Emotional Trigger

Emotions are triggered by the arousal and appraisal of anything that impacts on values. Ortony, Clore, and Collins view emotions as valenced reactions to stimuli, that is, as reactions tied to appraisals or evaluations of desirability. This is much the same as saying that emotional arousal arises from emotive stimuli being very positively or very negatively appraised against values.[36] As mentioned in chapter 1, Ortony, Clore, and Collins distinguish three types of emotive stimuli, viewed typically as the object of the emotion, that is, what the emotion is about, as follows.

1. *Consequences of events.* The emotions of hope and fear are associated with consumers being uncertain in their appraisals about buying consequences. If the consequences promise to be positive, there is hope, and if the consequences are judged likely to be negative, there is fear. The consequences of events are appraised or evaluated in terms of *goals.* The more desirable or undesirable the perceived consequences, the more intense the emotional reaction.

2. *Actions of agents.* When consumers, like people generally, appraise their own actions as agents, the associated emotions are pride and shame: *pride* if the action leads one to feel one has achieved more than expected and *shame* if one has fallen below community standards. When one of us was a preteenager, he was proud, on opening his first packet of cigarettes, when he found it contained the message: "You have bought the best." Anything that boosts self-esteem adds to pride. Obtaining what is perceived as a bargain can also give rise to a sense of pride, and so can finally managing, say, to obtain the status symbol of a sports car. In addition, there can be the emotion toward others of *admiration* or of *reproach.* Admiring others, we seek that admiration ourselves through imitative behavior. Similarly, there is a desire to distance from those we would reproach, and they become a negative reference group in buying. Actions are thus appraised in

terms of their *praiseworthiness*. As praiseworthiness assumes some standard for assessment purposes, it relates to achievement as against expected performance.

3. *Aspects, properties, attributes of objects.* Whenever the consumer appraises some emotional aspect or attribute of an object, like a product, there is a "gut reaction" of like or dislike. If an object's attributes are of concern to the consumer, there is no such thing as a neutral view but inevitably a judgment of liking or not. This immediate affective reaction is the core of the consumer's attitude toward the product (including service/experiences). Aspects, properties or attributes of objects are appraised in terms of their *appealingness*.

Ortony et al. are obviously talking about first-level appraisals, as the consumer can be interested in the aspects, properties, or attributes of objects because they give rise to certain consequences. But Ortony et al. would rightly argue that the interest lies in the immediate reaction to consequences, actions, or aspects of objects. The more important the values against which consequences are appraised, the greater the intensity of the emotion aroused (with "intensity" being a function of the size of the emotion times its duration.)[37]

If value systems are fairly stable, the same things retain their power to elicit emotions almost indefinitely.[37] Frijda (1988) claims that whenever something can be viewed in different ways, the tendency is to interpret so as to minimize the negative emotional load and maximize the emotional gain. This explains why consumers are not put off their implicit favorite model by unpleasant facts (e.g., problems of making the mortgage payments). But these are generalities. Research suggests that depressed people are more realistic about life. There are also consumers who force themselves to face reality; others who are masters of self-deception; and still others who seem constitutionally unable to be positive about any purchase but worry all the time about imaginary risks.

A controversial issue is whether imagining things known to be false, but felt to be true, generates *genuine* emotions. This is a key question for advertising imagery. As we have shown, Campbell (1987) claims that consumers do this all the time and that advertisers and film producers stimulate emotions via the appeal to the imagination, even when the alleged factual base is known to be false. This is true. Consumers are often asked to imagine what it would be like (what it *really* would be like) to be in a particular situation so as to conjure up an emotional experience. Gordon denies, though, that the imagination does generate exactly the same autonomic physiological effects, since emotions generated at the theater are different from genuine emotions.[38] Nonetheless, generated emotions can still be powerful. And even if *true* emotions *cannot* be elicited *solely* by imagining some event, action, or attributes, this still leaves open the question of whether true emotions can be generated by *imitating* the physical signs. Is there, for example, truth in the belief that making ourselves smile in adversity will help us feel happy? There is some evidence for it, as found by Laird[39] and Ginsburg and Harrington,[40] but not unequivocal support.

Carroll (1990) provides the most perceptive analysis of the relation between fictional events and the emotions. He accepts that people can be frightened when watching horror films and asks: How can we be frightened by what we know does not exist? Why would anyone be interested in horror films, since being horrified is unpleasant? As Carroll says, the answer to the first question is all of a piece with answers to such questions as how does the plight of Oedipus move us to pity and fear?" He might also have said it is related to such questions as: How does the plight, the joy, the fear, and so on of the actors in a TV commercial move the target audience?

Carroll claims that when we are moved by *real* situations (e.g., being indignant in the face of injustice), our emotions change if we find that the situation is not as we believed it to be. In other words, emotions typically (but certainly not always) rest on beliefs and change as beliefs change. Elster also stresses the following cognitive beliefs as the triggers to emotions.[41]

- Shame is a negative emotion triggered by a *belief* about one's own character. The emotion of shame is not only *a* support of social norms but *the* support.
- Contempt and hatred are negative emotions triggered by *beliefs* about another's character: contempt is induced by the thought that another is inferior and hate by the thought he or she is evil.
- Guilt is a negative emotion triggered by a *belief* about one's own action.
- Anger is a negative emotion triggered by a *belief* about another's action.
- Liking is a positive emotion triggered by a *belief* about another's character.
- Pride is a positive emotion triggered by a *belief* about one's own action.

In his *Strong Feelings* Elster adds emotions that are triggered by the belief that someone else deservedly or undeservedly possesses some good or bad characteristic:[42]

- *Envy* is a negative emotion caused by the deserved good of someone else.
- *Indignation* is a negative emotion caused by the undeserved good of someone else.

- *Pity* is a negative emotion caused by the undeserved misfortune of another.
- *Malice* is a positive emotion caused by the undeserved misfortune of someone else.
- *Gloating* is a positive emotion caused by the deserved misfortune of someone else.

All these emotions, according to Elster, are induced by beliefs that are firmly held. In contrast, emotions like hope, fear, love, and jealousy are held in terms of belief probabilities. Emotions like regret and disappointment are generated by thoughts about what might have happened or what might have been done. Since emotions can be triggered by nonconscious appraisal, giving rise to automatic "reflex" emotions, we accept Elster, but only providing that we define beliefs to include nonconscious default beliefs and imaginings that may lie behind "reflex"-type emotions. In addition, Elster's "definitions" take for granted that there is antecedent appraisal and subsequent "feeling toward" the object.

Carroll rejects the "illusion theory of fiction" that claims we actually do believe. He also rejects the notion that there is a willing "suspension of belief" that the monsters and so on are fiction. As we have shown, he argues that we cannot just suspend belief at will. Similarly, Carroll rejects the "pretend theory of fictional response," which denies we are genuinely responding with emotion and affirms that the fear is make-believe or "pretend-fear." This, he argues, would presuppose that the emotions can be engaged at will. Carroll advocates what he calls a *thought theory of emotional response* to fiction. As we said earlier, he argues that emotion can be generated just by entertaining the thought of (say) something terrible, something beautiful, something disgusting, and so on. With thoughts, the content is merely entertained without necessarily any commitment to its being the case. We can reflect on highly pleasant thoughts, say, of a car, and such reflection can generate feelings and be emotionally arousing. The implicit belief that just entertaining the thought can be emotionally arousing is why a politician (as in one case) might call his opponent a "sick, pathetic, permissive, tax-spending, bureaucratic liberal" and himself a "humane, visionary, candid, hard-working reformer." Carroll is right. Just entertaining a certain thought can be emotional, just as we can think of our car going over the side of a cliff into the sea and feel a certain fear. Advertisers, by stimulating certain thoughts—nothing more, nothing less—can generate feelings and emotions that can be highly supportive of a brand.

Patrons of horror movies can be frightened by what they know does not exist because horror films are symbolic. Just entertaining the thought alone can do it. While consumers know that vampires do not exist, evil, violent, predatory people do: the vampire is thus a vivid emotional metaphor. On the

question of consumer interest in being horrified, it provides relief from boredom, and consumers take pleasure in the contrast, appreciating their security
more, as when we step back into a warm house on a cold day.

Carroll speaks of *entertaining thoughts* rather than *imagining*, on the ground
that the latter implies that consumers themselves are the primary source of the
content of their thought when the fictional story or film itself provides all that
is needed. This may be so, but Carroll's entertaining and imagining are for
practical purposes much the same.

To link Carroll's views with those of Lyons,[43] we are horrified in films, and
so on, if and only if we are (1) in a state of physically felt agitation (e.g., shud-
dering), (2) which is caused by entertaining the thought that the monster is a
possibility and the evaluation that it is both threatening and impure (if only
threatening, the emotion is fear, if only impure, the emotion is disgust), and
(3) our thoughts are accompanied by some desire (e.g., not to touch the monster).
We can extend this way of identifying "if-and-only-if" principles to the development of commercials.

Appraisal of Emotive Stimuli: Dimensions Appraised

In figure 2.1, appraisal is shown to be at the core of the emotional process, in
that emotions are shown as responses to appraisals that link to:

- Value systems or the key concerns of the consumer
- Events, actions, or attributes (aspects) of objects
- Beliefs or imaginings of the consumer
- Wishes, wants, and desires of the consumer

Value systems constitute criteria against which appraisals are made. In fact, appraisal could be defined as an evaluation that concludes that some envisaged
state of affairs is worthy of approval or disapproval. The appraisal in figure 2.1
takes the form of a value judgment. Events, actions, and attributes (aspects) of
objects (real or imagined) constitute the stimuli that trigger the process of generating emotion, while beliefs and wishes shape the specific emotional responses that result. (While appraisal in figure 2.1 is at the core of the process,
it was listed as the third element (after value systems and emotive stimuli, already discussed) at the beginning of this chapter in setting out the process of
generating emotion.)

Appraisal is a necessary antecedent to evoking emotion. We typically take
this for granted and may omit it, as Elster does in *Alchemies of the Mind,* in

defining different emotions. Thus he defines shame as a negative emotion triggered by a *belief* about one's own character. But this is just a shorthand that leaves out appraisal. We should say that shame is a negative emotion triggered by an appraisal leading to a belief about one's own character and feelings toward self. But even this does not tell the whole story, since, as shown in figure 2.1, appraisal and the other elements in the process of generating emotion form an interacting system; although we think of appraisal leading to inferential beliefs, it is also true that initial beliefs can influence appraisal, just as the consumer with firm beliefs about the efficacy of some product will appraise the evidence accordingly.

Without appraisal, there is no emotion. This is sometimes denied, since we can find ourselves depressed without knowing what brought it about.[44] In other words we have no sense of any appraisal having taken place. But this simply means that *conscious* cognitive appraisal is not always a necessary antecedent to emotion: there can, however, be nonconscious appraisal. The eliciting context of an emotion can be nonconscious, without any sense of any cognitive appraisal of triggering stimuli.

Zajonc (1994) discusses the nonconscious *affective* influence that occurs after repeated exposures to the same stimuli. Repeated exposure to an ad or a brand strengthens verbal and visual memories of that ad or that brand. This means the *availability principle* is likely to operate. The availability principle claims that easy availability in the mind means easy recall so that when a particular product is wanted, the brand most available in the mind is the one most easily recalled from memory. The availability principle even explains why *not* rounding off a price to, say, $10 but using the price $9.99 creates the illusion of a price within the $9 range: it is the 9 that is most available in memory. However, the "repeated exposure effect" is something more: it is the increase in a positive attitude toward something as a direct consequence of mere repeated exposure.[45] This increase in positive attitude is independent of any *conscious* cognitive appraisal.[46] When consumers find themselves repeatedly exposed to some brand or ad, more liking is generated, providing that the stimuli were not unpleasant in the first place.

Appraisal is the process whereby the personal relevance of the event, action, or attributes to a person's concerns or values is apprehended. Consumers may be aware of a "gut" emotional reaction or reflex emotion but nonetheless have no sense of any conscious appraisal. Appraisal in fact need *not* be a conscious process. While an appraisal is a type of *evaluation* (an evaluation of the value or personal significance of some event or situation) it may not be a deliberate conscious act and instead may be an instantaneous apprehension. *Conscious* appraisal, as opposed to a nonconscious appraisal, is an *interpretive* act, that is, a sense-making process. A conscious appraisal results in beliefs that are positive or negative about the object. A nonconscious appraisal falls back on nonconscious default beliefs or imaginings.

Appraisals of emotional stimuli give rise to "feelings toward" the object (event, action, attribute). "Feeling toward" is thinking about the object with feeling. Thinking with feeling encompasses more than just thinking. There is a good deal of difference in content between just thinking about the attractions of a vacation resort in a detached way versus thinking about the vacation resort with feeling. As Goldie points out, many traditional accounts of the emotional process are perfectly consistent with experiencing no feelings at all.[47] Acting out of emotion is acting with emotion that includes "feeling toward" the object, and this, Goldie argues, helps to explain the difference between acting out of emotion and action undertaken solely for other reasons.

It cannot just be assumed that the object or stimuli appraised has a stable, constant meaning, as additional learning by consumers changes meanings for them. For this reason Livingstone recommends replacing the notion of the stimulus with that of the *text*.[48] She argues that the notion of a stimulus views the objects of appraisal (e.g., an ad or product) as either unstructured and amorphous or as something fixed in meaning, that is, as something that has invariant, singular, and unequivocal meaning. The metaphor of the text (as postmodernists constantly remind us) can be applied to anything that is being evaluated or appraised, not just to written material. The use of this metaphor is a reminder that "reading" any text makes sense only from a certain point of view. Using the metaphor of the text, whatever is appraised has to be "read" with the possibility that different readings may result in multiple possible meanings, given that the social context can be a major factor in any reading. This is true of all ads: there are multiple possible readings (interpretations), though cultural factors and belonging to the same market group are apt to produce somewhat similar readings. But popular interpretations can be very remote from academic interpreters, who are apt to bring close scrutiny and a mass of concepts to the reading.

Substituting the metaphor of the text for the concept of the stimulus implies a rejection of the two extremes (1) that the thing being appraised is of unequivocal, stable meaning and (2) that appraisal amounts to trying to make sense out of a "blooming, buzzing confusion." Livingstone claims that persuasion research in psychology evades the crucial problem of specifying the exact text prior to interpretation by taking unambiguous texts that no academic reader feels obliged to challenge. In fact, the nodel of cognitive psychology as a form of information processing tends to deny the complexity of texts in everyday life. Viewing emotional stimuli as texts with multiple meanings draws attention to the hazardous nature of ensuring that an ad will be interpreted as intended and of predicting the corresponding emotional responses. However, while bearing

Livingstone's caution in mind, we will continue using the term *stimuli* to refer to the object of emotion, whether it is an event, action, or attribute.

According to Frijda et al., the *dimensions* that are appraised, at the most abstract level, are relatively few: namely, pleasantness/unpleasantness; familiarity/unfamiliarity; expectedness/unexpectedness; beneficial/harmful implication; uncertainty about implications; personal responsibility for an event; whether what has occurred is relevant to our well-being or that of a significant other; controllability/noncontrollability; and conformity/nonconformity to social norms.[49] There are other lists. Thus Ellsworth claims that *appraisals* that *evoke the emotions* involve one or more of the following: novelty; valence; uncertainty; obstacles and control; agency; and norm/self-concept compatibility.[50] Only experience in using these lists can determine which (if any) is best for the marketer's purposes. However, the Ellsworth list seems more suited to marketing, and we consider here each of the dimensions.

Novelty. Perceptions of novelty relate to emotion, because novelty has the potential of excitement. Novelty is tied to emotional *curiosity,* which is exploited in teaser advertising, as when in advertising a yet-to-be-launched new car there is a cover over the actual car. There is an innate desire for novelty. Once humankind solved the problem of mere physical survival, it is argued, boredom became a problem, with rebellion against the constraints of the repetitive pattern of life. This is not to reject all routine. No one is able to cope with complete novelty or novelty with no link to the past. People, like other animals, find most interest in situations where there is novelty to be explored but where similarities to past experience can still be used to guide that exploration. As Simon says, people (and rats) find the most interest in situations that are neither completely strange nor entirely known—where there is novelty to be explored but where similarities and programs remembered from past experience help guide the exploration.[51]

Valence. This term, as it is used in psychology and first coined by Kurt Lewin, refers to the psychological value dimension of the object; high positive or negative valence indicates something highly relevant to one's concerns. (This seems all-embracing and could be said to be the overall class rather than a species, covering in fact all of Ellsworth's list).

Uncertainty. Uncertainty is a dimension of products, and so on, that, if positive, evokes curiosity or hope, while uncertainty about things perceived as negative leads to anxiety and fear. Promises in advertising generate hope in the face of uncertainty as to performance while generating uncertainty about negative events (e.g., illness) creates anxiety and fear.

Obstacles and control. Obstacles to goal attainment frustrate. A high sense of control provides a challenge, while a low sense of control results in fear and frustration. The significance of the word "cool" in youth-speak is its implication of being in control, that most admired of qualities. Consumer advertising commonly implies a promise to enhance the consumer's control of his or her life. In fact, a good deal of advertising is about control in one form or another. Advertisements depict the loss and restoration of control, for example, the loss and regaining of credit cards while on holiday. The loss and restoration of power is a strong emotional theme.

Agency. Highly negative events caused by others evoke *anger;* negative events caused by one's self provoke a sense of *shame or guilt;* and negative events caused by chance result in *sorrow.* A good deal of fund-raising for charities shows negative events caused by others (e.g., war atrocities) to exploit shame and guilt and negative events caused by chance (e.g., floods) to evoke sorrow leading to compassion.

Norm/self-concept compatibility. The violation of social norms gives rise to the fear of social disapproval and a feeling of shame. Advertising may attack the validity of any alleged social stigma attached to a product by showing it being endorsed by a celebrity (e.g., President Ronald Reagan using a hearing aid) or, on the contrary, showing some common practice (e.g., not using a deodorant) to be violating social norms. Advertising commonly exploits the power of embarrassment, as in the sudden discovery one has violated a social taboo. Although deodorants came into being in nineteenth century France and were advertised in the United States in the 1920s, deodorants were not extensively used until advertising exploited the fear of embarrassment ("and then a friend told me why").

Another way of looking at the appraisal of emotional stimuli is to ask about the *positive feelings* that might potentially be aroused. These feelings relate more directly to values and are more amenable to analysis than those in the previous lists.[52] (The analysis in the illustrative example section in chapter 1 draws on this list.)

- *Activation:* feelings of being alive and full of vitality, as opposed to bored and sluggish
- *Relatedness:* feelings of having warm, close, loving relationships with others as opposed to feeling lonely, isolated, and like an outsider
- *Hedonic tone:* feelings of achieving inner harmony, and relaxation, as opposed to being in a state of anxiety (fig. 2.4)
- *Competence:* feelings of being in control of life and having a sense of accomplishment, as opposed to feeling unable to cope.

These are the value-feelings that need to be projected by an offering. They should be built into the marketing to arouse appropriate emotions. This is not something to be done mechanically but requires a good deal of creativity.

Figure 2.4.   Hedonic tone: inner harmony, freedom from anxiety. Courtesy Ford Motor Company.

Some Key Assertions for Marketing

1. If the consumer's emotions are to be tapped, marketing management must recognize that emotions arise whenever there is an opportunity to enhance something consumers hold dear or there is a threat to what they hold dear.

2. If marketing is to link its offering with the ultimate concerns of the consumer, this means tying the offering—in product, price promotion, and distribution—to the consumer's system of values. Consumers are very conscious of the polarities in the human condition and prefer the most agreeable polar extreme, for example, having an enjoyable rather than miserable life, being socially accepted rather than rejected, and so on. In particular, consumers in their purchases are concerned to buffer their self-esteem; to protect some sense of personal integrity, as in rejecting an unfair deal; to enhance interpersonal relations; to avoid unnecessary risk; and to carry out their tasks. The relative weights given to the various values defines the consumer's system of values. However, values change from one generation to another through cultural drift. Yet values and lifestyles associated with earlier periods in the life of the consumer can, if aroused, give rise to a strong emotion of nostalgia. All consumer trade-offs involve criteria emanating from values, and all values are both emotionally grounded and emotionally nurtured. But values per se can be a poor predictor of buyer behavior unless we can assume certain beliefs about what the consumer regards as appropriate means for supporting and promoting them.

3. If marketing management is to harness consumer values, it must recognize that values cannot be proved right or wrong in any absolute sense but can only be defended. Yet changing value judgments (without changing values) is possible, since they are tied to descriptions of the item, person, or situation and of the anticipated consequences of choice. Marketing may redescribe events or situations to fit the consumer's values. One form of redescription lies in reframing the message, which is something less than attempting to change an entire perspective.

4. If marketing management is to do something new, then, unless it is concerned with just relieving discomfort, it should be sure to stimulate the imagination about the possibility of experiencing something novel. However, if imagining means the consumer *creates* the content of his or her thought, marketing management need not stimulate the imagination so much as get the target audience to simply entertain thoughts that link to the emotions.

5. If marketing management is to stimulate the adoption of its product, it should remember that *emotional* pleasure lies in fantasizing that involves anticipating and, by extension, attending to and contemplating the novel and that this can be the spur to buying. This means that marketing should feed the fantasy and stress curiosity to shape the anticipation. It should dramatize the consumption experience from which flow the contemplation and the feelings that induce buying action. One of the aims of market-

ing is to induce consumers to (1) anticipate/contemplate buying with pleasure and (2) buy without reservations, as otherwise we buy with anxiety, which makes us susceptible to postpurchase dissonance.

6. If marketing management is successful in tapping the emotions of its target audience, consumers are disposed (if reasonable interpretation permits) to believe whatever their emotions want them to believe. Tapping the emotions can be tied to the novelty of the product/brand/offering; the arousal of curiosity; alleviating frustrations; or the fear and shame of violating strong social norms. There can be a primacy of image over objective facts. Images and symbolic meanings are as much a real part of the offering from the consumer's point of view as the real stuff of which the offering is composed. A product may even be built around the symbolism of the name. There is a hunger, hence a demand, for new images that either delight the senses, allow us to indulge in fantasy, or hold out the hope of novelty. Consumers, like everyone else, are apt to reconcile hopes and ideals with harsh reality by wishful thinking to the effect that the ideal will be a reality some time, some place.

7. If marketing management adopts, say, slice-of-life advertising, it is too much to assume that the target audience identifies with the fictional characters. Instead the target audience needs to be assisted to assimilate the situation, coming to see the situation both from the point of view of the characters in the commercial and from the outside as well.

8. If marketing management is to form a truer view of consumer motivations, it should recognize that, contrary to popular opinion, the consumer can contemplate with pleasure the upholding of social norms or some system of uplifting values in buying.

9. If marketing's offering is to have maximum impact, this means that every part of the offering should be positively appraised by consumers, as the more positive the appraisal, the more positive the emotions that attach to the offering. Appraisal is the process whereby one apprehends the personal relevance of an object or stimuli (event, action, or attributes) to one's concerns. It is useful to explain stimuli in terms of consequences of events, actions of agents, aspects of offerings, and specific emotional dimensions. All dimensions of the offering have the potential to be emotional triggers.

10. If marketing is to generate liking for its offering, repeated exposure increases the audience's positive attitude towards the offering.

11. If marketing management is interested in arousing positive feelings tied to values, activation, relatedness, hedonic tone, and competence are useful classifications of types of positive feelings.

3

Generating Emotion: Beliefs and Wishes

Beliefs and Wishes/Wants/Desires

In the last chapter, appraisal was shown to be linked to the consumer's value system and feelings toward emotive stimuli. But appraisal is also linked to beliefs and desires, which are also connected to the consumer's value system. This is not to suggest that all relevant beliefs and desires are present in consciousness at the time of the appraisal. There may in fact be nonconscious appraisal. Perception can immediately be followed by emotional response, as Damasio's work (see chapter 1) suggests. This is the basis of the likability heuristic, where the consumer just goes along with gut feeling. Young children are attracted to many products without having acquired the evaluative concepts that are needed for the attraction to be tied to conscious judgment.

This chapter considers the role played by beliefs and desires in the process of generating emotion, the fourth element in that process as listed in the first paragraph of chapter 2 and shown in figure 2.1. There are limitations to this way of showing how emotion is generated, since, in a dynamic system, any emotion generated can lead to a chain of emotions. We agree with Elster that studies of emotion have a static character in that they merely explain, in a one-shot situation, how emotions arise or affect behavior.[1] Their weakness is that they do not help one to understand how an emotional event precipitates a sequence of emotional events. Elster is right. There is a need to study the dynamics of emotion.

Beliefs

A belief is a disposition to accept that certain statements (for example, about a product's performance) are more likely to be true than false or that certain things should be done (for example, to shop around before choosing) or not done. Beliefs can be true or false, unlike wishes/desires/wants, which can only be fulfilled or frustrated. Beliefs lie behind pursuing ends and can control and inform action, all the way from shaping wants to making specific brand choices to guiding postpurchase actions such as returning an unsatisfactory product. Hence marketing has an interest in what leads to favorable appraisals that influence beliefs.

Wollheim argues that beliefs map the world to provide a picture of it, while wishes/wants/desires target things in the world at which to aim.[2] Without the picture provided by beliefs, there would be nothing for desire to target and therefore no basis for emotion, as emotion "rides into our lives on the back of desire." Similarly, Searle argues that beliefs have a "mind-to-world" direction of fit because their aim is to represent how things are in the world.[3] In contrast, wishes/wants/desires have a "world-to-mind" direction of fit because their aim is to represent not how things are but how we would like them to be or how we plan to make them be.

Velleman, argues that the two distinct features of belief are *accepting things as true* and *aiming at truth*.[4] The fact of belief aiming at truth explains the difficulty of believing at will. No cognitive state that is not governed by mechanisms designed to track the truth can be a belief state. To accept a self-evident falsehood does not amount to believing it. Forming, revising, and extinguishing beliefs in accordance with new evidence and argument is the evolutionary function of belief. If such a function were not present, survival would be far more at risk. Belief thus contrasts with illusion and fantasy, which are not affected by objective evidence. To claim that beliefs aim at truth does not exclude being misled, but, unlike fantasy, a biased belief responds to new evidence, other things remaining equal. Valleman thus posits a strong role for beliefs in rejecting what is contrary to evidence. However, much depends on what we consider to be evidence, since what is considered evidence in favor of the existence of God is not of the same nature as evidence for the existence of atoms. Valleman acknowledges that indicators of truth will only count as reasons to believe if there is already a cognitive inclination that makes us susceptible to their influence. In other words, the indicators must fit the consumer's perspective or cohere with the way he or she currently views the world. But evidence first has to be selected and interpreted, and emotion has a habit of biasing the selection of evidence and interpreting it to favor existing beliefs. Perhaps Valleman exaggerates in talking about beliefs aiming at "truth" and might better speak of beliefs aiming at truthlikeness (verisimilitude), since truth is not something we necessarily recognize. We only know, from our perspective, what seemingly indicates the truth.

Beliefs can be viewed as being composed of internal mental structures that seek to direct actions in line with their informational content about what seems to be the truth. Expectations are beliefs about future states that are apt to be emotionally grounded. When the consumer talks about having high expectations about a product, he or she is disappointed if those expectations are not realized—a disappointment that is all the harder to bear because it undermines self-confidence about beliefs.

In chapter 1 we reported some of the emotional elements in cola buying and consumption for certain youths. The protocols or verbal statements were also used to identify:

- *Beliefs about the product.* Examples: "I buy a [cola] not just to relieve my thirst but to give me a lift when I'm tired and need to be refreshed." "The caffeine in the sugar in the [cola] gets me jumping so whenever I play a sport it helps me play better." "All [colas] are not equally as good."
- *Beliefs about brand attributes.* Examples: "Classic Coke has the original formula which is best. Other [colas] contain preservatives."
- *Beliefs about experiences with the brand.* Examples: "Classic Coke is not watery and has no unpleasant aftertaste." "Coca-Cola doesn't give me that terrible syrupy taste that is much too sweet." "I regard Coca-Cola as part of my life." "It has a unique taste." "Coke Classic does not satisfy my thirst." "Coca-Cola does not hurt my throat like other [colas] do when I drink it straight down and feel it settle in my stomach." "The gas in Pepsi causes burping. This can be eliminated by letting the can sit in the fridge for a while." "Coke rids me of all that tension." "TV commercials say it cools down your nerves at the end of the day and they are right."

Beliefs are tied to information, and new information affects beliefs: beliefs are in fact parasitic on the interpretation of the information that beliefs encode. As more information is acquired about an offering, beliefs become refined and more specific in steering action. When the output of an appraisal is new information, beliefs are changed, or at least modified. Of particular significance is information that adds to the consumer's repertoire of concepts. For instance, when beliefs about the long-term consequences of smoking cigarettes changed from the view that the effects were benign to the view that the long-term effects were lung cancer, people came to grasp the concept of carcinogens and to relate the tar in cigarettes to lung cancer.

While what one understands about a product is tied to how it is described, one first has to grasp the concepts in that description for that understanding to be meaningful. Consumers are aware of a great number of products but do not have always a sufficient grasp of the concepts needed to understand how they function. Thus we may be aware of digital cameras but without any clear idea of their workings, function, or advantages or what they could do to enrich our life. Typically manufacturers overestimate the knowledge possessed by the public about their product: they confuse awareness of the product with understanding of what the product is about and what it can do to enrich one's life. The learning of new concepts can lead the consumer to endorsing a new set of beliefs. Thus, in learning about the concept of the mouse as an add-on feature of computers, we come to endorse that feature, that is, we come to believe in its benefits. Where consumers fail to grasp the concept of the product and its differences from rivals, they cannot develop a genuine preference for it. Although consumers may profess belief in a product they have little conception of, a clear understanding is required for the belief to be firm.

All consumers wish their beliefs to be based on the best information available, but time pressures and cost factors usually rule this out. Consumers are likely to collect just enough information to determine a brand preference but not to become experts on the product class. If the consumer currently has emotional leanings toward one brand rather than another so that he or she has an implicit favorite, information search will be cut short. The interpretation of any information is colored by the consumer's emotional orientation. If it is possible to interpret new information to confirm the current orientation, that orientation is likely to stand. This is not to suggest that if someone *wants* to believe something, they will. Just as no one can make a person believe that black is white, one cannot make one's self believe it, even if it is a matter of life and death. Yet, as Haack says, "while, to be sure, one cannot believe at will, wishful and fearful thinking are a problem precisely because the will can get in the way of our judgment of evidence."[5] Beliefs aiming at truth or truthlikeness can be undermined by emotional influences.

Marketers should aim to get their brand accepted as the implicit favorite model before any search or evaluation is attempted. In this way new information is more likely to be molded to fit the existing desires of the consumer. This is aided by associating the brand with positive emotional experiences. There can be, contrary to Elster, cognitive impenetrability in emotional experience, in that emotions cannot always be changed by changes in beliefs. Thus consumers may now accept that the Concorde is as safe as any plane flying the Atlantic, but the emotion generated by the Concorde disaster in Paris may remain unaffected by such beliefs. More typically, emotional experiences are "cognitively penetrable" by beliefs, just as fear of the snake on the ground is removed by knowing that it is simply a toy.

Beliefs are seldom isolated beliefs but are part of a system. This is why some are more fixed and less easily given up or imagined to be false than others. It is also why attacking a single belief (e.g., that smoking is not harmful) may be ineffective when it is part of a supporting network of beliefs (e.g., many smokers live well into old age, and I'll be one of them). It is also the reason why the retraction of a false statement in an advertisement may not undo the damage. Those consumers who believe the falsehood are likely to retrieve other beliefs in support when these other beliefs remain in place. New beliefs are more easily endorsed when not in competition with other sets of beliefs. In any case, most beliefs involved in buying are tacit. Memory stores the resources out of which beliefs come into being, and most overt beliefs are "manufactured" from information already possessed, as when consumers arrive at their beliefs about the overall cost of shopping by calling on the rules of addition. And beliefs are not always based on objective facts but are linked, via the emotions, to loyalties, hopes, fears, self-interest, and social conditioning so that they relate only imperfectly to supporting evidence.

Some beliefs reflect wishful thinking. Self-deception occurs when false beliefs are unchecked for the sake of some goal to which the individual is emotionally attached. Wanting something to be true (e.g., a cure for baldness) is emotionally compelling and influences the selection of facts, so that the consumer selectively perceives, remembers, and interprets, filtering out assaults on beliefs that are emotionally held. Consumers do not generally have the time, the ability, or the desire to retrieve and canvass all their beliefs, so that when one is emotionally disposed to believe that there is a cure for cancer, the result can be an uncritical endorsement of choices in line with that belief.

Consistency theory in psychology talks about people's need to reconcile beliefs with each other and with feelings, though it is not uncommon for emotions to point in one direction and beliefs in another, since they are not necessarily present in the mind at the same time. Thus Campbell's (1987) expression (mentioned in chapter 2): "known to be false but felt to be true." Consumers are often pulled between the desire for something and the simultaneous knowledge that it is not for them—a high-powered car, for example. On the other hand, when emotion is strongly felt, selectivity in the choosing and interpretation of evidence can dampen the search for truth. Beliefs can be influenced by emotion, as when buyers get immediately excited about "the house of our dreams" and rush into believing that the poor condition of the house will not be a problem. Beliefs commonly trigger emotions such as anger, as when one believes, say, that a waiter is not treating one as well as expected. However, it is probably true that, in general, consumers seek to avoid cognitive dissonance by reconciling beliefs and feelings.

An untenable belief can be held in place by an emotion such as fear. Thus a consumer may believe in the magical properties of some product because she fears any doubt would take away her one chance of being cured. But beliefs supported by long experience are not likely to be overturned by contrary evidence. Even if the consumer has no rejoinder to the evidence and accepts the logic of experts about her favorite brand of antidandruff shampoo being relatively inferior, she is still likely to remain with her favorite brand if her own experience is supportive of its effectiveness. This is one reason why converting customers from rivals is so much more difficult than retaining existing customers. In fact, when experience with a brand is highly favorable, it is difficult to get the consumer to even think of changing at all. This is because such thinking cannot even begin without some energizing stimulation and cannot be sustained for long without a strong emotional urge to do so.

As already pointed out, the view that emotions are always triggered by conscious appraisal is undermined by findings that show that emotions can bypass cognition. Many now accept that when an event threatens values or what people hold dear, an emotional response can come from perception alone, without conscious appraisal. However, Elster (1999) claims that while this might be true of primal emotions like fear, it is an open question as to how extensive this bypassing is. Elster is reluctant to acknowledge that emotions can arise from appraisals that bypass cognition; yet perception and emotion can occur simultaneously without conscious cognitive appraisal. Goleman, taking into account LeDoux's work, points out that incoming signals arriving from the senses allow the amygdala to screen every experience ("Will it hurt or will it please me?") so that the amygdala acts as an emotional sentinel, able to bypass the neocortex: the amygdala has us spring into action, while the neocortex is still evolving its more "refined plan of action."[6] What all this means is that consumers can react to stimuli ("the incoming signals") with positive (approving) or negative (disapproving) emotions, without conscious reaction. This is the basis of the likability heuristic, whereby choices may be made purely on the "gut reaction" of liking. Finding something attractive does not necessarily imply any conscious cognitive appraisal or evaluation.

Wishes/Wants/Desires

If the consumer desires something, he or she contemplates bringing it about, just as in believing something the consumer regards it as right or true. To want product X is a disposition toward using, consuming, or possessing that product. To say John wants a Mercedes is to say something about John's potential future action. A want, unlike a wish, takes account of feasibility, so that neither wants nor goals are entertained that are impossible to fulfill. A "want" is represented in the mind as benefits sought, so the wanting for a product is not just wanting the product regardless (e.g., in poor condition) but is wanting it under some description of benefits promised. This is why description of the offering is so important and why marketing focuses not on a product per se but on benefits or potential experiences. Wants are always comparative, in that whatever is wanted is wanted through comparison with the alternatives displaced.

Wants and desire take account of what is believed to be achievable, whereas wishes do not, and incompatible wishes can be happily entertained. On the other hand, unlike beliefs, wants and desires do not aim at being in some way correct. Consumers may have strong desires for many products that they acknowledge to be undesirable, like cigarettes. They seek out many pleasures that conflict with their values, feeling propelled along by the desire itself. Such people may evince a desire not to desire but find resistance difficult. This is the case with many drug addicts.

Wishes, wants, desires and needs are often used as synonyms for each other, but for marketing purposes it is useful to distinguish their usage.

- A desire is a want that the consumer is acutely aware of not having realized. One aim of advertising is to elevate wants to desires so that the consumer thinks about the product, inquires about it, and is moved by facts about it.
- A need is an absolute requirement. On this basis we may need things we do not actively want (car safety belts) and want things we do not really need (cigarettes).
- A wish, unlike the typical want, is a yearning for some state of affairs regardless of the feasibility of attainment or the incompatibility of the wishes. Thus people may wish to be taller, more beautiful, more slim, and so on, and these wishes may have to remain unsatisfied. Yet consumers can imagine their wishes being satisfied, and advertising often exploits this fact. Emotional stimulation is often tied to an appeal to wishes in the use of fantasy in ads.

The demand for a product rests on wishes/wants/desires and beliefs. The wants consumers seek to satisfy are not necessarily the strongest but may cohere with beliefs about what is the wise or sensible thing to do. Thus we may long to smoke a cigarette but believe it to be harmful over the long term. There is this eternal conflict between the desire for "instant gratification" and beliefs about what is best for the future. Although changes in beliefs (e.g., about the relationship between health and weight) can lead to rejecting some specific product (e.g., ice cream loaded with calories), there will remain the corresponding longing that is still awaiting satisfaction. The longing remains to reemerge if the context is right. This is why a product may at first fail but be successfully reintroduced by eliminating or adding some ingredient, component, or feature. The automobile itself looked like being just a fad at the beginning of the last century until technical developments made driving easier.

Fantasies and Wishes as Motivators

In general we talk about reasons, in terms of wants/desires and beliefs, motivating an intention to take action like buying. But as Velleman (2000) says, we can be motivated by fantasies and wishes. In terms of motivating action via fantasy and wishes, Velleman substitutes "fantasies" for beliefs and "wishes" for wants/desires. Unlike a belief, a fantasy involves entertaining something as true regardless of whether it is in fact true. Fantasies are only true in the imagination, since fantasies are manipulated to feed the appetite and provide excitement and a substitute for the real thing. Fantasy does not attempt to track the truth. Yet in a way fantasies qualify as unconscious beliefs because they are what the unconscious has instead of beliefs. Wishes, unlike wants and desires, can be for anything, regardless of whether it is obtainable, whether it exists, or whether it would be approved by the consumer when not fantasizing. Velleman describes three categories of behavior that feature motivation by imagining:

1. *Behavior expressive of emotion.* Fantasies and wishes can motivate behavior that is expressive of emotion. Velleman quotes Hume (1711–1776), who pointed out that anyone suspended in a cage at a great height is likely to tremble with fear even if he knows that he is securely supported. He is fearful not because he thinks he is going to fall but because he imagines falling, and the imagination (fantasizing) arouses the same emotion as belief. This relates to Carroll's argument (see chapter 2) about emotion being activated simply by entertaining the thought itself. As Velleman says, the person in the cage is likely to take action—clinging to the bars of the cage, shouting for

help, and so on—just as if the fantasy was true. Wishes and fantasies give rise to behavior that is expressive of emotion—in our gestures, when we cower in fear, hide our face in shame, clench fists in anger, or shake the head in regret. But acting out fantasies and wishes, Velleman argues, goes beyond just gestures. A simple example would be setting one's watch a few minutes ahead to help prevent being late. We act on this fantasy and hurry accordingly, showing that we are motivated by cognition other than a belief. He quotes a great number of similar examples to demonstrate behaviors that cannot be explained by the wants-and-beliefs model. How often, he asks, does mere fantasy of disaster lead us to check if we have locked the house on leaving or worry about not having turned off the stove?

2. *Fantasizing about being others.* When consumers fantasize they are assuming another identity, such as that of some celebrity, it is a case not of saying "Let me behave as if I am Madonna" but of saying "I am Madonna" and proceeding from there into certain patterns of behavior (e.g., spending on clothes). The consumer acts out of motives she now imagines she has. As she cannot desire what is not obtainable, she falls back on wishes. When fantasy and wishes move the consumer to behave in a certain way, they carry out the same motivational role of belief and desire.

3. *Talking to ourselves* is defined as imagining ourselves in conversation with someone else. Some of us do it every time we read a book and have a somewhat one-sided conversation with the author about what he is claiming! While fantasizing about being someone else is a way of imagining that is wishful thinking rather than realistic, goal-pursuing action, talking to ourselves, Velleman argues, is wanting not just to imagine conversing with that someone else but rather wanting to actually converse with that person.

How does all this square up with what has already been said? Person (1996), as discussed in chapter 2, talked of fantasizing in terms of being an internal dialogue that serves some wish-fulfilling function. Velleman would not object but would regard this view as too narrow. With regard to Campbell's talk of belief-dependent emotionality—suspending or manipulating beliefs in respect to fantasizing—Velleman would reject the term *belief*, since beliefs aim at truth, and would substitute for it the word *fantasy*. He is right, since beliefs do need to be kept separate from fantasizing for the sake of conceptual clarity. Finally, with regard to Carroll's distinction between *entertaining* and *imagining* (that the word *imagine* implies that consumers themselves are the primary source of the content of their thought, whereas, because the fiction itself provides all that is needed, the word *entertaining* is more correct), we suspect that Velleman would argue that it would be difficult to conceive of entertaining a thought without input from the imagination. In any case all might agree that marketing should arouse or intensify the anticipation, attending to, and contemplation in fantasizing about the novel aspects of the product (including services/experiences) as this feeds the motivation to buy through self-persuasion via the imagination.

Velleman argues that mastering the distinction between fantasy and reality requires that we learn to seek what can actually be obtained and seek it in ways that will actually lead to its being obtained. As Velleman says, being able to separate desires and beliefs from wishes and imaginings (fantasies) is the first step toward mastering the distinction between fact and fiction. It would be difficult to cope with life unless the separation is generally made.

It is argued on occasion that consumers live in a world of wishes and imaginings. For some postmodernists, ads that evoke images of satisfaction aim at filling the consumer's mind with pure fantasy to stimulate buying in line with the fantasy. Baudrillard argues that our situation today is one of hyperreality, where distinctions are dissolved between objects and their representations, so we are left with only simulacra that refer to nothing but themselves.[7] For Baudrillard, a simulacrum is a copy of a copy for which there is no original. In the world of hyperreality, the only reality is TV ads and other signifiers, so media images become the reality, and any distinction between the real world and that of the pervasive media becomes eroded. Baudrillard argues that the use-value and exchange-value of products has given way to "sign-value," where products become primarily symbols to be consumed and exhibited. Thus, for example, the consumer, through designer labels, consumes the symbols of power, status, and prestige. Baudrillard sees consumer society as a constellation of sign-values that constitute a hierarchy of prestige. He claims that the distinction between reality and unreality, as a consequence, has been eradicated. There is a breakdown of the distinction between the real and the imaginary, as the consumerist society, and the technology that goes with it, creates its own reality for marketing purposes. Rejecting any stable relationship between the signifier (e.g., product) and the signified (symbols of prestige), signs do not have a distinct referent to any reality. There remains only simulacra, as signs (e.g., in ads) lose contact with the things signified. Consumers are said to create their own reality. The world of the consumer is seen as composed of pure simulacra, or the hyperreal, where just the signs themselves constitute the realm of experience. In a situation of strong hyperreality, the consumer is unable to separate reality from illusion. On the other hand, in a situation of weak hyperreality, the consumer separates the two but prefers to remain with the illusion, with no distinction between the real and the representation. Poster claims that ads tend to mirror the fantasies of social groups, so the academic analysis of consumption needs to shift from the analysis of technical/economic factors to the linguistic categories of sign and signifiers.[8] As TV controls the context of its message, even heroes can be created of villains.

We have no difficulty in seeing the role of fantasy in the life of the consumer. Women's magazines (and many men's) are all about fantasy and escapism. However, it is doubtful that readers are unable to separate the reality from the fantasy or that they read these magazines for their correspondence to the reality. If people could not distinguish between, say, the science fiction fantasies in films and reality, they would quickly find that life outside the cinema was impossible. And advertisers are not as influential as critics think, even among school children. There are always rival sources of information. Studies discussed by *The Economist* (January 6, 2001, p. 65) found that children as young as six years of age understood the purpose of commercials and distinguished them from entertainment, while fantasy was distinguished from reality.

Many would agree that modern media can help to form as well as to mirror realities, but this does not result in a situation in which sign or image is everything. It cannot all be done with mirrors. In addition, as Velleman makes clear, our imaginings are typically accompanied by countervailing beliefs, embodying knowledge of the facts one is imagining to be otherwise. These countervailing beliefs are in constant competition with imaginings, as is the recognition that wishes are not in the realm of the attainable. It is just not true that consumer behavior approaches being psychotic. But, of course, fantasies and wishes can lead to self-persuasion and action that is self-deceptive. One simple example is that of top designers putting small sizes on large clothes. The customer, pleased at finding she can get into a much smaller size of dress, is emotionally driven into purchase.

Factive Emotions

Not all emotions are generated in the same way. One distinction is between factive and epistemic emotions (see fig. 3.1 versus fig. 3.2), though both depend on what Gordon calls the belief-wish condition (BWC).[9] Gordon's model of the generation of emotion restricts itself to "wishes" and "beliefs"; hence his "belief-wish condition model of emotion." Factive emotions are grounded in a belief that, as a matter of fact, the emotive stimuli (events, action, or attributes of objects) have occurred, while epistemic emotions arise from the belief there is uncertainty about the likelihood of the emotive stimuli arising.

In the case of factive emotions, the BWC model consists of a belief that the relevant emotive trigger or stimuli did occur or is now happening. While Gor-

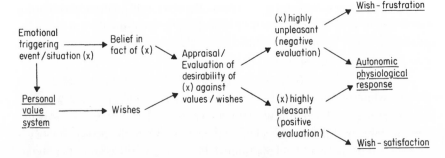

Figure 3.1. Belief-wish condition: factive emotions.

don talks in terms of the belief being true, the model does not require this. Fantasy/imaginings may substitute for beliefs and may not be based on any objective reality. Erroneous perceptions can excite the imagination into believing something that is just not so. In Prussia, dueling persisted until the end of the nineteenth century, often provoked by imaginings about slights upon honor. Similarly, consumer beliefs about the level of service at a hotel can emanate more from imagined indifference than the facts on the ground. Whether the corresponding wish is for something or against something relates to whether the belief or fantasy is positive or negative. We will go along with Gordon in speaking only of belief, with the recognition that, in fantasizing, fantasy substitutes for belief and wishes for desires.

The BWC may involve several beliefs. Thus, as Gordon points out, the emotion of "indignation" presupposes not only a belief relevant to anger (about some insulting action having occurred) but the belief that what occurred was unjust. In addition, since a person may at one time be emotional (e.g. annoyed) about a number of things, it is possible to frustrate several wishes and not just one.

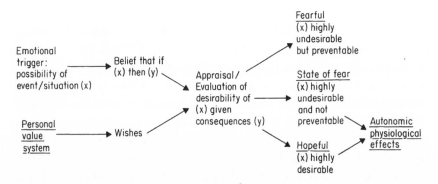

Figure 3.2. Belief-wish condition: epistemic emotions.

Is emotion congruent with belief, as the BWC model suggests? As pointed out earlier, emotions can lag behind beliefs. The model needs a little revision, since beliefs can be updated by new information without emotions immediately catching up. There can also be overbelief (believing beyond what is warranted by the evidence) and underbelief (not believing when the evidence warrants belief). This is still a problem with the bovine spongiform encephalitis ("mad cow disease" or BSE) crisis in Europe. There is now overbelief that eating meat is fatal; in an earlier period there was underbelief about the dangers.

As Lyons says, emotion need not be in line with belief at all. He points out that we can be conditioned to react (say) to some situation with fear yet believe, contrary to our reaction, that there is nothing really to fear.[10] This happens all the time with "white coat syndrome," which makes blood pressure readings unreliable. This is a variation of the thesis that consumers can feel something to be true while knowing it is false. We can be in a world of fantasy yet be pulled at the same time by beliefs that track the truth. It is a problem in air travel. Travelers know the statistical risk is negligible but still fantasize about disaster and feel too frightened to fly. This fear of flying is reinforced when wide publicity is given to an air crash, since the "availability principle" then operates, whereby what is most available in memory is what is most easily recalled as a belief. Gordon (1987) gets around Lyons by saying people sometimes react "as if" they believe something is the case rather than actually believing it. Consumers act "as if" they believe there is something to fear, worry about, and so on. For example, in buying a car, consumers can be full of anxiety even though they have trust in the dealer. But how can it be assumed that it is "as if" when consumers react without consulting their true beliefs? One answer is to claim that the initial surge of emotion is consistent with holding default beliefs that come into play at the time, before any reflection has had time to occur. After reflection, consumers no longer entertain the initial emotion, because the default belief is shown to be wrong.

Gordon seems to assume that everyone will go through a process of conscious reflection on the emotive stimuli giving rise to the emotion. But this need not be so. There can be "reflex" emotions or "gut" emotional reactions, as reflected in such sayings as "He just saw red" and as demonstrated by Damasio (see chapter 1). This is the objection Goldie levels at Gordon.[11] He argues, in line with Damasio, for what he calls "recognition and response" (what we earlier called perception and response) in that what comes first, after recognition (perception), is the emotional response itself—the feeling of excitement at seeing the new house—and not relevant beliefs about costs. The cognitive reflection comes too late to explain the emotional response.

Belief systems can be affect-driven, with likes and dislikes being the glue for bringing about a coherence. Beliefs may track the truth but be sidetracked by liking, providing the evidence allows this, which it usually does, given the scope for interpretation. With affect-driven belief systems, emotion becomes a major influence on what is believed. Sniderman et al. claim that affect-driven belief systems are more common among the less educated.[12] Many consumers move directly from feelings to brand preferences and then reason backward to establish supportive beliefs, if need be, to justify that preference. This happens all the time in buying. The consumer may be moved to buy a puppy because of its appealing looks but justifies the purchase on the ground of needing a guard dog. Reasoning backward uses a chain of reasoning to justify choice rather than employ some crude rationalization. In line with this, TV advertising may use an emotional appeal first and only later supply reasons to justify it. We suspect that affect-driven belief systems are common among all consumers, though more common among the less educated. It is estimated that up to 20% of adults are functionally illiterate in Western societies. They represent a substantial slice of consumers. Yet marketing knows little about them, since marketing research tends to ignore them as difficult to contact and interview and their behavior as difficult to record.

An allied problem lies in explaining emotional responses to fictional characters in TV commercials and films. Can we claim that consumers are acting "as if" they believe (say) the monster in a horror film is a real threat, as Gordon's position would suggest? To answer in the affirmative leaves us open to Carroll's objections to the illusion theory, or the pretend theory, of emotional response (see chapter 2). When Carroll argues that genuine emotions can be generated by just entertaining the thought of (say) the monster, he is rejecting any assumed belief in the existence of the monster. He argues that to have a belief is to entertain a proposition assertively (e.g., I believe X as a fact), whereas a thought is merely entertained without any commitment to the case that X is true. In other words, one can entertain some thought (e.g., of jumping off a cliff) and be emotional as a result without having any corresponding supporting belief (e.g., the belief that one is in fact about to jump off the cliff).

In line with Carroll, marketing promotions may aim at getting the target audience to entertain emotionally charged thoughts about the product, suggesting certain emotionally satisfying experiences in, say, driving a certain car or whatever. Newspapers often follow this formula. One British newspaper engaged its audience with fantasy projections of a new Europe dominated by a German "fourth Reich"—as a way of arousing its audience to the danger of further European integration. However, it may be wrong to assume, as Carroll does, that to hold a belief is always to consciously entertain a proposition assertively. Beliefs are not always firmly held, while we cannot rule out the possibility that nonconscious beliefs act as default beliefs, though it was suggested earlier that such may be more in the nature of fantasies.

Carroll denies that emotion always links up with a desire (want or wish). Thus one may feel saddened by the sudden realization that one will die someday without that leading to any desire, such as wanting to live forever. We would question Carroll's claim, as this illustration (the only one he gives) is not very convincing, since a desire or wish would be involved, for example, to be able to choose how and when to die. The same goes for any similar examples. We can assume there is always a link between emotion and desire, since emotion energizes desire.

Drawing on the work of both Lyons and Gordon, the process of generating factive emotions when developing ads or sales appeals (as shown in fig. 3.1) consists of:

1. A *belief* (consciously held at the time or some default belief) that something is so. Thus the consumer may believe as a fact that he or she will be able to afford a remodeled kitchen.
2. A *wish* for some state of affairs, like wishing to have a new kitchen.
3. A strongly positive or negative *appraisal* of what is believed as either in line with wishes or out of line with wishes, as occurs when the consumer finds he or she cannot afford to remodel the kitchen.
4. An *autonomic physiological arousal* following the appraisal, like strong disappointment.
5. The physiological arousal is accompanied by: a *feeling of wish-frustration* if there is a very negative evaluation, as in this case when the consumer finds he or she cannot afford the kitchen remodeling; and a *sense of wish-satisfaction* if there is a very positive evaluation. Either of these will cause a positive or negative emotional state.

Gordon uses the term *wish* rather than *want* or *desire,* in recognition that "wish" suggests a yearning with less concern about feasibility. A wish may be entertained even when incompatible with other wishes. Wishes can operate with fantasy to motivate action. This is a distinction we have already made, but it is an important one for marketing. In marketing surveys, respondents are frequently asked what they want (whereby they take account of feasibility) when the marketer's interest really lies in respondents' "wishes"; it is the manufacturer who has a better sense of what is practical.

Wish-frustration is a state in which someone simultaneously wishes something were not true yet believes that it is. Wish-satisfaction is the state in which someone simultaneously wishes that something were the case and believes that it is. Appraisals leading to actual or anticipated wish-satisfactions and wish-frustrations cause factive emotions.

Gordon accepts that emotions like "surprise" involve expectation-frustration rather than wish-frustration while words like "disappointment" involve both expectation-frustration and wish-frustration. But this limitation is less valid than appears. Although words like *surprise* or *disappointment,* out of context, do not signal whether they are negative or positive, they do so within a specific context, in that to arouse emotion, there must be a negative or positive appraisal of the object or emotion-arousing stimuli.

Epistemic Emotions

Epistemic means pertaining to knowledge. Epistemic emotions involve fear and hope. If we fear X happening, we wish X not to occur because X brings with it undesired consequences Y. Similarly, if we hope X will happen, we wish it to be so, as we anticipate consequences Y to be pleasant. Spectator sports typically generate epistemic emotions associated with the hope of winning and the fear of losing. Spectator sports are an interesting demonstration that consequences need not go beyond the intense emotional feelings that can arise from a loss or a win.

There are four cognitive appraisal processes that mediate the choice of how an audience is going to react to a fear appeal:

1. The perceived severity and nearness of the threat
2. The perceived probability that the threat will occur
3. The perceived ability of a coping behavior to remove the threat
4. Perceived ability to carry out the coping behavior.[13]

This being so, advertising would find it advantageous to give the target audience information on some or all of the following: (1) the severity and nearness of the threat; (2) the probability of its occurrence; (3) the effectiveness of certain coping strategies; and (4) the speed and ease with which the coping response can be implemented. Thus ads for investment services might stress the probability of losing money in equities and suggest that money can be quickly transferred to "safer" alternatives.

The generation of epistemic emotions (see fig. 3.2) includes the first four conditions listed for factive emotions, namely: (1) a belief (consciously held or some default belief) that something is so; (2) a wish about some state of affairs; (3) a strongly positive or negative appraisal of what is believed as either in line with wishes or out-of-line with wishes; and (4) an autonomic physiological arousal following the appraisal. However, the actual type of emotional state generated by epistemic emotions differs from factive emotions in that epistemic emotions depend on:

- Attitudinal reasons (AR) for wishing X to occur or not to occur. These AR for wishing or not wishing X to occur relate to why consequences Y of X are viewed as desirable or undesirable in terms of the consumer's wishes. Thus one consults a physician because one may fear a heart attack (X), because consequences Y might be death, and because one values life. Attitudinal reasons refer to the consumer's attitude to consequences.
- Epistemic reasons (ER) are the reasons for believing the likelihood of X. Epistemic reasons refer to the reasons for believing the likelihood of the occurrence or nonoccurrence of X.

The ER might objectively be more supportive of not believing in the likelihood of a heart attack than in believing in it. Nonetheless, the patient commonly acts as if she believed otherwise. This is a key point made by Gordon about epistemic emotion: the evidential base for X occurring (e.g., an accident) may be very small indeed, but the intensity of epistemic emotions may have only a weak relationship with either the probability of X occurring or with the expected value (probability X weighted by consequences Y) since people can get extremely emotional over what even they admit is a negligible probability of the event, or whatever, happening. This was dramatically illustrated after the terrorist attack of September 11, 2001, when so many people avoided air travel, bought gas masks, and demanded vaccination against anthrax. Being very concerned about an issue makes us exaggerate the risks involved: fantasy/imaginings take over. The fear of nuclear war is very real for many people even though the probability is small. In fact when the Reagan-era television film *The Day After* showed people actually surviving a nuclear Holocaust, support for Reagan among viewers actually rose because the dramatized consequences of it were not as dreadful as they had imagined. Another example was over the issue of passports in Great Britain a few years ago. In only 80 cases over many months were passports actually delivered late, yet an extraordinary national panic arose as people began to imagine what it would mean to miss their vacation. This is interesting, since if we were to assume that consumers were acting according to the norms of rationality, the degree of concern would coincide or be positively correlated to what the evidence indicates. This commonly does not happen, as people get emotional by just entertaining the thought.

People get emotional not only about potential disaster but also about potential gain and are equally unconcerned about probabilities. Thus if people really took seriously the probability of winning the lottery, they would be much less likely to buy a lottery ticket. But the fantasy of winning is emotionally compelling, and hope replaces any sober calculus of probability. The fear of harm

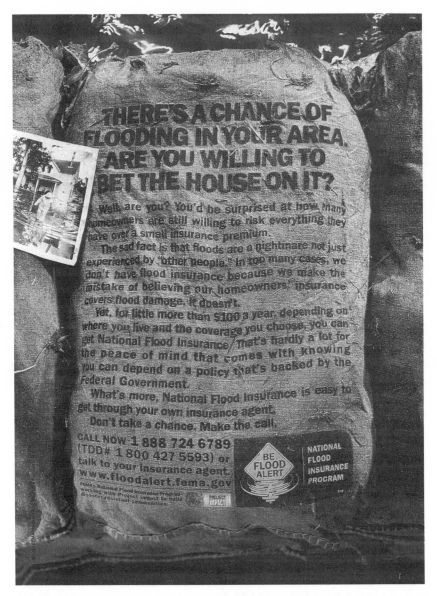

Figure 3.3. An appeal to fear. Courtesy FEMA/National Flood Insurance Program.

and the hope of gain are emotions that can close out assessments of probability.

When entertaining a thought is highly pleasant or unpleasant, people (consumers) have AR for wishing or not wishing something, and the accompanying emotion does not necessarily take much account of likelihood (ER).

In fact, people may have no ER and still get emotional. This is to suggest not that demonstrating the probability of an event does not affect emotional response but simply that the degree of emotion arising need not correlate directly with probabilities. For example, America in the 1950s faced no real danger of a communist invasion, but fear nonetheless was tangible, as expressed concretely in the McCarthyite witch hunt and abstractly in such Hollywood horror movies as *Invasion of the Giant Killer Ants*. This means that advertising would have to overdramatize the probabilities of consequences for the probabilities themselves to play a major role in affecting behavior. For example, in antidrug campaigns, many users regard the probability of serious consequences as negligible for them, just as soldiers in the trenches dismissed the likelihood of their own death. The dramatization of consequences has been a traditional staple of antidrug campaigns since the film *Reefer Madness* in the 1930s, which claimed that using marijuana would lead to grotesque insanity. The problem lies in getting people to believe it could all happen to them. Consumers do not wish to think about being unable to work, but insurance advertising may get them to do so, though more by dramatizing what it would be like than quoting probabilities. Epistemic reasons are typically easier to change than attitudinal reasons. It is much easier to get people to accept low or high probabilities by quoting statistics than to change attitudes regarding the consequences. The probabilities need to be highly dramatized to hit home.

If we wish to avoid consequences Y of X (e.g., heart attack from high blood pressure) and believe the X cannot be prevented, then the emotional state will be one of fear. If, on the other hand, it is believed that X can be prevented (e.g., by drugs to lower blood pressure) we may be fearful but not necessarily in a state of fear. In either case, the subject's focus will be on reducing vulnerability (e.g., by following the doctor's advice). On the other hand, if we wish X to occur and also have some expectation that it will occur to produce the desired consequences Y, then the emotional state will be one of hope. Thus if we wish to lower our weight and expect it to produce an improved appearance, we will be emotionally hopeful.

A distinction between primary appraisal and secondary appraisal is relevant here. Lazarus claims that two kinds of appraisal are at work in influencing the type of emotion experienced.[14] Primary appraisal assesses the relevance of the state of affairs for the person's well-being (that is, relevance to values or key concerns) while secondary appraisal assesses the capacity for coping with the event after its occurrence. Lazarus argues that it is the combination of these two appraisals that affects the emotional outcome. Thus if the primary appraisal is negative (e.g., signs of aging) and the secondary appraisal of coping potential is low, then sadness or depression may result. If the primary appraisal is negative but the secondary appraisal of coping potential is high (new antiaging cream) then the emotion will be one of hope. What advertising commonly does is to enhance perceptions of being able to cope and so to provide hope.

Moods

Can the BWC model accommodate "mood" as an emotion? Moods can be the lingering effects of events that are emotionally charged. We may no longer be angry with an investment service that failed to live up to expectations, but something lingers on in mood. Yet the link between mood and action is not clear, as moods themselves lack specificity about their object. Moods can range from very positive to very negative and in this way influence *expressive* action, like showing laughter or tears, or affect how actions are carried out, like acting wearily or energetically. In any case, they are capable of influencing appraisals and, as such, influence feeling toward the object.

Positive emotional experiences are found to be recalled more when a person's mood is positive, while negative emotional experiences are found to be recalled more when a person's mood is negative, though the evidence for this claim is not unequivocal.[15] Since a positive mood favors buying, many service organizations are concerned with putting customers in a good mood. This raises the question: What affects mood?

A person's mood is said to be affected by four factors:[16]

1. negative affective (emotional) happenings, like stressful events, and positive affective (emotional) happenings, like an unexpected bonus. It is easier to induce a positive mood by getting customers to actively do something (e.g., getting the prospective customer to drive the car) than through just stimulating thinking, whereas it is easier to induce a negative mood through just thinking than through actively doing something. Hence the importance of the tactic of getting customers in some way involved in doing something, like testing a product for themselves.
2. Positive affect is generally higher in the morning and in spring and is lowest in winter.
3. Traits and temperament: people differ in their predisposition to moods. Happy people are attracted more to pleasant things, while sad people prefer serious stories, nostalgic stories, and nostalgic music. This explains why nostalgia returns in bad times, and advertising exploits it.

4. Characteristic variability in the individual. People seek a TV program corresponding to their mood, and since ads congruent with mood are more likely to be absorbed, advertisers should select ads that are congruent with the TV program.

There is interest in the marketing literature in how moods can be engendered or manipulated, taking into account these four factors. Cantril's classic study of deviant social movements like the Nazi party shows how national moods develop.[16] Major cultural change anywhere is accompanied by uncertainty, fear, anger, and greed. Innovations can be major sources of cultural turbulence, with social change in particular generating emotion because there can be no nonusers. In times of cultural turbulence, social values are under attack, expectations are not being realized, and people face uncertainty. As a consequence, they lose the informational anchors that help them understand what is happening. The result is a sense of lost competence and a mood of life being unmanageable. This often happens on a minor scale.

Advertising's antidote is to exploit nostalgia—by using the symbols of an earlier period; its celebrities, songs, brand names, and even brand slogans ("Timex takes a licking but keeps on ticking"). On the other hand, appeals to the optimistic young might be deliberately antinostalgic, condemning the past (e.g., for its lack of freedom for women) and pointing to the advantages of the present ("You've come a long way baby"). Where social values are rigid and predictable, the result may be a national mood of boredom; an antidote in advertising is to project brands as adding excitement to life. And on occasion advertisements deliberately jeer at social norms when their target audience is doing the same.

Cantril's work can be fitted into the BWC model. When people wish to maintain social values that they believe are being undermined, there is persistent wish-frustration and a corresponding negative mood. People may be fearful or be in an actual state of fear about the future with their AR, hating the changing social values that threaten their status and self-esteem and accepting ER for believing in the likelihood of an erosion of social values. The net result is vulnerability-avoidance action to stop the tide of change or to seek protection from its consequences. It is easy thus to see why advertising reflects current values more than it creates them. Williamson shows how closely advertising reflects the values of the era.[18] She gives exhaustive examples of how greed and individualism can be embodied in advertising, for example, in an ad showing a taxi splashing a bus line of people. And advertising can also represent the public arena as a place of threat or failure, as when Arthur the cat hides his cat food and rings the doorbell of his yuppie master to escape danger on the street.

Illustrations of Factive Emotions

We have talked about wishes and beliefs, not saying much about what might be wished and what might be believed. We can depict the factive emotions commonly exploited in advertising, drawing on Taylor's work on the *self-assessment emotions* (pride, envy, shame, guilt, integrity, etc.) that are directed toward self, personal status, and the need to believe in one's self-worth.[19] More specifically, the emotions of pride, guilt, shame, and embarrassment are all tied to maintaining self-esteem. The rule in all service activities is never to undermine the customer's self-esteem.

Advertising frequently fuses images, symbols, and brand, thus suggesting that the brand will bring pride of possession, result in the envy of others, remove guilt or shame, or give the buyer a glow of integrity. Advertising promotes the idea that how one appears to the world is a result of what one buys. On the other hand, as Douglas argues, saying what the brand or company is against may have considerable appeal, as in the Sprite ad that says: "Sprite is not a status symbol or a badge that says who I am. . . . Image is nothing. . . . Thirst is everything. . . . Obey your thirst."[20]. Douglas claims that people generally are more aware of what they hate than what they love. This is generally so, though it is exploited more in political advertising than in advertising to the consumer.

Emotions of interest to marketing typically occur in a social context where an audience is present or felt to be present. If we look at the emotional appeals exploited in marketing, they are more commonly tied not to biologically driven emotions like anger or fear but to the cognitive/cultural emotions such as appeals to self-image, duty, or self-esteem. These are the ones of interest to Taylor.

The self-assessment emotions are factive in that they presuppose as a fact (1) that a person has risen above or fallen below some personal expectation or standard and (2) that in so doing there is a change in status or standing in the world. If, as one of his or her values, the consumer wishes his or her status in the world to be increased, or at least maintained, then an increase in status leads to wish-satisfaction, and a decrease in status leads to wish-frustration.

Taylor views beliefs as the core of what makes an emotional experience what it is. Lying behind the beliefs that identify an emotion (the identificatory beliefs) are a number of supporting beliefs that explain one's being in a certain emotional state and that stem from one's appraisal of the triggering stimuli (events, actions, or attributes). Explanatory beliefs make the emotional state understandable or intelligible; inferences from the explanatory beliefs support the identificatory beliefs. Taylor sets out both sets of beliefs that lie behind each of the self-assessment emotions. But can emotional responses lag behind beliefs and so be out of line with beliefs? Taylor would answer that beliefs still play the central role, but in this case the relevant beliefs would be the relevant "default" beliefs that have prominence until the new beliefs were internalized.

Taylor focuses on belief rather than belief plus wishes (wants/desires) because she claims that wishes are reflected in the beliefs themselves. Gordon (1987) denies that this is so—on the legitimate ground that it presupposes that "desiring" is always equivalent to "believing desirable," which is just not so. As pointed out earlier, beliefs refer to how the world actually is, while wishes relate to how we would like the world to be. This is important for marketing. For example, consumers desire to eat many food products that they do not believe are wholly desirable. A problem, therefore, is to ensure that customers see what they desire as also desirable, as when the candy manufacturer reduces the calories in a chocolate bar. This is at one with trying to get the consumer to buy without reservations so that there is no postpurchase dissonance. Finally, Taylor's focus on beliefs would presumably treat fantasies as perceived beliefs, though this ignores the claim that the biological function of belief is to track the truth.

The last section of this chapter sets out the BWC model for each of the self-assessment factive emotions, incorporating Taylor's identificatory beliefs and explanatory beliefs. We have added the epistemic emotions of fear and hope, as these can be of crucial importance in persuasion. A brief note is also given of the types of ads that link to these emotions. But ads need not seek to arouse strong emotions. Think of a current ad in Europe for American Express: "handy if you get robbed in America." The fear message is there, but touched with humor. Advertisements can put an audience into an emotional state (think of the anger aroused by ads showing the killing of baby seals); more typically, consumer ads seldom arouse strong emotions to the extent that autonomic physiological changes are consciously felt. In what follows, we discuss the self-assessment emotions in sufficient detail to provide the understanding needed for promotional purposes.

Pride, Self-esteem, Envy, Conceit, and Arrogance

When consumers experience the emotion of pride, they feel they shine in the reflected glory of what they are proud of, because they believe that it is something esteemed in their social milieu. On the other hand, taking great pleasure in a possession does not mean necessarily taking pride in it. Something can give a great deal of pleasure (e.g., certain types of films or magazines) while one feels ashamed about the purchase. This means that one is buying with reservations. Goldie (2000) argues that pride involves "feelings toward" but not desires; this is just not so, since to take pride in something means we desire that state of affairs, as it is tied to self-esteem, in that whatever supports self-esteem is something of which to be proud. Ads that boost self-esteem are very common. One American political fund-raising letter sought to appeal to the self-esteem of its audience by saying: "This letter is not going to just anyone, only proud flag-waving Republicans like you."

Pride is involved in securing a bargain. Obtaining what is perceived as a "bargain" is emotional. Consumers feel pride in having come out on top— beaten the system. There is also the excitement of shopping for a bargain. Similarly, when consumers obtain something that is scarce, they take pride in achievement. The more a seller suggests that something is scarce or unavailable, the more attractive it is. Some consumers will buy anything that appears to be "only one left." Scarcity enhances desirability. Football tickets and the new, not-yet-generally-available car can increase their perceived value by seeming to be scarce. The recognition of scarcity as a selling point leads to the practice by retailers of ensuring that display boxes of merchandise are never actually full. As Cialdini says, opportunities are more valuable to us when their availability is limited.[21] As he illustrates, an imperfect postage stamp would have no value were it not for stamp collectors prizing scarcity. The emotional focus is on the loss, as we are more concerned with losses than corresponding gains. Thus it is much more effective to emphasize the loss from not insulating a home than to say how much could saved by insulating. Cialdini points out that when an item is scarce, we want it even more if there is competition to get it; witness the battles when department stores first open their doors at sale time. What is particularly interesting is Cialdini's claim that the joy lies not in experiencing the scarce product but in possessing it. In other words, the pleasure lies purely in possession, with the consumption experience very much secondary. This is an important caveat to the general rule stressing the consumption experience only.

When a consumer has pride in a possession, others are thought to envy him or her. Williamson claims that advertising often induces consumers to imagine themselves transformed by the product into an object of envy by others, which, in turn, justifies the buyer loving him- or herself![22] Veblen's theory of the leisure class held that the desire to be wealthy arose because wealth helps one achieve esteem and the envy of others.[23] This, of course, is not universally true. There are many wealthy people who go out of their way to avoid envy; they do not want to put themselves in a position of superiority to others and incur dislike and resentment. Elster regards envy as unique in being the only emotion that no one wants to admit to others, as envy generates the suspicion: "I am less because I have less." For Elster, the cognitive antecedent of envy includes the belief that someone has something I want, together with the counterfactual belief that it could have been me. If this is so, what does Elster make of the sayings "How I envy you" or "I'm green with envy," which are common usages of the term "envy"? He would argue that the meaning of any word is tied to context and that in these contexts the sayings are simply suggestive of admiration and not the emotional state of envy. An alternative is to make a distinction between malicious and nonmalicious envy, as Goldie (2000) does. Elster is, however, right to argue that many "cut off their nose to spite their face" by excluding the most competent from holding office because of envy. On the other hand, many consumers do seek to attract nonmalicious envy: it is good for promoting a sense of self-worth.

Pride as an emotion, as opposed to being a character trait (as when we speak of someone being a proud person), when excessive, leads to "conceit" or "arrogance." A conceited person, for example, contrasts his or her achievements with what he or she believes to be the typical achievement of others within his or her social milieu and feels superior as a result. If one just takes such superiority for granted without seeing any need for evidential support, one is regarded as arrogant. An arrogant person may resent praise as implying that he or she went beyond what others might have expected him or her to accomplish. Thus we have Sartre refusing the Nobel Prize with undisguised contempt for those who felt themselves in a position to do him honor. Advertising that is directed at our conceits and arrogance takes the form of assuming that its target audience knows what constitutes the "best" and takes it for granted as their due.

The BWC model (see the last section of this chapter) for the emotion of pride shows that if sellers wish to arouse pride, they must aim at subtly demonstrating that the brand is:

- Highly esteemed by the target audience's social milieu and/or relevant reference groups
- No longer beyond the target audience's aspirations and merely symbolizes their aspiration level
- Socially visible
- Enhancing of self-esteem and status

Advertisers may wish to overturn pride in possession. In this case, the aim is to get the target audience to reinterpret the facts so what is currently esteemed is no longer esteemed by those "in the know." This is the strategy of British Knights athletic shoes. In a $15 million campaign created by the Deutsch agency, the theme was: "Your mother wears Nike—choose change," to make the point that Nikes were no longer on the cutting edge. As the young always seek to distance themselves from their parents in clothing, music, fragrances, and so on, this campaign resonated with its target audience.[24] Denim, once very much the cloth of the young, has become less popular for the moment among the young as they seek to detach themselves from the symbols of their parents' generation. Combat pants are much preferred. Only firms that have managed to nuance contemporary youth culture, such as Diesel, manage to prosper in such a market.

Shame, Embarrassment, and Self-respect

To feel shame is to feel exposed to condemnation by some real or imagined audience for breaking a taboo that people feel obligated to uphold. Such taboos are tied to culture. As Elster (1999) says, the Greeks felt shame over losing any competition and felt little shame in inducing shame in others in circumstances that would not be justified today. Elster points out that in shame, the tendency is to hide or run away. With guilt, the tendency is to make repairs, though it could be argued that this only occurs if the guilt is accompanied by remorse.

The alleged difference between Western culture and that of Japan has often been stressed in terms of the difference between guilt and shame cultures. In Japan the emotion of shame is potentially pervasive, and the radical act of hara-kiri, or ritual suicide, is associated with it. When former taboos are no longer taboos (e.g., children outside marriage), there is no longer any sense of moral obligation or shame. To feel shame is the reverse of feeling proud. However, both emotions view the situation as it is imagined that others might view it: as circumscribed by social norms. And what lies behind all social norms? Elster argues that social norms are enforced by the emotion of shame. People are indoctrinated to act in accordance with the social norms of society, or at least the norms of their social milieu, or otherwise feel shame. Elster gives the key role to shame in bringing about compliance with social norms. This is important, as Lal claims that non-Western countries, like those in Asia, can import the best of American technology and practices without undermining cultural values, as has occurred in Western societies. This is because Eastern cultures like Hinduism, Islam, and Confucianism are "shame" cultures with cultural mores enforced by social norms.[25] On the other hand, Western cultures are "guilt" cultures, which depend on belief in God and Christian teaching for the enforcement of social norms. Once such beliefs no longer hold, social disintegration begins to occur. Elster would disagree, as he argues that social norms in Western societies operate equally through the emotion of shame and accepts that shame is typically more intensely painful than guilt. There has simply been a cultural drift in Western cultures, with a change in what is subject to social norms. When there is no longer any shame in violating some traditional taboos, shame does not cease to occur but transfers to upholding emerging new values, like concern for animal "rights" or the environment, because people want to identify themselves with creating a more caring society.

Shame is a complex act, in which physical expression plays a part, for example, in the lowering of the eyes, covering of the face, or hanging of the head. Shame relates to self-respect and thus to self-esteem, since a person who has done nothing to invite condemnation (i.e., no shame) maintains a sense of self-respect. Self-esteem is also tied to humiliation, in that humiliation involves a loss in self-esteem, as those who feel humiliated believe that they have not been given the recognition to which they are entitled. With the emotion of humiliation, there is a belief that one is being pushed into a lower-status position.

The exploitation of shame in persuasive communication assumes that the target audience is committed to the relevant social norms, as the strategy is to demonstrate condemnation by relevant reference groups. World War I posters traded on shame ("What did you do in the war, Daddy?"). In World War II, appeals to shame were enlisted in maintaining secrecy ("Careless talk costs lives"). There were also the poster cartoons by Fougasse that depicted Hitler sneaking and eavesdropping under chairs, sitting behind talkers in train carriages, or staring from a portrait in a club. Of course, the relevant reference groups must have credibility. This has been the problem in using entertainment and sports celebrities in antidrug campaigns. Few are believed, as they are collectively viewed as secret drug users. Unfortunately, many reference groups for the young show contempt for traditional values, with the result that shame no longer operates so extensively with respect to antisocial behavior.

If advertising wishes to remove a sense of shame in the use of a product, the strategy is to show relevant reference groups indulging in the activity without shame. This was the strategy of the American cigarette ads in the 1920s that showed cigarettes being endorsed by the most socially prominent women in Europe. But commercial advertising is not generally involved in arousing feelings of shame, though it is common in not-for-profit and public service advertising that seeks (say) to stop abortion, cruelty to animals, drug-taking, and so on. Yet commercial advertising can be slanted toward triggering shame, as when ads make ethical claims about what constitutes responsible behavior, like taking out a life insurance policy, with the implicit suggestion that the target audience should feel shame at not having done anything so far.

The desire to avoid embarrassment through being socially maladroit lies behind many actions. Even the so-called principle of reciprocity, whereby people feel an urge to repay any form of social debt, may be based on a desire not to be embarrassed. Embarrassment is commonly exploited in commercial ads, as it is intimately tied to personal morality, respect, and a sense of integrity. Shame is the deeper and more disturbing emotion. While a person can feel both shame and embarrassment at the same time, embarrassment is always tied to a social context. As a consequence, embarrassment requires a socially appropriate response to remove it. It is this failure to respond appropriately that perpetuates the embarrassment, since it is essentially a failure in perceived image management. Ads recognize this by suggesting ways of responding appropriately. In contrast, shame is not localized to any particular social context. And whereas embarrassment arises from someone perceiving that an action will be judged by others as socially maladroit, in the case of shame there is the feeling that one's self as a whole would be condemned.

Advertisers trade on the desire to avoid being judged as foolish by, say, smelling bad or wearing the wrong clothes. Entire industries have arisen to alleviate embarrassment that advertising has done much to arouse in the first place. Deodorants are a case that readily comes to mind. It is not that advertising "created" the want for deodorants. This would suggest that people had no underlying appetite for such a product or were motivationally empty until advertising came along to promote deodorants. Advertisers simply persuaded consumers to give more weight to the problem. Advertising highlighted and dramatized the function a deodorant could perform in removing smells that could cause potential embarrassment ("Even your best friend might not tell you"). Advertising has been very adept at exploiting the social consequences of bad breath, acne, body odor, and so on. And advertising can dramatize the worst social nightmares, such as the ex-girlfriend marching into a restaurant and pouring a plate of spaghetti over the head of the former lover and his new paramour!

Embarrassment is contagious. We identify with an embarrassed person's failure to respond in a way that removes his or her embarrassment. There are many potential situations for embarrassment. Thus, while attaching sexual associations to a brand can be appealing, aggressive sexuality (as in the Calvin Klein ads) can be embarrassing to many potential customers. The initial Woolworth "buying inducement"—that no product in the store was more expensive than a few cents—worked well in poorer times because it reduced the potential embarrassment of asking the price and being unable to afford it. Even when the target audience is the educated elite, ads can still appeal to the avoidance of embarrassment. The *Financial Times* with its "No *Financial Times*, no comment" ad, suggests the paper saves its readers the embarrassment of being unable to make intelligent comment. The *Economist* asks: "Would you like to find yourself sitting next to you at dinner?" against a scene of finding yourself sitting next to Henry Kissinger on the plane. Here life is presented as a series of knowledge tests, with the potential embarrassment and blow to self-esteem of failure to know. To avoid showing ignorance of current and international affairs, reading *The Economist* is a must!

Many ads exploit the viewer's vicarious embarrassment arising (say) from not using the more effective dish detergent. A good deal of "slice-of-life" advertising draws on the consumer's capacity for vicarious embarrassment. Saatchi and Saatchi acquired their original reputation through social advertising, as in, for example their famous picture of a pregnant man in an ad for the Health Education Council in Britain ("Wouldn't you be more careful if it was you that got pregnant?") (fig. 3.4). Shame, on the other hand, is not catching, though people may feel shame over the actions of those with whom they are related ("significant others") or might be thought to be related, just as we might be ashamed of the actions of our compatriots when we are abroad.

Many social norms are followed to avoid embarrassment and not just shame. One is the principle of reciprocity. This is the obligation to return a favor. Scratch my back and I'll scratch yours. It is this principle that lies behind charities sending fund-raising letters that contain a little gift, like address labels, and why market research firms send out questionnaires in envelopes containing a dollar bill. Manufacturers follow the principle every time a salesperson leaves a little gift or sends out a gift to clients at Christmas time or, more commonly, simply shows enormous courtesy and makes great efforts to be obliging.[26] Showing courtesy affirms another's worth and obliges a reciprocal gesture such as being prepared to listen to a sales pitch, as well as inducing a favorable disposition to please in return. In all these cases, the prospective buyer feels obligated to make a positive response.

Guilt and Remorse

People who feel guilty believe they have broken the rules of an accepted authority, either human or divine—rules they believe it is their duty to uphold. Although guilt is typically associated with violating the laws of God or civil government, the authority could be some authority figure from the past or present whose rules we have been conditioned to obey. A good many emotional "hang-ups" about spending money can be traced to early childhood conditioning by parents. Older people exhibit a stronger sense of duty and willingness to accept authority, which means they are more prone to guilt than the young, who question the rules. There is a generation gap. In the last century, a British monarch said: "Yes, we do enjoy opening hospitals, and no, we are never bored." This can be contrasted with the ethos of a later generation, as embodied in Princess Diana, who expressed the supremacy of personal feeling over austere, externalized duty, which is why she caught the imagination of so many, sharing their values in this way.

We do not feel guilty for the actions of others but feel shame for what oth-

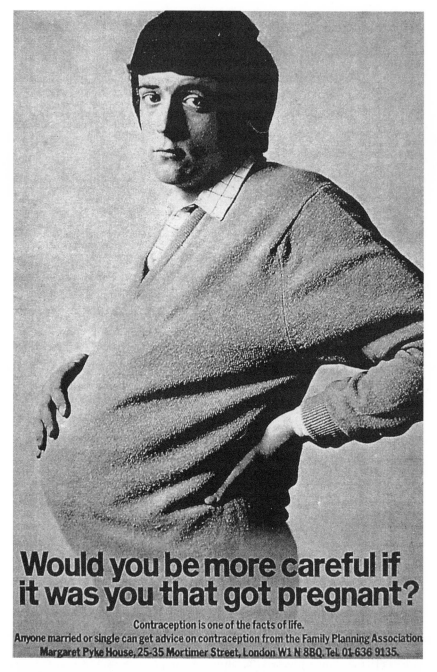

Figure 3.4.   An appeal to shame/integrity. Courtesy M. C. Saatchi.

ers do if they are associated with us. Only if we believe ourselves responsible in some way does guilt arise. With guilt, unlike shame, restitution or atonement is typically demanded. If guilt is accompanied by a wanting to compensate for wrong done, the emotion is that of remorse. This explains why amnesties for the tax evader can be effective. Shame is associated with a submissive demeanor, guilt with self-punishment. Shame inhibits action, while guilt may also interfere with positive action with its capacity to haunt its victim. Negative emotions like guilt and shame exercise greater hold than positive emotions like pride because they tend to impose themselves on the mind, as they are less optional emotions than (say) joy. Greenspan also points out how the emotion of guilt can serve as a substitute for action as an indirect way of satisfying perceived obligations to take action without actually doing so.[27] Emotions get their motivational force from their role as rewards or punishments. Emotion drives motivation and explains why building emotion into all aspects of marketing is the most effective way of fixing attention on the brand.

Arousing guilt is common in public service ads that focus on the importance of upholding the law (e.g., like not drinking and driving) and the expressed remorse of those subsequently found in violation. One ad showed photographs of all those who had been killed in a random week. Guilt is a powerful appeal in social marketing ("Ignore the hungry and they'll go away" or "It takes twenty dumb animals to make a fur coat but only one to wear it.") The Puritan heritage, the idea that those at leisure are idle and idleness means trouble, is still strong, and there is a continuing American suspicion of time spent away from work—so vacations are taken with a laptop computer. TV evangelists arouse guilt for past sins, though offering help to relieve guilt is more likely to expand the market!

Guilt appeals are not uncommon, even in consumer ads like those designed to make people feel guilty about not feeding their family the very best. Commercial ads may seek to assuage guilt through reinterpretation, particularly in relation to the rules acquired from past authority figures like parents, so what might initially be perceived as extravagance is reinterpreted as an investment. A key problem for Kentucky Fried Chicken was guilt, so the problem was defined as how to sell the notion of guilt-free fast food. This gave rise to the advertising slogan: "It's nice to feel so good about a meal."

There are many studies showing the relationship between guilt and compliance. In one experiment, subjects who were made to feel guilty were three times more likely to comply with a request than subjects who were not.[28] Removing feelings of guilt is such an emotional imperative that the merits of the recommended course of action may hardly be considered.

Integrity

Immanuel Kant (1724–1804) based a theory of morality on the distinction between acting from inclination and acting from duty. A person of integrity does not seek to satisfy the most pressing desires but gives priority to ethical values. In general, people (including consumers) are not wanton in simply doing what they feel most inclined to do but exercise some scrutiny and control over their desires. Without control over the ordering of desires, Frankfurt argues, integrity would be meaningless in guiding action.[29] Ethical considerations frequently do lead to a rejection of initial impulses. Maintaining standards of personal integrity is tied to maintaining self-respect. However, while self-respect and integrity always go together, people can have high personal self-esteem without having much integrity, as having integrity (unfortunately) is not an important value for everyone.

An appeal to integrity is an appeal to the values that define where that person stands on certain ethical issues. We expect people to have an emotional commitment to their ethical principles, and we assume that this commitment will give rise to a corresponding consistency in their behavior. In fact, one tactic of persuasion lies in getting public commitment to some position and then pointing out that being consistent with that position necessitates taking a certain action. A high degree of consistency in a person's behavior is regarded as indicating character, trustworthiness, and high integrity. Ethical commitments adopted are a major factor entering into a person's self-image, and building up a commitment to a particular position (e.g., the relief of Third World debt) can lead to a revised view of self (e.g., as one who is concerned with Third World poverty). But there is pressure generally for commitment and supportive action to go together. When consumers are induced to make favorable statements about a brand in public or in written "competitions" sponsored by companies, this can act as a commitment, with the result the consumers begin to act in a way consistent with their praise. Thus we may make a public commitment at Weight Watchers to reduce weight and feel uncomfortable in not going along with what others demand as behavior (e.g., regularly attending Weight Watchers) that is consistent with that commitment. In much selling, an attempt is made to get the buyer to accept a commitment to a certain ("logical") position and then to point to how this conflicts with his or her current behavior—"This is what you claim to believe but this is what you are actually doing"—in order to bring about changes in buying behavior. Failing to be consistent with commitments results in embarrassment and a sense of diminished self-image.

When a company acts unethically, it violates trust and undermines its reputational capital, in turn undermining consumer loyalty, which rests on trust. It is because total trust is lacking with strangers that contracts are backed by a legal system to enforce them. Trust is basic to loyalty. This is why it is easier to be loyal to a person than an institution. Thus customers are likely to be more loyal to their hairdresser than to the hairdressing establishment. As a consequence, staff may take their customers with them when they leave the company to work elsewhere. This suggests, however, that not enough has been done to sell the institution itself. A failure to sell the institution has commonly led to salespeople in Wall Street, taking their customers with them—after being paid telephone-number salaries to stop them doing so in the first place. In contrast, the institution may on occasion be the natural focus of loyalty, just as there is likely to be more loyalty to a favorite restaurant than its waiters, other things remaining equal. Service providers need to ask themselves where the natural focus is for loyalty from customers and act on this information.

In personal relationships, trust means "sticking to friends through thick and thin," while in business it leads to forgoing demands for immediate reciprocity or equal exchanges because it involves a belief that things will even out over the long term. Firms that have the trust of their customers can weather a storm of competition until they are strong enough to respond. Old brand names, even if rejected as no longer "with it," may still retain an image of being a brand one can trust, which facilitates a revival. Corporate advertising, not uncommonly, seeks to link the company with moral values. However, consumers are cynical about any company advertising its moral virtues. Actions in ethics speak louder than words.

There are many ways for a company to project integrity. It can relate its virtues to the personality of a charismatic founder. Virgin became a label symbolizing integrity, energy, youth, enterprise, and dynamism through Branson's personality, but Virgin's poor performance in trains in Britain and claims made about Branson's personal life have diluted his image and the image of Virgin. Being consistent is one aspect of integrity. This can explain the success of the "foot-in-the-door" technique, whereby salespeople commit buyers to a cause by asking for a small favor, which then facilitates asking for much more. Once a person accedes to a small request, they are more inclined to go along with the next-bigger request.[30] The "door-in-the-face" technique, on the other hand, is to make a big request first; when, inevitably, rejected, a small favor is asked. Acceptance of the rejection is viewed as a concession that invokes the principle of reciprocity by the other party. Agreeing to lower a price from some initial inflated "anchor" price can be made to appear a concession that invokes the principle of reciprocity.[31] Whenever salespeople are given some discretion over price, this principle tends to be exploited.

It is impossible for the world to function without trust. In the complete absence of trust, people would find it difficult to step outdoors. From the makers of pills to food manufacturers, trust is a necessary condition for buying. Lack of consumer trust, for example, led to the near collapse of Britain's beef industry. The crisis has had enormous impact on attitudes to food, government, and scientists. Consumer services generally need high levels of trust. The traditional design of banks (now changing)—the mahogany, the intimidating layers of marble, and so on—were all aimed to inspire trust. But consumers seek integrity today not only in reliable products but in perceptions of the firm itself as a moral agent that does not, say, exploit the Third World, use child labor, abuse the environment, and so on. Behavior must suggest the trust is not ill placed. Many businesses arising out of the 1960s counterculture have sought to present themselves as ethical businesses, such as the Bodyshop, Ben & Jerry's, Virgin, and so on. This is never easy, given the prevailing skepticism about all attempts at ethical image-building that is not fully backed by verifiable, unmistakable actions.

Love and Hate

The term *love* is used in several senses. There is first what Leavy calls the principled love that characterizes discussions on Christian love that stress a duty to do good works and desiring goodwill for all humankind.[32] There is also the use of the term *love* to represent pure desire for physical sexual union. "Gifts" are offered here, with the expectation of reciprocity, which if not forthcoming arouses a loss of self-esteem and generates anger. Finally, there is "true" love, in the sense of so identifying with another that his or her key interests become a priority.

Each of these senses of "love" reflects human longings, and much advertising presupposes that these longings are strong. Advertising trades on the emotion of eros (associated with sexual desire), promising a sensual utopia free of the consequences of actions and competitive relationships. There are ads that associate a brand with goodwill toward others (Benetton ads), with the promise of increasing the chances of physical love, or with the possibility of a close loving relationship with another. Freud viewed most emotions as resulting from disappointment in love. A loss of love is a threat to self when the self completely identifies with the object of its desire. Love, as an emotion, finds its expression in attachment, liking, and caring but is also closely associated with jealousy and hate.

Lewis et al. argue that the neural systems that are responsible for emotion and intellect are separate and that we cannot choose who lures us any more than we can will ourselves to play an instrument we do not know.[33] It is the limbic brain with its attendant chemicals—serotonin, opiates, and oxytocin—that makes mothers rear their young, makes children want puppies, and allows all mammals to form attachment bonds with each other. For these authors, the neocortex does the thinking and the reptilian brain does the breathing, but love is definitely limbic! The limbic brain does not diagnose or self-correct; all it does is feel.

In the last section of this chapter, the focus is on love as identifying fully with another. Both this type of love and physical love are subjects of daydreams, fantasies, and longings, with people constantly on the lookout for ways to enhance the role of love in their lives. Appeals in advertising commonly promise the product will attract or enhance love relationships with others.

Unger regards love and hate as extreme ways of resolving the conflict between the longing for others and the dangers arising from being involved too closely with others.[34] Because hate is such an intense emotion and so easily aroused at an encounter with the hated, people are much more conscious of what they hate than what they like. This is the point made by Douglas (1996) and mentioned earlier. What we endorse, buy, or vote for may be more of a symbolic stand against what we hate than for what we like. Hate involves the feeling that it is impossible to reconcile the other's existence with one's own. It is the emotion at work behind ethnic cleansing and the barbaric acts that characterize the so-called paramilitary groups in Northern Ireland and the white supremacist groups in the United States. It is tempting and easy for the media and politicians to whip up the emotion of hate, particularly among the less educated, and then absolve themselves of any responsibility for the consequences. While the educated may rein in action tendencies because wider consequences come to mind, the less educated are more likely to go along with the emotional disposition aroused.[35]

The popular press long ago found that to be loudly against the potentially unpopular touches a raw nerve and sells papers, but at the cost of social division. You can often ask about many a newspaper: What hate are we being asked to share this week?—the appeal to solidarity in hate is a powerful way to sell newspapers. Hatred can be socially created by the media and will be if the media are controlled by dictators like Stalin, Hitler, and, more recently, Milosevic, who whipped up hatred against Albanians and other groups. The novel *1984* by Orwell depicted a totalitarian regime with a fictitious dictator, Big Brother, and an invented enemy called Goldstein for the purpose of whipping up popular anger, with followers screaming at a film of Goldstein in regular hate sessions. People gain better self-definition if propaganda creates a "hateful" other: the construction of some two-dimensional dehumanized enemy. In this sense, journalists can be propagandists. During the Gulf War it was alleged that Iraqi troops had disconnected the incubators of Kuwaiti babies; the story had actually been invented and spread by a public relations firm. War typically demands the denial of a shared humanity with the enemy so that killing becomes more acceptable. In *Homage to Catalonia,* Orwell describes the shattering of such illusions of hatred when a man he is about to fire on proceeds to relieve himself, thus reminding Orwell of their common humanness.

Jealousy occurs with a belief that the only way to keep a loved one is by domination to exclude relationships with others. While malicious envy occurs between two people, jealousy assumes there are three people involved. But both are tied to a lack of self-esteem.

Anger and Indignation

Anger is over the current or proposed actions of others and their likely consequences. When we are angry with ourselves, we are viewing part of the self as a separate person threatening the interests of the whole self. Anger is provoked by a threat to self-esteem or self-interests. Self-interest is interpreted broadly as embracing some inclusive concept of self, such as the family or community, since people get angry toward those who pollute the environment, act cruelly to children, or violate social norms covering the "rights" of others.

Anger involves indignation when the provoking situation involves perceived injustice. Public service advertising and not-for-profit advertising seek to arouse both anger and indignation. The campaign against killing baby seals in Canada is a classic example. But commercial ads also exploit these emotions when, for example, they suggest that competitors are currently "ripping off" the public with their high prices.

Epistemic Emotions

As with factive emotions, epistemic emotions involve wishes and beliefs: a wish that Y should or should not be so, accompanied by the belief that if X occurs then Y will be the case. What is unique about epistemic emotions is a lack of knowledge about whether X will or will not happen. Even though there is uncertainty over the occurrence of X, people act as if they believe X will happen. This can arise even though they accept that the objective evidence or their own common sense suggests that the likelihood of X occurring is negligible. This can happen with nations also, as when they justify their behavior on the ground that they are vulnerable to enemy attack when there is no such risk. Prophets of doom always find an audience. While the probability of X is objectively low, people are nevertheless fearful. Fear of violent crime has had far-reaching effects on political climate, quite out of proportion to what the objective facts warrant. These and other fears are exploited in one way or another by advertising.

Figure 3.5.   An appeal to anger and indignation. Courtesy DeVito/Verdi, New York, NY.

Fear

The paradigm case of an epistemic emotion is fear. Being in a state of fear motivates the strategy of vulnerability avoidance. When people act out of fear they act as if they believe X will occur and are motivated to avoid vulnerability so that when X does occur they will avoid the inevitable consequences Y. However, when people believe X can be prevented, they act to prevent it, for fear that unless they do so, the consequences Y are inevitable. The former is likely to be less emotional than the latter because vulnerability-avoidance is generally less certain in the latter.

The essential point about fear is that the occurrence of X must be uncertain. When consumers are persuaded to buy suntan lotion to reduce the effect of the sun's rays, they are not acting out of fear, as they usually deliberately expose themselves to the sun. They are acting to prevent sunburn X with its painful consequences Y. Although such fear can be aroused by dramatic advertising, it does not work if the "solution" is not regarded as feasible.

To put people into a state of fear, advertisers need to dramatize the unpleasant consequences and stress the high probability of their occurring. If X has the highly negative consequences Y, and the target audience believes that there is nothing that can be done about preventing X occurring, it is hoped they will be motivated to avoid vulnerability by taking action that will break for them the link between X and Y. If, on the other hand, advertisers wish to relieve people from fear, they will dismiss the likelihood of X or try to change beliefs about Y by showing what might be done to reduce or eliminate Y.

Empirical studies show that, in general, the more fear is aroused, the more likely people are to take preventive measures.[36] But specific recipients of the message may reject it because it is too frightening. Fear messages that are constantly hammered home can make people rebel and end up tuning out the messages. This is what occurred in Britain when the government at the worst stage of the crisis overdid the scare tactics with respect to BSE by banning beef on the bone. This led to defiance that was shown by an actual increase in sales of beef on the bone. When a warning is given too often, there can be "warning fatigue," to the extent that people become desensitized. While the truth in the warning might be accepted, it is pushed to the background and out of consciousness. It is no longer easily available in memory. Those most likely to be moved to action by ads that arouse a high degree of fear are those who have high self-esteem; those with low self-esteem seem slower to react, as if they have difficulty in coping with anything threatening.[37] If people are not shown how to cope with the threat in an efficient, feasible, and socially appropriate way, they may just ignore the threat. In any case, any fear appeal should be specific about what action should be taken, by whom, and how, when, and where.

Not-for-profit antidrug campaigns typically lack the credibility to arouse a high level of fear, while many drug addicts lack the "will" to stop. Fulfilling a goal to stop taking drugs is, as for any other individual performance, a function of: (1) motivation (fear), (2) beliefs about the recommended action being desirable, (3) ability to take the action (feasibility), and (4) opportunity to act. All these need to be taken into account, which seldom happens in antidrug campaigns.

Commercial advertising may show how X, that produces the unpleasant consequences Y, can be prevented. Thus the ad may say that bad breath, body odor, and so on have unpleasant social consequences that can be avoided by using the advertised product. But just as often ads promote the emotional consequences Y of not preventing X, so consumers act for fear that unless they do so they will be embarrassed. Commercial advertising can also intensify the consumer's latent fears. Insurance ads are a case in point, with such appeals as "Have you ever stayed awake at night thinking about . . . ?" "How secure is your job?" and then suggesting how insurance might disconnect one from the consequences of loss of job, disability, and so on. In "normal times" the consumer may not listen to outrageous claims and predictions of dire consequences, but in anxious times such claims are a matter of concern. For example, one ad for American trade unions reminds people of the bad old days before the advent of trade unions ("If you don't come Sunday, don't come Monday"). Like the Fat Boy in the *Pickwick Papers*, such advertisements seek to "make yer flesh creep."

A stress on the emotion of fear can be a conservative force, disfavoring change because the consequences are unknowable and therefore fearful. In politics, fear of change (often deliberately promoted) tends to favor the government of the day or the incumbent currently in power; people fear losses much more than they desire equivalent gains.[38] Perhaps the reason for this has a good deal to do with the perceived greater "unfairness" of losses: the negative emotion of making a loss outlasts the positive emotion of making an equivalent gain. In any case, fear can turn into a mood of free-floating anxiety (Roosevelt's "We have nothing to fear but fear itself"), leading to a need for reassurance. Hence in such circumstances the popularity of authority figures (often supplied in the twentieth century in the form of dictators!).

Hope

Advertising promises and promises raise hopes. As already pointed out (but worth repeating), consumers may doubt an advertising claim but still have hope when the promise deals with matters of concern. Hope is the opposite of despair. Hope, like fear, is an epistemic emotion, so people who are hopeful act as if they believe that what is yet to be will be. When a person accepts that X is not very likely, hopefulness slides into wishful thinking. This explains why anyone promoting cures for deadly diseases that are not currently curable has a ready audience. It explains why so many intelligent people seek "cures" that the objective evidence suggests are useless. Some (but by no means all) alternative medicines, therapies, and the larger lunacies of astrology and other superstitions connect with the consumer's hope of something better. It goes without saying that a good deal of consumer advertising harnesses a hope that springs eternal: the implicit message that the product will change the consumer's whole life and not just one trivial bit of it. People may then be shown to be completely renewed and rejuvenated through the agency of the product.

Hope is the stock in trade of magazines and self-help books. Perhaps the power of hope to defy reason is best illustrated by the flourishing of state and national lotteries. Whether the promise in an ad gives rise to the emotional state of hope depends significantly on the importance to the consumer of the perceived consequences of something, since those with a very strong need are unlikely to reflect too much on the rational credibility of the message, for instance, that all disease results from improper diet.

Illustrative Example: Obtaining a Homeowner's Mortgage

A study described in this section shows the concerns, beliefs, and emotional issues that arise in taking out a home mortgage.

In a study by one of us (J.O'S.) of consumers obtaining a homeowner's mortgage, the *factors that were of most concern* and so most likely to arouse the emotions were:

- The time required to obtain the loan (since the property might be sold to someone else if there was delay)
- The mental and physical effort needed to understand the various options available, their implications, and the procedures involved
- The emotional stress accompanying the uncertainties attendant on seeking a mortgage from "strangers"
- Present and future cash outlays

Commonly held beliefs that were taken into account in the choice of lender were as follows. About commercial banks:

- Banks are premium price lenders.
- Banks are bureaucratic organizations that have fixed policies and so are inflexible about negotiating rates.
- Banks charge more to borrow.
- Banks are not competitive on rates.
- Banks are out to get the maximum.
- Banks that are tied to big business have little interest in making loans to individual home buyers.
- Large banks will be efficient and credible in terms of expertise.

About mortgage firms and brokers:

- Mortgage firms are not as safe as banks.
- Mortgage firms work with several banks and are not just tied to one so are able to carry a lower rate and to work quickly.
- Brokers are needed only when there is difficulty in getting a loan.

About costs:

- Closing costs are generally the same.
- Points are like a second interest rate.
- The lower the interest rate, the more the points.
- Costs, as advertised, are misleading, as the low rates you see are not what you get.

The *emotions most apparent in the borrowing process* were fear, arising from uncertainty; anger, arising from frustration with the process; and blows to self-esteem, as a result of imbalance of power. These can be detailed as follows. A good deal of fear arises from uncertainty about:

- Hidden costs and closing costs that could be beyond what was expected and allowed for in the couple's budget
- Whether payments can be met
- Whether the lender's terms are a "rip-off"
- Whether future interest rates will justify current choices
- Whether the lender is sufficiently established to remain in business for the period of the loan to remove the uncertainty of repayment terms changing
- Whether it is wise to tie oneself to such payments, given the lack of knowledge about future conditions

Anger from frustration with the process arises in response to:

- Delays in obtaining a loan, which postpone the gratification of owning the new home and symbolize the possibility of rejection and missing out to a rival buyer who can come up with the money sooner
- The length of the process
- Not being informed of progress
- Vague and ambiguous questions in questionnaires

Blows to self-esteem occur because of the imbalance of power between buyer (borrower) and seller (lender) as perceived by the borrower—a situation that distinguishes mortgage buying from other buying. Lenders are fairly certain about the behavior of borrowers, but borrowers are uncertain about the probable demands of lenders. When people I am dealing with are fairly certain about my behavior but I am uncertain about theirs, this pushes the balance of power in their favor. Borrowers are also conscious of their ignorance when it comes to mortgage options and mortgage procedures and are very conscious of the fact that only the lender can deal with what are critical uncertainties. This gross knowledge imbalance in itself can lead to borrower perceptions of being the much less powerful partner in the relationship. It is the lender who controls resources (money) the borrower needs within time constraints. In return, the borrower simply promises to pay back the money and pledges his future home as security. At the time the promise and the pledge seem less substantial, which again enhances the borrower's perceptions of lender power. In addition, the borrower is dependent on the lender not just for a loan per se but also for the satisfaction of being accepted as worthy of a loan. A loan rejection symbolizes a negative judgment of the applicant's prospects of repaying the loan, which can be a blow to self-esteem. Borrowers in an unbalanced power relationship will, in general, seek to "lean over backward" to be on the good side of the lender but can be expected on occasion to "let off steam" in some emotional outburst as suppressed emotion reaches the surface. This seemed to always come as a surprise to the mortgage staff, who felt things were going well, not realizing the emotional nature of the transaction. Alternatively, borrowers escape altogether by turning to some other lender. Everything needs to be done to alter perceptions of this power imbalance between lender and borrower.

The desire to protect self-esteem leads to the borrower avoiding the risk of rejection and backing off from any deals that cast doubt on his or her standing and creditworthiness. Where the borrower has a strong desire to protect self-esteem, this was shown to lead to a number of tactics: (1) choosing a friendly bank or a bank where someone is known and liked; (2) preferring to deal with a local bank; (3) avoiding institutions viewed as bureaucratic; (4) avoiding those using a hard sell; (5) preferring to deal with one "understanding" person rather than a group of anonymous bureaucrats—and, most important, (6) seeking a lending institution that has an image of caring. Consumers react with anger and indignation at any sharp practice, as sharp practice would undermine self-esteem if one were to be taken in by it. As a consequence, there is a desire to avoid unpleasant confrontations by seeking honesty and openness in dealings with everything up front. One indicator of likely sharp practice for the consumer is misleading advertising. "Too good to be true" advertising creates distrust right from the start in dealing with mortgage lenders.

Some Key Assertions for Marketing

1. If marketing management is to direct emotions into actions that favor its brand, it must pay attention to beliefs. Beliefs dictate what means (brands) are most in line with the emotions. Beliefs lie behind attitudes and steer and inform action all the way from shaping wants into specific brand preferences to guiding postpurchase actions, such as returning an unsatisfactory product. Hence marketing has an interest in developing stimuli that lead to favorable appraisals that influence beliefs. In other words, marketing is interested in bringing about favorable value judgments with respect to the firm's brand.

2. If marketing management focuses on emotional appeals through, say, novelty, emotion can pressure beliefs to fall in line with emotional longings, and action may arise purely from emotional conditioning or impulse. Beliefs can be affect-driven, with likes and dislikes giving beliefs whatever coherence they possess. But generally beliefs have an independent role to play in buying. This is because the consumer's beliefs aim at truth and represent how things are in the world and how things work, in contrast to desires, which target the things in the world and how we would like them to be, with emotion providing the orientation (negative or positive) toward

these things. Without the representation provided by beliefs, desire would have nothing specific to target, and without such targets there would be no emotional arousal. In any case, beliefs are not always based on objective facts but are linked, via the emotions, to loyalties, hopes, fears, self-interest, and social conditioning, so they only imperfectly relate in an unbiased way to supporting evidence. Consumers can react to stimuli ("the incoming signals") with positive (approving) or negative (disapproving) emotions, without that reaction being a conscious reaction. This is the basis of the likability heuristic, whereby choices are made purely on a "gut reaction" of liking.

3. If marketing management is to change beliefs, the focus should be on offering information to the consumer. The more information one acquires about a product, the more one's beliefs become refined and specific in steering buying action. However, the interpretation of any information is colored by the consumer's emotional orientation. The learning of new words to describe a brand or the meaning of product features can lead to the consumer endorsing a new set of beliefs. Where consumers fail to grasp the concept of the product and its differences from rivals, they cannot develop a genuine preference for it. Consumers may profess belief in some product of which they have little conception, but a clear conception is required for the belief to be firm. Companies all too often overestimate the consumer's knowledge of the product, confusing awareness of the product with conceptual understanding of what it is all about.

4. If marketing management stresses information, it must recognize that consumers wish their beliefs to be based on the best information available but that time pressures and cost factors usually rule this out. Consumers are therefore likely to collect just enough information to make a choice but not to become experts on the product class. If the consumer has emotional leanings toward one brand rather than another so that there is an implicit favorite, the information search will be cut short. What marketers would like to do is get their particular brand accepted as the implicit favorite before any search or evaluation is attempted. This is helped by associating the brand with positive emotional experiences.

5. If management is to give attention to beliefs, there is a need to recognize that beliefs are seldom isolated but are usually part of a system of beliefs. This is why some beliefs are more fixed and less easily given up or imagined to be false than others. It is also why attacking a single belief (e.g., that smoking is not bad for the health) may be ineffective when it is part of a supporting network of beliefs. The whole set of relevant beliefs must be undermined.

6. If the marketing is to take account of all relevant motivation and not just that arising from reasons and reasoning based on want/desires and beliefs, it must be recognized that fantasy can substitute for belief and wishes for wants and desires in motivating behavior. However, while beliefs have the biological function of aiming at truth (or truthlikeness), fantasy is free to support whatever it wants. Similarly, while wants/desires take account of what is feasible, wishes do not. In any case, fantasies and

wishes can be aroused in getting the consumer to anticipate, contemplate, and attend to novelty in products or experiences, and this can lead to self-persuasion via imagining.

7. If marketing management is offering a product (including services/experiences) that promises excitement in its consumption (e.g., the theater), then promotion that associates the product with that excitement can arouse consumers to buy for the emotional experience. The emotional message and context is presented first, with reasons for buying added to allow the consumer to better rationalize the purchase.

8. If marketing management is to match the expectations of the buyer, it must recognize that the action of buying rests not just on beliefs but on wishes/wants/desires tied to values. A "want" is represented in the mind as benefits sought, so a wanting for a product is not just wanting that product regardless (e.g., in poor condition); it is wanted under some description of benefits sought. Understanding is understanding based on the chosen description. This is why marketing focuses not on marketing a product per se but on marketing described benefits or described potential experiences. The wants of the consumer are always comparative, in that whatever is wanted is wanted in comparison with the alternatives displaced. *Wishes, wants, desires,* and *needs* are often used as synonyms, but it is useful to remember that wishes take no account of feasibility; desires reflect an awareness of the want and its intensity; and needs suggest an absolute requirement.

9. If marketing management is concerned with generating factive emotions (i.e., emotions grounded in a belief that, as a matter of fact, the emotional event or whatever has occurred), the aim should be to arouse a strong positive appraisal of the brand by showing that, as a matter of fact, the brand is in line with beliefs and wishes (wants, desires). The self-assessment emotions of pride, self-esteem, envy, shame, embarrassment, guilt, and self-respect are factive emotions, in that one takes it as a fact that (1) one has risen above or fallen below expectations and in so doing (2) has changed one's status or standing in the world. Hence all appeals to such self-assessment emotions will aim at presenting the brand as restoring or enhancing self-esteem or standing in the world.

10. If marketing management is concerned with generating epistemic emotions (i.e., emotions that arise from the belief that there is uncertainty about the likelihood of the event arising), the aim should be to arouse a strong positive appraisal of the brand. This involves showing that attitudinal reasons (i.e., attitude to consequences) for wishing X to occur or not to occur are in line with the buying of the brand and epistemic reasons (i.e., reasons for believing the likelihood of occurrence of X) also favor the buying of the brand. The classic examples of epistemic emotions are fear and hope. However, attitudinal reasons are much less easily influenced and more determining of action than epistemic reasons. In any case, fear motivates people to act to avoid vulnerability. With fear appeals, the target audience must be shown how to cope with the threat in an efficient, feasible, and socially appropriate way (via the firm's product?) or otherwise there is a danger of the target audience just ignoring the threat.

11. If the heart of an advertisement is a promise, this promise raises hope, and people cling to hope when the alternative is despair. Hope is fully compatible with doubt (whose opposite is credulity).

12. If marketing management is to appeal to nostalgia, it will find a more ready audience when times are hard rather than when times are good; but appeals to nostalgia always have emotional potential in marketing.

Belief-wish Condition Models for Understanding the Emotions, Based on Taylor (1985)

Pride

Wishes: Whatever has occurred by way of achievements, possessions, or personal qualities, they are states that would have been wished.

Explanatory beliefs: (1) what has occurred would be perceived as worth having by relevant reference groups; and (2) what has occurred is connected in some way with self through ownership, kinship, or whatever.

Inferences from explanatory beliefs that support identificatory beliefs: (1) what occurred would be normally beyond one's expectation and capabilities as based on one's past experience and own sense of limitations and the expectations that others have of one; (2) what occurred is something that one cares about and values highly and that will increase one's standing; and (3) that of which one is proud did in fact occur.

Example: the Aston Martin ad: "Every Aston Martin motorcar is hand-built for its owner. Every chassis is identified by its owner's initials."

Shame

Wish: to uphold certain internalized cultural or social norms.

Explanatory beliefs: (1) others would condemn one (or those with whom one identifies) for what has been done; and (2) one is in fact connected and accepts that connection with what occurred.

Inferences from explanatory beliefs that support identificatory beliefs: (1) one's standing or status is reduced in one's own and other's eyes; and (2) one has lost self-respect, self-esteem, and self-worth.

Example: the antidrug campaign: "Anyone taking drugs is fostering crime and destroying society."

Anger and Indignation

Wish: to uphold self-esteem and other interests of self or quasi selves.

Explanatory beliefs: (1) action X carried out by Y threatened interests of self or quasi selves; and (2) action X is a slight or insult.

Inferences from explanatory beliefs that support identificatory beliefs: standing or status had been reduced.

In the case of indignation, there is (1) a belief that action X created an injustice and (2) the sense of a need to hit back. *Example:* the ad against the killing of baby seals in Canada.

Fear

Wish: that either *X* could be prevented or that one could be protected from its consequences *Y.*

Explanatory beliefs: (1) a situation or event *X* has unpleasant consequences *Y*; and (2) either *X* may occur, unless preventive action is taken, or *X* cannot be prevented, so protection against *Y* is needed.

Inferences from explanatory beliefs that support identificatory beliefs: (1) the self is threatened; and (2) uncertainty about the occurrence of *X*.

Example: the ad for hair restorer: "If you're concerned about hair loss . . ."

Embarrassment

Wish: for one's own behavior and that of others to be socially appropriate.

Explanatory beliefs: (1) one (or others being observed) has done something that would be viewed by the audience as gauche or in some other way socially maladroit; and (2) the audience is as in fact viewing one's behavior that way.

Inference from explanatory beliefs that supports identificatory beliefs: one (or others being observed) seems unable to respond in some socially appropriate way to remove embarrassment.

Example: the ad for Close-Up toothpaste: "When he's this close, you'll be glad you used the new improved Close-Up."

Guilt

Wish: that one had not violated the taboo, rule, or law.

Explanatory beliefs: (1) one has broken the rule of some authority; and (2) that authority is a voice of conscience (even if one rationally rejects that authority, as emotional reactions are not always in step with current reasoning).

Inference from explanatory beliefs that supports identificatory beliefs: one's standing or status is reduced in one's own eyes.

Example: the ad on behalf of the homeless: "Isn't it time you stopped looking away?"

Integrity

Wish: to uphold one's values.

Explanatory beliefs: (1) a threat or appeal has been made to one's sense of integrity; and (2) unless one's values are upheld by oneself, one will lose self-respect and sense of standing in one's social milieu.

Inferences from explanatory beliefs that support identificatory beliefs: (1) action *X* does or would lower one's own sense of standing in one's social milieu; and (2) there is a need to defend personal values (integrity) against *X*.

Example: the wartime recruitment poster: "Your country needs you."

Love

Wish: to continue and further the relationship with individual *X*.

Explanatory beliefs: (1) one believes *X* is the right partner for him; and (2) the relationship is or will be enhanced by some events or situation.

Inference from explanatory beliefs that supports identificatory beliefs: belief that the interests of *X* are his concern.

Example: any ad showing how to attract a partner by focusing on her concerns.

Hope

Wish: for consequences *Y* of *X*.

Explanatory beliefs: (1) if *X* occurs then consequences *Y* will occur; and (2) uncertainty about the possibility of *X* happening.

Inferences from explanatory beliefs that support identificatory beliefs: (1) consequences *Y* are of high value; and (2) *X* can yet happen.

Example: cosmetics advertising.

4

Generating Emotion: Emotional Responses

In figure 2.1, the following factors are shown as entering into the generation of emotion:

1. The consumer's value system
2. Emotive stimuli (events, actions, attributes of objects)
3. Appraisal of stimuli, leading to a feeling toward the object
4. Wishes/wants/desires and beliefs, forming the background against which the appraisal takes place
5. Responses of the consumer to the appraisal made, cognitive effects, arousal of feelings, behavioral expressions/displays, and action readiness: choice processes

This chapter is concerned with the final category: the responses of the consumer to the appraisal made.

Cognitive Effects

There is a tradition, going back to Plato, that views emotion as the enemy of reason. For example, the emotion of fear is associated with inhibiting learning, as people are likely to forget newly acquired information after an emotional experience. Swift (1667–1745) was obsessed with the tension between reason and emotion. In his satirical masterpiece *Gulliver's Travels* he juxtaposed the Houyhnhnms, equine creatures of pure reason, with the Yahoos, hairy humanoids dominated by sensual emotion. The Houyhnhnms have no word for "lie" but use the phrase "the thing that is not," and their way of death is totally rational, with all the Houyhnhnms lining up to say a reasonable farewell to the dying. For Swift, reason alone does not make life meaningful, but emotion without the discipline of reason degrades us. This is insightful, as there is no way that emotion and reason can be considered totally independent. Emotion energizes and influences the process of deciding, while even hard reasoning involves emotional pressures. On the other hand, as Frijda points out, emotion is apt to be closed to judgments about consequences other than achieving the goal of the particular emotion (e.g., revenge).[1] With intense emotions there is a self-righteous absoluteness of feeling, with the emotion so occupying center stage that other concerns can get ignored. In this situation people seem quite prepared to "cut off their nose to spite their face." Complaining customers not uncommonly appear in this state. The usual reaction is to cut off communication with them, by walking away or putting down the phone. But once sympathy is shown by acknowledging the complaint, and in a manner that suggests a willingness to make amends, the customer is apt to calm down fairly quickly. This is a better approach than losing a customer.

What de Sousa says in *The Rationality of Emotion* bears repeating.[2] While agreeing that emotion can limit the range of information and the options taken into account, he argues that emotion fills the gaps left by pure reason in the determination of action. Without emotion, decision-making would be in paralysis, for the decision-maker would be unable to make up his or her mind. This is because emotions link to values that are crucial for making trade-offs. Emotions determine the salience of things and act as arbitrators among reasons, assigning values to options to determine trade-offs. This means that what objectively appears the weaker motive can prevail through the consumer throwing her emotional weight behind the weaker motive. Rationality can proscribe but cannot prescribe. In real life there is no man or woman of pure rationality uncontaminated by emotion, as he or she would be unable to make a decision on anything that really concerned him or her. In sum, emotion deals with the insufficiencies of reason by influencing the selection of, and controlling the salience of, the factors reason takes into account. In this sense all trade-offs that occur in making a serious decision are rooted in feelings as well as beliefs.

Preferences, however, can be purely *affect (feelings)–driven*. Feelings have the advantage of being immediately accessible and save cognitive energy when used to determine a preference. Affect-driven choices are more common among the less educated and the ill informed, since cognition-driven reasoning depends on a certain level of education.[3] Consumers may cope with a lack of information on a product (e.g., automobiles) by simply basing their choices on likes and dislikes ("gut" feel). The more difficult it is to obtain advice or absorb available information, the more prone is the consumer to use the *likability heuristic* to determine choice. Liking can fill the gap left by the paucity of information. The likability heuristic is a rule of thumb ("buy that which is intrinsically most appealing" or "if it feels good, buy it") that is appropriate when brands seem otherwise equal. If a consumer's likes and dislikes form a coherent system, they provide the consumer with a means to make choices without much reflection. A good deal of buying is less reflective than is claimed in postpurchase interrogation of consumers, where post-purchase rationalization occurs.

Solomon, while claiming that emotions are typically purposive choices, agrees that emotions can prompt action at variance with long-term interests.[4] Emotions can be multiple and conflicting, with some emotions pressing for instant gratification and other emotions pushing for long-term benefit. But consumers, like people generally, typically exercise some forbearance. It is not all pure pleasure-seeking. Without some control over inclinations, integrity would be meaningless in guiding action. Thus earlier (in chapter 3) we quoted Darwall, who points to the close connection between judging that there are sound reasons for taking some action—like buying "green" or giving to charity—and, as a consequence, being motivated to take such action.[5] We all have a strong disposition to be guided by reason. There is nothing contradictory in saying that someone has an emotional commitment to be rational, a person of integrity, or a good citizen, as these are key values for many people.

An emotional response may alter future wants and actions. Someone seeing the plight of refugees may be emotionally upset and change from viewing them as just a nuisance to doing something about it. A constant theme throughout the ages has been the "energizing" effects of the emotions, by which is meant not just that the emotions can act as motives but that strong emotions fuel drive and sustained effort (persistence).[6]

Action and not just emotion can lag behind the updating of beliefs. For example, a consumer may no longer believe that there is an advantage in using a high-premium gasoline but continue to buy it. Here, beliefs about premium gasoline have changed, but one still acts as if one believes in the consequences of the original belief. It may be that the two incompatible beliefs are in memory but are recalled at different times. There is an echo of this even in the natural sciences. Deutsch points out that in the natural sciences "It is perfectly possible for a person to discover a new theory. . . . but nevertheless to continue to hold beliefs that contradict it. The more profound the theory is, the more likely this is to happen."[7] But, more generally, individual beliefs form part of a constellation of supportive beliefs.

Sometimes the notion that beliefs are ordinarily part of a network of supportive beliefs (see chapter 3) is denied. Thus Converse claims that for most people the interconnection of political beliefs is triply lacking (1) *horizontally,* that is, between opinions on an issue; (2) *vertically,* that is, between higher-level concepts like liberalism and conservatism and specific preferences on specific concrete issues; and (3) *temporally,* that is, between political positions taken at different times.[8] This claim implies that the individual constituents of belief systems are only minimally connected so that each has only minimal influence on the others. Sniderman and his colleagues question this, claiming that Converse's results arose from the limitations of the questions respondents were asked, which assumed that belief systems contain only opinions on *specific* issues, with values excluded.[9] The authors argue that one way the less educated hold together their beliefs is through *affect.* In such cases belief systems are affect driven, with likes and dislikes providing an overall coherence. However, the authors agree it would be wrong to assume that, while the unsophisticated fall back on "gut feel," the sophisticated rely on "head think." The well educated are not always cognition driven. What the well educated more commonly do is take account of a wider range of consequences in evaluating alternatives. This can lead to a certain indecisiveness when things are not clear-cut—a not unusual characteristic of many academics!

Beliefs, even when not part of a closely knit set of beliefs, are not necessarily easy to change. An experiment by Nisbett and Ross illustrates the persistence of beliefs.[10] Experimental subjects were persuaded that they were skilled at distinguishing real from fake suicide notes, and the belief remained with the subjects even after being shown that the evidence for the claim was completely false. Whether such experiments weaken the case for claiming that the evolutionary function of beliefs is to aim at the truth is debatable.

Beliefs and action are not always in harmony. Factors like habit intrude. It takes time for people to change their voting patterns, even when a party may no longer serve a voter's interests. The same is true of products. There is sentiment for a brand, which can be at variance with current beliefs. Brands often have a highly esteemed social identity that exists to some extent independently of beliefs about effectiveness. This is certainly true of some high-priced cars!

Actions triggered by emotion are not *generally* just brute emotional reactions, since the ways chosen to achieve the goals of emotion involve beliefs. This is important to remember when considering advertising that exploits emotion. Thus the success of one cereal firm in getting consumers to be fearful about colon cancer did not guarantee that these consumers bought the firm's brand of cereals, or any other brand, as a means to allay their fear. Consumers' beliefs led to different ways of allaying their fear. Hence in using emotional advertising to stimulate buying, the ad must subtly suggest why the brand advertised is the best option. A common error among advertisers is to assume that arousing the relevant emotion in an ad is sufficient without the need to direct beliefs to be supportive of the brand.

People commonly, as in religion, seek a coherent set of beliefs rather than necessarily the set of beliefs that are most evidentially supported. They may interpret evidence through the lens of a coherent set of emotionally held beliefs and, on this basis, decide what to them is true. Consumers want to believe what their emotions (feelings) tell them to believe. When the consumer is emotionally attracted to a purchase, opposing beliefs may be put on the back burner. Nonetheless, new information can and does change beliefs. This is particularly true when the information refines beliefs and adds to the consumer's repertoire of concepts relating to the product so that the consumer gets a better idea of the product's potential for meeting some want.

Arousal of *Feelings:* Feelings Toward and Bodily Feelings

In thinking about emotional responses, the arousal of feelings comes most readily to mind. Highly positive or highly negative appraisals arouse feelings toward the stimuli or the object of emotion. But the arousal must reach some threshold level of intensity to be experienced bodily as emotion. The consumer identifies his or her emotion by taking into account feelings, situational factors, ongoing social interactions, and roles adopted[11] as well as self-attributions.[12] As an influence on emotions the role adopted is not obvious, but it can be crucial: for example, when dressed in the uniform of a nurse, a person may be less aggressive than when dressed normally. Similarly, wearing a Ku Klux Klan outfit results in more aggressiveness. This is why the tougher military regiments get appropriate uniforms! The trickle-up effect of aggressive dressing from tough street kids to middle-class teenagers encourages middle-class teenagers to adopt more aggressive behavior. Service organizations should pay attention to how the role their service provides is described and how personnel should dress, because both influence service behavior. The "casual Friday" phenomenon may be welcome to staff, but it is likely to be deleterious to overall performance, in that informality in dress encourages a casualness in work.

The pleasure, arousal, dominance (PAD) model of Merabian and Russell is based on the claim that a person's *feeling state* after an appraisal is positioned along three dimensions:[13]

- Pleasure/displeasure
- Arousal/nonarousal
- Dominance/submissiveness

On this basis, every highly positive or negative appraisal of emotive stimuli (events, actions, attributes) gives rise to feelings covering:

1. a feeling of pleasure or displeasure
2. some bodily feelings of arousal
3. a feeling of increased or decreased standing (dominance/submissiveness) vis-à-vis the world at large.

If this is so, it offers guidance in choosing the advertisements most likely to elicit the emotions of interest, since not all ads seek to engender merely feelings of pleasure. The utility of the model has been demonstrated by Foxall.[14]

Physiological measures of arousal are one way to measure emotional responses. The mind-view method monitors basal skin response to stimuli like a TV commercial, and this data is combined with other data to detail a viewer profile. Another method uses headsets to measure brain waves. (This method is also used to gauge the alertness of commercial airline pilots; it shows the rise and fall of attention levels.) There are also nonphysiological measures such as the method that asks consumers to indicate the pictures shown that best reflect their feelings after watching a commercial. There is less vagueness and ambiguity in using pictures than words alone. The problem, however, with all such measures lies in (1) establishing that the ad is the only causal factor at work producing the arousal and (2) the significance or meaning of the measure in terms of buying action. There is wide scope in interpreting significance.

Averill asserts that "feelings" of arousal are neither necessary nor sufficient for being in an emotional state, so people are not always aware of being angry; this would not be true if feelings were a necessary condition for anger.[15] This is misleading. Because people do not recognize they are angry does not mean that they have no feelings of anger but simply means that they do not accept that they are angry or the anger is not at the level to draw attention in consciousness. Commonly consumers deny that they are angry, say, with restaurant service, when both their nonverbal behavior and their subsequent behavior tell a different story. Observers are often better judges of whether others are in an emotional state than they are themselves. There can be many physiological effects (e.g., raised blood pressure) as well as emotional displays without consumers being aware of them. Averill further claims that a person can *feel* angry without *being* angry, which would not be the case if feelings were a sufficient condition for the generation of emotion. We have feelings of all sorts (e.g., of pain from a pin prick) that do not evoke emotion, so it is true that feelings are not a sufficient condition for emotion. But the claim nonetheless seems strange, since "feeling angry" is sufficient evidence for accepting that we are, as a matter of fact, angry. What other evidence would Averill require before accepting a person's statement as being that of being angry? In fact, an essential element of the acting out of emotion is a "feeling toward" some object.[16]

Frijda (1988) quotes research findings showing that the continuance of pleasure is contingent on *change*. This is because change suggests novelty. This might explain variety-seeking (a species of novelty-seeking) and why variety puts off the point of satiety. One characteristic of amorality is uninhibited variety-seeking; the drama of action to counteract boredom. On the other hand, we can have variety without real choice, as with current TV channels! Constant change is a major appeal of fast action movies. In fact, Hollywood's dominance of the movie industry was helped by its early mastery of fast-paced action. Constant change is also a way of grabbing attention in advertisements and avoiding boredom on the part of the audience.

While pleasure tends to quickly fall off, Frijda reminds us that negative emotions are apt to persist, though not with the initial poignancy. This explains why purchases or services that fall well below what was promised arouse long-term emotions accompanied by a resolve never to deal with that company again. We seldom forget discourteous service. On the other hand, a purchase that rises above expectations is highly pleasing, but the pleasure is felt less intensely over the long term.

Feelings generally are seldom monotone but embody complexities and contradictions. It is this subtlety that great literature seeks to nuance and that makes understanding emotions so complex.

Behavioral Expressions/Displays/Symbolic Expression

Emotional responses can take the form of *expressions of emotion:* these exclude bodily changes—not only heightened heartbeat or the raised blood pressure that might accompany emotion but also any actions that are taken "out of emotion." Expressions of emotion fall somewhere in between such bodily changes and such actions. Expressions of emotion relate to facial expressions and such reactions as jumping for joy. As Goldie (2000) says, bodily changes just happen to us, and actions are explained in terms of wants and beliefs (or, we might add, fantasies and wishes), but genuine expressions of emotion are not enacted as a means to a conscious end.

Emotions can appear in facial expressions too quickly to be blocked by conscious effort. In Damasio's terms, the *somatic markers* have their effect first.[17] This seems to conflict with the observation that an accused in court can be said to have displayed no emotion when sentenced to long-term imprisonment. This is because we expect emotion on such occasions to be extended and not to be a momentary reflex. But sometimes there is only a momentary emotional reaction before conscious control takes over.

Body posture, gestures, facial expressions, and tone of voice all suggest an emotional state apparent to observers but not necessarily to the person in the emotional state. But no singular nonverbal sign is as an isolated signal box. The total context has to be taken into account in interpreting nonverbal behavior. Just as the meaning of a word is tied to context (e.g., drugs at a pharmacist as opposed to drugs in the context of the street), gestures are tied to the context in which they appear. Context is always important in the interpretation of what things mean, as things frequently look, smell, sound, feel, and even taste different in different conditions. The same dress in a local store does not impress as much as when it is displayed in a boutique in the best part of town.

A *symbolic expression* is undertaken simply as a gesture to indicate where one stands on an issue. Thus a crowd may burn an effigy of some hated politician as a symbolic expression, when attempting to do the real thing could lead to a murder charge! A consumer may refuse to buy any clothing emblazoned with the designer name as a symbolic expression of values. Sometimes a symbolic expression may have no end in mind except letting off steam, as when a consumer turns his or her back on the person making an unsatisfactory offer. Symbolic expressions are common in protests against "hated" international companies.

Action Readiness and Choice Processes

Emotional responses can take the form of action readiness or action itself in choosing or deciding what to do. Smith and Ellsworth regard emotions as *motivational states* that serve an evolutionary function in taking action for survival.[18] For instance, fear is a motivational state leading to escape from a dangerous situation through the impulse of "fight or flight." Since any active motivational state is a predisposition to action readiness, these two are linked.

Yet if the action is consciously adopted, the specific action taken depends not just on emotional state but also on beliefs. An emotional state, as a motivational state, does suggest a want, but a consumer's beliefs suggest the specific means for meeting the want.

Reasons for action involve both beliefs and wants (desires), and either beliefs or wants on occasion can be more determining of the action taken. This does not mean that the reasons must be earnest. Consumers may only need a trivial reason to do what they feel like doing anyway. However, the consumer can be moved by the belief that something is a bargain as much as by desire for the product itself, since belief in a bargain is emotionally energizing. Traditionally there is dispute over which is more determining. Kant argued that one can act against one's desires, but Hume (1711–1776) claimed that action always occurs at one time rather than some other time because a particular desire has force at the time. We now accept that beliefs alone do not motivate a specific intentional action without a corresponding desire, while conscious desire itself does not lead to a *specific* action without a corresponding belief about how to satisfy the desire. But if desires (wants) and beliefs enter into all action, emotion enters into *all* decision-making, since decision-making implies trade-offs, and trading off one thing for another involves values, which link to the emotions. Hence we inevitably return to values and the emotional episodes (in de Sousa's language, the "paradigm scenarios") on which they are grounded. Whether or not people *consciously* formulate or debate their values, they are the bedrock of all human activity, with emotions linked to values at every level.

All consumer choice processes are influenced by emotion and not just those involving trade-offs. The choice processes (discussed later) that do not involve trade-offs are (1) random picking; (2) simple liking; (3) habit; and (4) singular evaluation. There is no conscious deliberation of alternatives in these processes. What is interesting about the four processes is that they are apt to favor the brand leader.

If marketers want to understand how consumers reason when buying, they need to examine how consumers reason about the actual choices before them. In marketing we cannot, like the economist, just be interested in revealed preferences (actual choices made) but are vitally interested in the motives (wants), beliefs, and the emotions that moved the consumer to buying action. This is often forgotten even by market researchers. We often see some program on TV showing some researcher behind a camera hidden from view as the consumer is filmed walking around the store and making her purchases. We are then told a long story about what is motivating her, but there is no way of moving from watching people go about shopping to what their wants (motives) and beliefs are. It is all speculation, even if informed by some social science concepts. Of the three constituents wants, beliefs, and action, we need to know two of them to even make a reasonable guess at the third. Thus if we note the action and know a person's wants, we can make a good guess at beliefs. Similarly, if we note the action taken and know a person's beliefs, we can make a good guess at wants. But to know preferences alone rules out the individual psychology.

What follows is informed by findings from the social sciences and refined from analyzing consumer protocols, where consumers just talk "off the top of their head" before buying, during buying, and after buying.[19] This "talking off the top of their head," as consumers go about the job of buying, is important, since just asking ex post facto can be misleading. Ross and Nisbett show that when they are asked ex post facto to name the basis of their choices, people cannot do so correctly.[20] While focus groups are extremely useful, they are no substitute for protocols that record thinking before, during, and after buying. What is said at a focus group is influenced by (1) what has occurred during the period since the purchase; (2) the questions being put, in that questions stimulate thinking about things not previously thought about; (3) recall (a participant's recall is always a selective reconstruction of the past); and (4) other participants and what they have to say. If marketing wants to know about the dynamics of reasoning and choice, it can also be misleading to make judgments on the basis of how consumers make choices in experiments or in artificial settings like mall trailers. With major purchases, there is a need to see how consumers choose under the pressure of time and the emotional climate of an actual purchase, where they have to rely on a mixture of experience, imagination, likes/dislikes, and vague indicators in respect to likely product performance.

What puzzles many marketers is how consumers make intelligent decisions when commonly they are so badly informed. The answer is that, as in politics, they use heuristics (judgmental shortcuts)—particularly the likability heuristic.[21] This does not mean that all reasoning about what to buy is affect driven rather than cognition driven. While the tripartite model of the concept of attitude (cognition → affect → conation) found in marketing texts assumes a cognition-driven process and while there can be either cognition-driven or affect-driven processes on occasions, usually both cognition and affect are at work at any one time.

Picking

When brands seem alike or their differences are of no interest, or investigation of the differences would take too long or be just not feasible, consumers may choose on whim or at random. This is called *picking* behavior, as it is analogous to what occurs in picking a cigarette from a packet.[22] Whatever reasons enter into buying, they are so instantaneous that they remain unknown. It may be that some buyers minimize differences among brands while others accentuate the differences, or it may just be that the purpose for which the product is being bought differs among buyers. However, what is picked is probably less random than appears, as consumers are apt to choose the brand that resonates best with their emotional memories. Typically, this is the brand with which they are most familiar, as the most familiar brand falls under the *availability heuristic* in being more easily recalled or available in the mind.

Consumers have an emotional aversion to simply picking and so may come to *rationalize* a purchase after buying. Practical thinking is dominated by a concern for acting in accordance with reasons. Velleman regards the desire to act in accordance with reasons as a strong motivational force in all practical endeavors.[23] We would argue that this force is emotional at base. What this description of picking behavior implies is the need, when brands appear to be tokens of each other, to give the consumer a reason for preferring a specific brand. There is an emotional compulsion to seek reasons for preference. When brands look alike and are in the same packaging, and so on, they get grouped together in the mind as identical in both function and in quality—that is, they are viewed as tokens of each other, like commodity products. The two most basic questions in marketing are: Why buy from us? How do we compete? Answering either question points to the need for a differential advantage—that must, preferably, declare itself.

When the consumer is faced with a large choice of options that cannot all be evaluated, he or she may (1) reluctantly adopt a picking strategy or (2) not buy at all. When consumers are overwhelmed with choices, it becomes an approach-avoidance situation. On the one hand, consumers like to think they have many options from which to choose. This is the approach side. On the other hand, consumers hesitate to choose, as the wide range of options makes consumers anxious that they will not choose the best for their purposes. This is the avoidance side. As in all approach-avoidance situations, there is the tendency to indecision, which means postponement or abandonment of the purchase. The trick for the marketer is to suggest a choice that is wide but not wide enough to encourage this indecision.

Intrinsic Liking and Other Affect-Driven Choices

We think of buying as working back from what the consumer wants the product to do and drawing up the requisite technical specifications to form buying criteria. This cerebral account of buying underplays the role of affect, or feelings. Consumer reflection on buying is very much influenced by likes and dislikes. In some cases, the consumer just buys on the basis of liking. Consumers do not always plan their buying but may simply react to a product that catches their fancy. And a good deal of influence on behavior occurs at the nonconscious level. As Velleman (2000) says, a good deal of our behavior is regulated with the goal of avoiding pain, even though pain avoidance becomes an end-in-view only on rare occasions. This means that behavior can be regulated by aims that consumers are not aware of and that are not their conscious goals.

One way for a situation to be meaningful enough to get a buying reaction is for the consumer to have a liking for what he or she perceives. Liking may be all that is needed to generate a purchase, as liking is linked to excitement. Strong liking gives rise to affect-driven choices. This does not mean that things like price have no influence but simply that liking dominates the purchase.

Intrinsic liking: In conditions of pure intrinsic liking, consumers choose on the basis of taste, aesthetics, feel, smell, or sound. Anticipation of enjoyment is emotional, reflected in such expressions as "it makes my mouth water to think about it." In choosing on the basis of intrinsic liking, there is no deliberation on trade-offs but only reflection to establish which option coheres most with tastes. In fact, when the sole purpose of purchase is enjoyment, it makes no sense to ask a consumer why she or he chose this dessert rather than that, unless we are interested in the form of enjoyment sought (e.g., creamy taste). Appraisal in the case of intrinsic liking is confined to sensual appraisal.

Other affect-driven choices: In conditions of information overload, consumers may fall back on the likability heuristic, that is, they may choose on the basis of liking. Even expensive consumer durables are often bought on this basis. It is suspected that the poorly educated make wide use of the likability heuristic. In other words, the less educated are more apt to first check their feelings in making a choice. The option that is most liked or has the most instant appeal becomes the "implicit favorite model," and subsequent efforts are made to justify the choice. In the buying of services in particular, the attractiveness of the service provider is always important, as we all like to deal with people with whom we are comfortable. In general we like those who are physically attractive and seem similar to ourselves in terms of values, personality, interests, and background. Many a choice of doctor, dentist, insurance agent, financial advisor, and so on is made purely on "feelings toward" that person on first meeting.

In spite of what was said earlier, we suspect that the likability heuristic and the implicit favorite model are widespread in every social strata and every aspect of society. In jurisprudence, legal realists claim that judges commonly make "all-things-considered judgments" about who should win the case and then rationalize their judgment in terms of some legal rule.[24] In other words, it is not uncommon to go along with initial gut reaction or feel drawn to a product that resonates emotionally and then think of reasons why the choice is most defensible. This is not to suggest that consumers simply act according to the impulses of the moment: consumers may live with a strong sense of the individual moments in their lives but also have a sense of the overall narrative of their lives.

Habit

Englefield points out that if we hear from a news bulletin that it is going to rain, we may decide to carry an umbrella or take some other action without any mental representation of steaming windows or puddles.[25] When the situation is familiar, we go straight to a solution. What occurs in the mind is simply the idea of achieving some result (e.g., to keep dry) allied to a feeling of confidence that the result can be achieved by a certain course of action. This captures the concept of habit. When the consumer continues to buy the same brand, by definition, it is a habitual buy. Even when all brands in a segment are objectively the same, the consumer may stay with the habitual brand because:

- There is no uncertainty and no fear of feeling regret about making a mistake. Those buying for the family, for example, want to please family members and cannot afford to experiment, say, with new foods. As Gronow says, change is often accomplished by introducing the new item initially as an extra luxury.[26] However, while the habitual buy provides stability, reliability, and predictability of outcome, buying on habit is a conservative stance, which means forgoing the opportunity for something better that might come along.
- There is always the possibility of potential losses in choosing another brand, and consumers weight the potential loss from brand switching disproportionately, as losses are more emotionally charged than corresponding gains.
- Change demands mental and emotional energy, and consumers are cognitive misers. Buying on habit means speed in buying, minimum mental effort, and freeing of time for more worthwhile endeavors—all of which may be part of a rational buying strategy. Nonetheless, any such savings may not compensate for a suboptimal purchase.
- To buy the familiar adds a predictable element in life and contributes to a sense of comfort and control over one's life. Familiarity and liking are positively correlated, as that which is familiar becomes more and more part of a valued way of life. This is typically why we stick to "the tried and true," whether it is a detergent or a religion. People's daily

lives are constructed out of the familiar, as is illustrated by daily rituals and routines.

Consumers are not easily tempted away from habitual buys: if they do switch, it is commonly to a similar brand, which is why brand switching is more likely within than between market segments. The many habits in life add a certain hedonic tone to it. As with religion, preferences tend to become stronger with consumption. This is another reason why it is easier to retain customers than to convert them from rivals.

An *entrenched* habit can be merely *precedent governed*, in the sense of "buying as before." Behavior that is precedent governed may not get beyond looking at what was done in the past. An entrenched habit can instead be *rule following*, in that a rule determines what the consumer does, for example, "always buying my husband's favorite." This contrasts with buying being rule *governed*, which is simply descriptive of some regularity in buying. In the case of rule-governed action, it is the behavior itself that fixes the rule, not vice versa. The action is in accordance with a rule only in the sense that a rule can be devised that represents the regularity in behavior. In contrast, rule-following behavior is typically rooted in social norms or some justifying generalization. In any case, it seems that advertisers generally assume (not without reason) that the older a person is, the more entrenched he or she has become in buying habits. Hence the focus on youth. However, in being generally ignored, older consumers become more open to the few advertisers who make the effort.

Habits respond to new information. If prospective customers justify their habitual buy on grounds no longer tenable, this can be exposed, or if the habit is precedent-based, advertisers can appeal to the social norm of not being an "old stick in the mud," giving people the motivation to select the new over the habitual buy. The bigger problem arises when habit is rule following in a way that is tied to social norms. The problem then lies in elevating the confidence of the consumer in taking action that is inconsistent with these norms. This can be done by making appeals that stress how a role model no longer adheres to such norms. A good deal of cosmetic surgery was encouraged by reports of celebrities having it done. There is always word-of-mouth and other information about new products that tempts consumers to experiment. Novel products always have great appeal. People have a latent appetite for changes as far as they meet the desire for novelty to put off boredom. When one is seduced into trying something new, one may come to prefer that which was initially rejected. Hence marketers of rival brands have every incentive to tempt the consumer to break away from habit and hang in there until the consumer is truly sold.

Recognition-Primed Decision-Making

The traditional view is of the consumer simultaneously evaluating several brands to assess relative benefits. This may not be so, in two ways:

1. One may buy a product without evaluating alternatives, simply following the rule: "If I like it and it is within my price range, I will buy it," thus buying the brand the consumer *feels* he or she would like to have. The focus is on *perceptions* of a product's potential to enrich the consumer's life, not on whether other products or brands might do better. Alternatively, the consumer has in mind what would fit his or her desires to fulfill some function or use-occasion, in effect following the rule: "If I see something like what I have in mind, and the price is right, I will buy it."

2. If the buyer does seriously evaluate rival brands and adds up the pros and cons, he or she may evaluate options serially (and not simultaneously) until finding something approximating what he or she wants. This is a much more comfortable way of doing things.

Klein studied experts making decisions in conditions of (1) time pressure; (2) high stakes in the outcome (high-involvement decisions); (3) missing, ambiguous, or erroneous information; and (4) ill-defined goals and rules.[27] Not uncommonly, there was also a problem of integrating the decision-making of team members (team coordination). These conditions put decision-makers into an emotional state of mind. Such conditions are not uncommon in consumer decision-making and commonly operate in industrial buying—as well as in decisions taken by marketing managers in new product development!

How, according to Klein, are decisions made in such conditions? What surprised Klein was the extent to which *no* alternatives were considered beyond the one actually chosen, that is, *comparative evaluation* did not take place. The absence of comparative evaluation surprises many marketers, because the marketing literature stresses that consumers value being able to choose from a wide range of options. We should distinguish, however, between consumers wanting the opportunity to choose from a wide range of options and what they actually do. The consumer commonly does forgo comparative evaluation, that is, evaluating rival brands. Even when the consumer does comparative evaluations, it not uncommonly consists of just comparing prices, not relevant attributes. Much else is taken on trust.

Because no simultaneous evaluation of rival brands takes place does not mean that no evaluation of any sort occurs. The consumer may make mental comparisons of rival brands when, say, receiving advice from others. But this is a long way from the sort of evaluation typified by the multiattribute model (concerned with listing attributes, weighting them, and rating the rival brands on the extent to which they have the attributes to obtain each individual brand's score), which is so unfaithful to everyday shopping experience. An extreme example is the choice of personal physician. Mostly choice is based on recommendation. The fact that consumers today have far more choices to make on what to buy, combined with fewer women who are not in full-time employment, means less time can be spent on making decisions about what to buy.

If decision-making always involves deliberation of trade-offs in comparing alternatives, then decision-making in this sense did not take place in the cases discussed by Klein. In other words, there was *choosing without decision-making*. Although people often speak, following Herbert Simon, of programmed decisions, this is a loose way of talking. If we are to exploit the richness and nuances of the language, decision-making per se always involves weighing up the pros and cons and making trade-offs. We should speak of programmed choices, not programmed decisions.

In the Klein studies, fire ground commanders had no time for considering options but had to come up with an effective course of action right at the start. The option chosen was ranked as number one for the situation without any conscious evaluation of alternatives. From sizing up the situation, some solution sprang to mind. Although at the conscious level no alternatives need have been considered, many options would in fact have been rejected at the nonconscious level. Damasio shows that many options are rejected at the nonconscious level. Bad outcomes connected with an option instantly generate an unpleasant gut feeling; the feeling is "somatic" because it relates to the body and a "marker" because it "marks" an image, however fleetingly.[28] The unpleasant "gut feeling" leads to the immediate rejection of many alternatives, as if we nonconsciously act in accordance with the *conjunctive rule* (only accept as an option that which passes minimum standards) to eliminate alternatives that lack positive emotional resonance.

According to Klein, experienced fire commanders and similarly placed decision-makers evaluate situations, even if they are nonroutine ones, as examples of a *prototype* that point to what action to take. There is a recognizable pattern in situations that suggests a prototype to fit a particular situation. This sort of pattern recognition is a skill resulting from experience. If a prototype comes to mind that matches the situation, it allows an immediate choice to be made. The consumer, too, may be faced with a problem that results in a prototype (product or brand) coming to mind that he or she thinks will meet the situation. She then buys that product. There is no further search or comparative evaluation. Klein calls this approach *recognition-primed decision-making*

(RPD), though a better term might be recognition-primed *choice*, since no deliberation on trade-offs is involved.

One puzzle with RPD arises because many terms used to describe a product are relative, so when the consumer speaks of a high-quality brand, we naturally conclude it must be high quality relative to *evaluated* rival brands. But in RPD, quality is relative to the prototype, not to alternative brands or products. The prototype becomes the standard for comparison purposes. The consumer seeks to meet the standard demanded by the problem, and that standard is the prototype product. This is in line with consumers simply buying a particular product, without making comparisons, if it matches what they have in mind. Confronted with a problem (e.g., a headache), its "pattern" brings to mind the prototype (product/brand) that seems like a solution. Similarly, if a consumer wants a new dress for some occasion, some vision of what would be suitable comes to mind and she looks around until she finds something that fits the vision.

The danger with RPD lies in thinking that the prototype will always be an apt solution to a new situation. But Klein would argue that in such cases there are no experts, so errors are to be expected. Consumers make errors this way when (say) they erroneously misdiagnose a situation and choose some over-the-counter drug for a serious medical condition.

Choosing in RPD means first recognizing a situation as one suited to a particular course of action and then evaluating the course of action (or product) by imagining how it would work. If it seems suitable, it is chosen. So what is involved in this context when we talk about "evaluating" each option? Evaluation here means using *mental simulation* to run through a course of action to judge likely effectiveness and feasibility. If the first option is "seen" as not likely to work, the decision-maker moves on to the next option until an option appears feasible. Decision-makers in effect use Herbert Simon's *satisficing* strategy and choose the first option that would appear to work.[29] Simon suggested that this term is more appropriate than "maximizing." While the maximizer would look at the whole set of options to find the best buy, the satisficer settles for the first option that is "good enough." While the maximizer has the satisfaction of knowing he has chosen the best buy, the satisficer knows she has saved herself a good deal of time and trouble. This might erroneously suggest that "satisficing" is simply maximizing within constraints, but this is misleading, since the consumer is not thinking about constraints but just what would adequately do the job.

Klein presents, in fact, three variants of RPD. The first involves a simple matching of the situation with a prototype that fits. The second variation involves the additional factor of having to diagnose the situation before recognizing a suitable prototype. But does not sizing up a situation and matching with a prototype (the simple matching case) suggest some form of diagnosis, in that the selection of the prototype says where the solution is thought to lie (the essence of diagnosis)? Klein argues that problem diagnosis is an *elaboration* of (going beyond) *problem representation,* which may be all that is required, without any diagnosis. Klein is stressing instantaneous appreciation in the *simple matching case*—of situation with prototype. Third, RPD may involve having to evaluate several prototype options one at a time by imagining how each would work and maybe even having to make adjustments to any suggested option to better fit the situation. This is called *singular evaluation.* Thus even when Klein's decision makers did consider options, they never simultaneously compared them but evaluated each in turn, that is, serially, each on its merits. Klein contrasts this singular evaluation approach with the *comparative* (simultaneous) evaluation method. Singular evaluation contrasts with the *multiattribute* (compensatory) model.

Klein stresses that RPD applies to experienced decision-makers. Only on the basis of experience can they; (1) recognize a situation as familiar; (2) think of a prototype situation and evaluate it by imagining how it would work in practice and so spotting likely weaknesses; (3) be confident enough to select the first workable option; and (4) evaluate options one at a time (if need be) without feeling obliged to compare the pros and cons of each of the options before choosing.

Do the three variants of RPD have any applicability to consumer buying? The simple matching case of RPD may appear close to habit, where there is a one-to-one correspondence between problem and solution. But not quite. With habit there is no need for any matching. As to the second variant, consumers may also have to diagnose the problem before selecting from memory a suitable prototype to match with a brand. Finally, as in the third variant, consumers do on occasion imagine possessing and consuming the options that serially come to mind using mental simulation. This can be an emotional process leading to self-persuasion as to what to choose. The problem, however, lies in assessing the incidence of RPD in consumer buying. Klein is right in arguing that RPD assumes experienced decision-makers, which in consumer marketing means mature shoppers.

Out of the 156 cases of decisions made by experienced decision-makers, in 127 cases the RPD was used, as opposed to only 18 cases using comparative evaluation. These RPD decisions were made in conditions of (1) time pressures, (2) high investment in the outcomes, (3) inadequate information, and (4) goals being ill defined. Traditionally, such decision-making, under uncertainty and high risk, was considered ideal for using rational choice models that stress comparative evaluation. Klein claims such approaches are more suited to the novice. This is because deliberating the pros and cons of options makes more sense for novices who start from scratch. A person is more likely to follow some rough approximation to the rational choice model in buying a house than in buying a car, which is a more frequent purchase. Klein is right to argue that something like the rational choice (compensatory) model of comparative evaluation is more likely when, as in business-to-business buying, there is a need for conflict resolution, a need for justification, and a pretense at optimization.

Klein refers briefly to the noncompensatory models of decision-making (conjunctive rule, disjunctive rule, elimination by aspects, and the face-off procedure), but apart from viewing these models as simpler models than RPD, he does not draw out resemblances. He is skeptical of all "rational problem-solving" methods on the grounds that they do not prepare a person to improvise, act on imperfect information, or cope with unreliable data or shifting conditions. On the other hand, Klein points out that RPD is inadequate for explaining team (group) decision-making, where some approximation to the comparative evaluation approach (the rational model) may have more applicability.

Consumers are always seeking ways to reduce the complexity of buying, as complexity generates anxiety. Evans and Wurster present an unusual perspective on this. In arguing that buying can be time-consuming, difficult, and inevitably incomplete, Evans and Wurster view product suppliers as creating navigational tools, "everything from branding and advertising to relationship building and merchandising—to help consumers short-circuit the complexities of a comprehensive search and find products they're willing to buy."[30] This is a good perspective for many marketers.

Decision-Making: Deliberation and Trade-offs

Decision-making involves refraining from action while a person reasons out the best option. It occurs when no single option is superior in every respect and there is a need to deliberate the relative merits of the options to calculate trade-offs. Marketers typically assume more consumer deliberation on options than actually occurs. Time limitations and the absence of relevant knowledge force the consumer to take much on trust. There can be trust in the brand name, trust in advice, or trust that no product in a competitive market would even be competing unless certain requirements were being met.

Emotion always plays a role. Even if a consumer followed something like the multiattribute model, emotion linked to values would still enter into making the trade-offs. Models such as the multiattribute model, however, reflect the academic's desire to mold buyer behavior into something highly rational, when in fact the behavior of the buyer may be intelligible without following the norms of rationality. Contrary to the way it is sometimes presented, the multi-attribute model is not something optimal. Most versions of the model assume that we can measure differences in options like we measure a piece of cloth (i.e., on a ratio scale), and no attempt is made to measure dysfunctional consequences while the fact is ignored that there can be double counting when criteria overlap.

As Scriven points out, the weighting of scales cannot be given the significance intended, as relative importance is controlled by the number of criteria involved.[31] For example, assume the weights given to the criteria for each product attribute ranged from 1 to 5 and the ratings given to the alternatives being evaluated for the amount possessed of an attribute ranged from 1 to 10; then the most important criterion can only contribute a maximum of 50 points to any one of the products being evaluated. This maximum of 50 can be completely swamped by the accumulation of only five minor criteria, each weighted only 1 but each rated a 10 for the alternative being evaluated. Scriven points to numerous other deficiencies before advocating his own qualitative approach. There is also the implicit assumption in models like the multiattribute model that the consumer can specify the product wanted by getting out an inventory of attributes. In fact a sense of the whole can be lost by concentrating attention on the separate items in turn. In addition, there is the question of interaction effects. It is not enough to talk about the multiattribute model having had some predictive value in laboratory studies (it is easy to feed subjects the information in a way that offers little option but to follow the model). As Deutsch says, although prediction is part of the *method* of science, the main reason theories are rejected is because they are bad explanations (and the multiattribute model is a bad explanation of consumer decision-making), not because they necessarily fail experimental tests.[32]

It is difficult to believe that consumers build up an idea of what they want from listing individual attributes. To list all the attributes of a car would quickly overwhelm us. Just seeing a range of alternatives is better. A product is essentially a system, that is, a set of interdependent parts that together form a unitary whole for meeting some function(s). This means that any product attribute only has meaning in terms of the visualized whole. A buyer cannot just think about the size of car engine he wants unless he already has in mind a vision of the whole car of which the engine will be a part. And buying something new is a learning experience, which means that the attributes consumers initially claim to be seeking may be considerably modified or abandoned as they learn more about what they really want. Buying, as opposed to filling in questionnaires about buying, can be an emotional experience (even just looking at the packaging) that colors outlooks and prejudices buying decisions. Although we can take any person's purchase and work back to a multiattribute model of the process, this in no way indicates the way the information was processed.

An analysis of around 4,000 protocols since 1972, consisting of a record of what the consumer says before buying, during buying, and after buying, involving every conceivable consumer product, has involved only one case resembling the multiattribute model of buying, and this was in the buying of a calculator by an MBA student, who deliberately followed the procedure as taught! Nor was there any suggestion in the protocols that it was "as if" the buyers were adhering to something like the model. It is not even clear as to what the truth conditions are for the "as if" label to apply. If "as if" simply means "appears analogous to" or is a "model of," there is not the slightest evidence that anything analogous to the multiattribute model takes place unless it is prompted in laboratory experiments. In fact, few of those buying an infrequently bought product or buying for the first time knew exactly what they wanted, and, certainly, few had fully ordered preferences. An expressed prepurchase preference may be no more than a "ceteris paribus" saying that buying will only proceed if all else is equal. Buying is a learning experience, and initial preferences can be outweighed or overridden as learning takes place. As Underhill says, more and more purchasing decisions are being made in the store itself—with shoppers being susceptible to impressions and information acquired while in the store—rather than being dependent on advertising.[33]

In any rational choice model, there is the assumption of a means–end model of decision-making, where buyers have certain goals/wants to be met and then search for the best means. While consumers may have no difficulty in listing goals/wants, they may have difficulty in (1) saying how much of the goal in question is required or (2) gauging how much of the goals to be achieved is provided by various brands.[34] There is a problem of trade-offs as the consumer trades off, say, convenience-in-use for greater technical performance, aesthetics, or whatever. It is because trade-offs can seldom be measured on a common scale like money that trade-offs are made against values that link to the emotions.

The most often quoted way of measuring the relative importance of various attributes to undertake trade-offs is conjoint analysis, but this assumes consumers know what attributes they will want and that what they want is some sum of *tangible* attributes.[35] But the sum of several things together need not be the sum of their individual values. As Velleman says, even if we could establish the equivalence of value between a helping of financial benefit and a helping of physical well-being, these measures of financial benefit and physical benefit would not reflect potential interactions between the values of the underlying commodities.

Even when consumers know what they want, their preferences are rarely absolute and usually conditional. Shopping around is a learning experience, and new trade-offs occur all the time. The conjunctive rule in consumer decision-making suggests that certain minimum levels on attributes can be a necessary condition for the brand to be acceptable. Thus, for example, one necessary attribute for a particular consumer on a car may be that it is a four-door sedan. But such conditions seldom turn out to be absolute and are constantly traded off at the point of sale. Thus one woman in a protocol statement who had insisted on the four-door attribute actually bought the two-door version of the car on seeing how much more streamlined and stylish the two-door version of the Chevy Cavalier was. Consumers who are knowledgeable about what exactly they want will act as if choosing in line with conjunctive rules, but this applies less to new buying situations when shopping becomes a learning experience that does not lend itself to premature closure on what attributes to exclude.

In any case, symbolism and aesthetics and not just tangible attributes can be all-important. And they are assuming increasing importance in marketing.[36] In affluent societies the choices of consumers are becoming increasingly aesthetic, though Marder shows that the relative importance of product versus image varies from product category to product category and from customer to customer.[37] Given the problems associated with making decisions on every aspect of the product, it is not surprising if the consumer abandons setting out precisely what he or she wants in favor of just seeing what is available.

Many rational choice models of decision-making implicitly take for granted that consumers are a bundle of fixed, explicit wants that act as a filter determining what attributes they prefer and what they will buy. But in respect to new products, consumers have only notional wants that give rise to *latent* wants, that is, wants that are activated when consumers are made aware of how what is being offered can enrich their lives. Consumers typically remain open to persuasion right to the point of sale. They are open to persuasion because what induces people to believe something about a product is always a matter of how things are presented, the tangible evidence available, and the conflicting forces of emotion. Consumer beliefs are seldom firm but coated with doubts.

As regards meticulously collecting and analyzing information, consumers only collect enough information to have the confidence to form a preference. As to the claim that consumers are becoming well informed, this assumes consumers have the motivation and ability to become well informed on whatever product is being bought.[38] With 20–30% of adults being functionally illiterate, much buying of new products is inevitably tied to trust in advice or brand. Even the very educated find there is a problem of information overload, time pressures, and so on that requires that they adopt some coping strategy that avoids the spending of too much time in searching for and analyzing information. Ignorance is more the rule than being highly informed. In any case, consumers are far from making themselves experts. In buying a new product, the multi-attribute model in particular seems remote from reality, in that consumers are being asked about preferences for experiences they have not tried in conditions outside the emotional context of buying. Consumers are not given courses on deciding how to decide, so their approaches are far from optimal.

Decision-making arises whenever the consumer evaluates various options in order to make a choice. The process involves trade-offs, and trade-offs involve values and the past emotional episodes that determined those values in the first place. The set of brands considered is the *competitive frame* or *evoked set*. Different consumers make up their minds in different ways, as they come to the task of buying with different expectations, information, and understandings of consequences and take account of different considerations. They also come to the task with different amounts of product sophistication. Some have a poor conceptualization of the product. Yet having the right conceptualization of the product is vital, since conceiving the potential of the product comes before actively seeking it. And conceptualization is tied closely to presentation in promotion. Even where two consumers have the same choice criteria, they may choose different brands when faced with the same choices. This happens when they (1) use different indicators for the presence of attributes; (2) are attracted to different symbolism and aesthetics; or (3) are in different emotional states. One consumer may depend on brand reputation to indicate the quality of the product while another may just take advice. Any buying decision embraces wants, emotion, beliefs, symbolism, and buying intent, and a comprehensive model pays respect to each.

Consumers are emotional beings, and, as Elster says, emotion subverts the rationality of action in three ways: (1) through belief formation, as in wishful thinking; (2) through information acquisition, as in jumping to conclusions; and (3) through (most important) the lack of regard or neglect of thought about consequences, including a lack of concern for more information.[39] Rationality in consumer buying is typically flawed. Consumers commonly seek evidence that confirms what they already believe and avoid thinking out the consequences of unwelcome information. They are influenced particularly by what information most readily comes to mind. They tend to be overconfident in buying when confidence is high and underconfident when confidence is low. They have emotional preferences that typically lead to self-deception or wishful thinking. They have an emotional dislike of losses that counts more than the pleasure of winning equivalent gains, as it is emotionally more damaging to lose than it feels good to win—with the consequence that people are ordinarily risk averse.

If we were to make some generalization as to the stages of the decision-making process of the consumer, these would be in line with Velleman's earlier work, as follows.[40]

- Ruling out of options disliked
- Reflection on the descriptive image of each option considered and its fit to the descriptive image of ourselves and the situation
- Rationalization to further justify an emerging implicit favorite model
- Formation of buying intention
- Postpurchase behavior

1. **Ruling out of options disliked.** Consumers rule out many options at the nonconscious level that resonate as having a negative brand image or as inappropriate in some other way.[41] Emotional memories (via Damasio's somatic markers) tells us what we hate or dislike more strongly than does rational analysis. Consumers unconsciously rule out products or brands that conflict with values anchored in emotion.

Douglas and Isherwood generalize about the goals directly tied to buying in arguing that consumer buying expresses social goals that reflect the following emotional aspirations:[42]

- Community with others
- Making sense of what is happening in the surrounding world

Both these goals involve the exchange of information, and consumer products can be viewed as being bought in order to transmit and receive information about the social scene, specifically information to help build bridges or erect social fences, since consumer products:

- Serve as a live information system to signal to others the user's self-image, rank, and values, as these are tied to personal self-esteem. Products like cosmetics, clothes, watches, shoes, cars, and life insurance fall into this category.
- Mark social events that are emotional occasions like marriage and time intervals like births. Cameras, expensive wines, wedding dresses, and so on are bought to mark social occasions.
- Increase the time available for the pleasures of social involvement. Lawnmowers, washing machines, telephones, and TV dinners come under this heading.
- Give order to events to meet the emotional need to be aware of what is happening in the world outside. Under this heading come newspa-

pers, magazines, and other products that help make sense of what is happening in the surrounding world.

2. Reflection on the descriptive image of each option. Consumers focus on options that attract their attention and seem promising at the gut feeling level. Emotion is always involved here. If several options are considered, serial evaluation rather than simultaneous comparative evaluation typically occurs. In deliberating on an alternative, consumers conjure up *descriptive images* of the product and its *fit to themselves and their situation* (e.g., use-occasion, etc.), imagining what it would be like to possess and consume the product. Descriptive images are likely to take account (however impressionistically) of some combination of the six criteria discussed in chapter 1: (1) technical functions, (2) economic factors, (3) legalistic factors, (4) integrative considerations, (5) adaptive (risk avoidance) factors, and (6) intrinsic appeal or degree of liking.

Trade-offs are made among these six criteria, and all link to feelings with emotional overtones, as discussed in chapter 1. The six criteria apply not just to the product itself but to the whole offering of product, price, availability, and branding (embracing packaging, name, graphics, and the symbols or associations that have been acquired by the brand). This entire stage illustrates the importance of how products are presented and described to ensure that a positive and exciting image is recalled that fits the persona of the consumer, even if this persona is somewhat fantasized. Promotions need to help in the self-imagining of feelings arising from buying, possessing, and consuming the product.

The six criteria determine what attributes (e.g., car engine) and level of attribute (e.g., size of engine) are considered, after which the necessary trade-offs are made. Consumer values are not so consciously identified and ranked as always to make clear the preferred trade-offs. It is not always easy, for example, to decide whether to trade off a bigger engine for the saving on price. Luce, Bettman, and Payne claim, on the basis of their experimental simulations, that undertaking trade-offs can be very emotional, with some arousing more emotion than others.[43] For these researchers, minimizing the likelihood of negative emotions (e.g., of regret) enters into making trade-offs for consumers and modifies any view suggesting that consumers act purely for technical and economic reasons. Their interest lies in establishing (1) what makes some trade-offs more emotionally demanding than others; (2) how variation in emotional trade-off difficulty influences how decision-makers go about deciding; and (3) what decisions are ultimately made. Any conscious appraisal of alternatives makes clear the trade-off difficulty involved, with the consumer taking into account not only the relative importance of the various attributes, like quality and price, but also the associated emotional implications and the cognitive difficulty of mastering what needs to be known. In respect to how emotional trade-off difficulty affects the way decision-makers go about deciding, these authors accept that the emotional trade-off difficulty can lead the consumer to be problem focused (deliberating how to bring about an improvement in the situation) or emotion focused (seeking to change the meaning of the situation for him or her or perhaps trying not to think about the problem at all). Finally, on the matter of the decision itself, these authors point out that fear of regret or loss, for example, promotes a strategy of sticking with the status quo, or the habitual buy.

Thagard writes that making sense of the world we live in is an activity of fitting something puzzling into a coherent pattern of mental representations made up of concepts, beliefs, wants, and action.[44] Thagard would claim that buyers find pleasure when an offering has the coherence that is sought, as incoherence contributes to anxiety and the possibility of an unpleasant surprise. All the elements of the offering should cohere both among themselves and the functions for which they are being bought. For Thagard, coherence becomes key to making an offering meaningful.

For all consumers, the presence or quality of some attributes may have to be (1) inferred from proxies or surrogate indicators, as when a car is judged on how well the doors close; (2) assumed on the basis of some heuristic (like the likability heuristic); or (3) simply accepted on trust. Trust in a brand or store substitutes for evidence in choosing what to buy. What particular heuristics are used will depend somewhat on how much knowledge consumers presently possess. In any case, as Marder says, the consumer has beliefs and desires about attributes, whether he or she is able to observe them directly or not.

3. Rationalization to further justify an emerging implicit favorite. Once one knows how to (1) describe the options and (2) how to describe oneself and one's situation in relation to the options and simulate what it would be like to buy, possess, and consume the product, one will know the most promising of the alternatives and will probably have an emerging (implicit) favorite that has emotional resonance. As Velleman (1989) says, rarely do the pros and cons remain to be computed. One seeks further information often in order not to reject the favored but to make a case for a choice already made.

4. Formation of buying intention. The output of a decision is a preference, which is a comparative desire for one of the options, and a preference is tied to buying intention. Consumers form their intention to buy in line with their reasons for buying, but there is a need to act in accordance with that intention. To say I intend to do X is not the same as to say I promise to do X or I will do X. If the consumer fails to carry out an intention, it is the prediction that is faulty, not the consumer. If, on the other hand, the consumer fails to keep a

promise, this is different, since promises carry a moral imperative. A promise is a socially defined obligation. To actually buy involves the "will to act" or the will to authorize it. A state of intending to buy is a state of the will, while acting on that intention is an act of will. Having an intention to buy is like going into gear, whereas having the "will to buy" is like pressing the accelerator: it provides the emotion behind the motivation to buy. This is why promotions can be so important in providing that final trigger.

5. Postpurchase behavior. Consumers seldom make major purchases without reservations. Where social reality is involved, one can never be sure one has bought the best product or chosen the best dentist or selected the best hairdresser, and so on, until others validate the choice. Validation is an emotional "must" in the buying of products that are socially visible. We commonly speak of cognitive dissonance as arising at the postpurchase evaluation stage. As developed by Leon Festinger, *cognitive dissonance* occurs when a person holds inconsistent cognitions (beliefs) at the same time.[45] Thus the belief that I am doing action X, though I believe that this is wrong, can cause emotional discomfort, so people try to reduce the conflict. Anyone who makes a difficult decision, particularly one that cannot be reversed, it is assumed, afterward will try to strengthen that decision so that it will come to seem more justified than when it was first made. Every choice made by a buyer is a potential source of dissonance, as the perceived loss of an attractive displaced alternative is dissonant with the knowledge that another product has been chosen.

Cognitive dissonance may be reduced by the individual lowering the value placed on some aspect of the product sacrificed (for example, being told "the 586 has yet to be tested") or enhancing the advantages of the product bought (for example, "since you bought, the price has risen 25%") or stressing the similarity between the product bought and the one sacrificed (for example, "in practice you'll find there is no real difference between the two"). When some not-for-profit organizations deliberately seek to arouse feelings of guilt, behind that guilt is dissonance: the belief that the receiver of the appeal for funds is a person who is generous to the less fortunate is inconsistent with any belief that the appeal must be ignored. It is the same with those begging in the street: to refuse a request can challenge beliefs about the type of person one is. The response, of course, may be not to donate but to argue to oneself about the unworthiness of the cause relative to others.

Cognitive dissonance is often used to explain market behavior. One study found that buyers of new cars paid more attention to advertisements promoting the brand they had bought than to advertisements for other brands.[46] Cognitive dissonance is usually quoted to justify "keeping the customer sold" by reassuring him about the wisdom of the buy. However, the theory of cognitive dissonance has lost some of its shine. The disposition toward the reduction of dissonance can be very weak when other interests are at stake. A more teasing problem has been the fact that we cannot predict before an experiment which mode of dissonance reduction a person will employ, so it becomes difficult to think of an experiment that would test (seek to try and falsify) the theory, as we do not know what predictions are to be confirmed or disconfirmed. However, cognitive dissonance as an explanation makes a great deal of intuitive sense and, although rival theories have been put forward, to many this still makes the most sense.

In any case, the tendency after buying is to think of further justifying reasons so as to ward off any emotional unease. A comforting rationalization helps to overcome the fear of regret.[47] It is not uncommon for people to turn what were initially objections to the purchase into advantages: the disadvantage of (say) smallness in an automobile or a house becomes an advantage in terms of maneuverability or ease of maintenance.

There can be many ambivalent feelings after purchase. The consumer may feel she has made the best buy possible, but the best buy still leaves many of her goals unsatisfied. If such a position is common, it presents an opportunity to fill a market gap. Consumers may find their purchase exactly what they had wanted and ordered yet be disappointed, because (1) important considerations were not considered before buying; (2) different consequences come to be weighted differently after buying; or (3) consequences were not as anticipated, as frequently happens with investments. Disappointment is particularly common with products that involve effort, like correspondence courses (long-distance learning) or health centers. For many purchases, it is difficult to know how things will turn out, as in the case of investments. Often the only way to find out whether something is suitable is to buy it, but even this may be little help when the benefits (if any) take years to realize. Getting to know a house, as well as its location and neighbors, takes time, so it takes time to know whether the purchase has been a success. Disappointment is more emotional than achieving a surplus on expectations. Yet for the seller to go beyond expectations is important, since it can lead to a surge of positive word-of-mouth communication that can be crucial for a new product.

Organizational Buying

We have ignored organizational buying except to say that it is likely to be a process involving comparative evaluation if it is a new and important product. Organizational buying is typically distinguished by several people being involved in the decision and no one person deciding. It is meant to be a shared decision: each participant is supposed to regard the buying decision as something to be jointly determined. The key decisions to be made are in (1) specifying the offering to be bought; (2) listing the suppliers who will be asked to make a bid; and (3) selection of the product/supplier. However, participants in any buying decision bring with them emotional baggage—for example, a desire to get even for past battles lost.

When several people are involved in a buying decision they form a decision-making unit (DMU). When members of a DMU represent different departments of a firm, they come to the DMU with their own individual responsibilities and departmental attachments. Each position (e.g., purchasing, engineering, production, etc.) represented by a participant has affixed to it certain normative expectations. The whole process has the potential for conflict. Each participant plays a role, but the rules are never fully scripted to cover every contingency in advance. The goals that are formally attached to each position (that give rise to the role to be played) constrain behavior enough to allow the participant's general thrust to be objectively defended but not anything beyond that. Actual behavior in the role will be saturated with feelings tied to self-assessment emotions, like pride and anger.

Economics avoids the problem of organizational decision-making by assuming that participants are just unitary individuals, instead of people who form coalitions that have mixed goals. Differences in viewpoints among the participants are likely to result in different weights being given to various choice criteria. Thus the purchasing department is likely to focus on the commercial aspects of the purchase and so be more interested in the economic aspects than engineering. Members of a DMU will also have varying influence on the buying decision depending on their role, their position in the management hierarchy, their technical expertise, and their position in the communications network; a central position close to top management adds to influence.

But often participants in a DMU do arrive at a unanimous decision. The concept of the *group polarization effect* is sometimes used to explain how a group like an organizational buying group does move unanimously to approve some decision. If each (or the great majority) of the participants to a group decision is (or is persuaded to be) even moderately in favor of some decision (e.g., a preference for a certain offering or supplier), the tendency is to become more so after discussion. The group polarization effect is tied to the emotional gratification arising from that agreement, as it is accompanied by a sense of group *affiliation,* affirmation of beliefs, and the emotional sharing of the decision. Mayhew defines the affiliation need as involving searching for and finding gratification in a show of solidarity with other people.[48] The idea of group polarization conflicts with the idea that groups converge and compromise on the average position of the group.

Some Key Assertions for Marketing

1. If marketing management is to anticipate emotional responses, it is useful to classify responses into cognitive effects, arousal of feelings, behavioral displays, and affect-driven actions.

2. If marketing management is to anticipate the *effects* of its actions on the consumer, it needs to: acknowledge that any strong negative emotions that are aroused (e.g., when the consumer feels cheated) can give rise to a self-righteous absoluteness of feeling that pushes out more reflective consider-ations; recognize that the emotions aroused are key to determining the salience of attributes and, in acting as arbitrators among reasons, to as-signing values to options to determine trade-offs; be mindful that the arousal of positive emotions toward a product can on occasions be suffi-cient to lead to buying that product, since choice can be *affect driven*, par-ticularly when relevant information is in short supply and uncertainty is high; be attentive to consumer beliefs—since, while the firm's promotions may have activated an emotional preference for the firm's type of product/ offering, the consumer's beliefs may direct him or her to buying a rival brand, unless the firm's promotion subtly suggests why the firm's brand is the best option; envision the possibility of a strong emotional response changing future wants and loyalties; be aware that, while emotions influ-ence beliefs, beliefs influence both the activation of emotions and the level of their intensity; and be familiar with the fact that the emotions can aid in learning the repertoire of concepts that illuminate what the product can do to enrich the consumer's life.

3. If marketing management is to understand the feelings aroused by the firm's actions, it must both: be aware that any highly positive or negative consumer appraisal arouses feelings in the consumer and these feelings in-volve a sense of decreased or enhanced standing vis-à-vis others in the world at large; and appreciate that the arousal of negative feelings lasts longer than the arousal of positive feelings.

4. If business is conducted face-to-face, the seller should look for emotional responses in the immediate facial displays and other nonverbal behavior before these are consciously blocked, bearing in mind that all such signs need to be interpreted within the context.

5. If marketing management is to devise strategies that take account of con-sumer choice or decision processes, it is helpful to assess how many con-sumers: just pick the firm's brand at random rather than select; make purely affect-driven choices or act on the basis of intrinsic liking; act on precedent-governed, rule-following or rule-governed habit; adopt singular evaluation by acting on some variant of RPD (recognition-primed decision-making), where the consumer uses, as criteria for buying, some mental prototype of what is wanted, so that simulated comparisons are made against the proto-

type rather than the comparison of options against each other; and actually undertake the trade-offs that characterize true decision-making. Here the consumer rules out emotionally disliked options; reflects on the descriptive image of each option and its fit to his or her wants and beliefs and situation; and finally often justifies some emerging implicit favorite model in arriving at the buying intention.

5

Predicting, Changing, and Influencing Emotional Responses

Every element of a firm's offering (product, price, promotion, and distribution) has the potential to generate emotional responses *if* the consumer's appraisal suggests that personal values or concerns are at stake. Any sort of novelty can lead to the emotional anticipation and contemplation of possessing a product; price can arouse emotion through being perceived either as a bargain or a rip-off; promotion can generate emotion by associating the product with desired images; and distribution can cause the emotion of frustration in buying or the emotion of excitement at the point of sale. This chapter is concerned with predicting emotional responses and gauging the extent to which they can be influenced and changed.

Predicting Emotional Responses

For Barlow and Maul, emotions tell us how customers are likely to behave in that, if they are angry, they feel primed to attack, and so on.[1] These authors endorse the view that if you can identify the emotion, you can identify the "emotional script" that goes from the triggering event, to thought, to feeling, to action. Thus, they argue, it is logically possible to predict likely customer behavior once the specific emotions are identified. While it is true that emotions, like all motives, have a dispositional tendency (e.g., frustration has a disposition to aggression), such tendencies can remain just that, dispositional tendencies. We cannot confidently predict specific action from emotion alone without knowledge of beliefs, no more than we can predict behavior from beliefs alone.

Everyone has some ability to predict emotional responses, given the circumstances. This is illustrated by an experiment conducted by Kahneman and Tversky.[2] The subjects in the experiment were given a scenario involving a Mr. Crane and Mr. Tees. These two gentlemen were scheduled to leave the airport at the same time but on different flights. They traveled to the airport in the same limousine, were caught in the same traffic jam, and arrived at the airport 30 minutes late for their flights. Mr. Crane was told his flight had left on time, but Mr. Tees was told that his had been delayed and had just left. The subjects in the experiment were asked: "Who was more upset, Mr. Crane or Mr. Tees?" Not surprisingly, 96% believed Mr. Tees would be more upset.

It is not always this easy to predict emotional responses, and researchers cannot just go out with a questionnaire and ask. A limitation of all questionnaires concerned with future buying is that they cannot capture the emotional context in which future buying takes place. Responses are dominated by rational replies, shorn of emotion. Predicting emotional responses by asking people how they will behave in some future situation is unlikely to incorporate the emotions that are evoked in real-life buying situations. In surveys, the pressures of shopping are unnaturally minimized.

Choices in real life are always the result of both individual preferences and situational pressures. This is one reason why it is easier to explain consumer behavior after the event than to predict it in the first place. The survey method has the additional limitation of being ill equipped to measure variation across contexts; yet the researcher often needs to appraise responses in contrasting situations. Contexts and background are important. This is why Underhill criticizes store designers for skimping on dressing rooms which operate as an effective selling tool by providing an attractive background.[3]

One prediction that can be made is that *emotional* experiences will be the ones remembered. This is why we may act purely to savor an emotional experience. Entertainment is the classical example, but shopping for something new and exciting is an emotional experience in itself. Impressionist painters focus attention on the experiences they have had with objects rather than on the objects themselves, and it is this that resonates with audiences. And emotional experiences do influence actions. Past emotional experiences become etched into emotional memory to determine what receives *attention*.[4] Strong emotional experiences are recalled and relived, refreshing and strengthening the emotional memory of them. Thus when the question is asked: *What were you doing when President Kennedy was assassinated?*" we get a ready answer. People remember events that evoke emotional memories, whether positive or negative, and any situation that resonates with these memories manifests itself in highly negative or positive appraisals. This is not to claim people do not reevaluate past experiences. Reevaluating experiences is part of growth and maturation. Nonetheless, at any one time there are emotional memories that influence current decisions.

Approaches to Predicting Emotional Responses

Emotional experiences have a privileged position in memory. But, as Bower (1994) says, emotional experiences do not heighten memory of *all* the details of an emotional event but only the key elements; peripheral details may be forgotten. This explains why an emotional ad may be remembered without the brand name being recalled at all. The mental capacity used up in absorbing, memorizing, and remembering the emotive elements takes away from what can be a "peripheral" element, namely, the brand name. This happens all too often. Thus every effort has to be made to link the name in an inseparable way with the key emotional elements.

While *explanation* looks to the effect to identify what brought it about, *prediction* asserts what happens as a consequence of some set of conditions. People are reasonably good at predicting emotional responses, given knowledge of the circumstances. How is this done? At the broadest level there are two approaches. The first is to draw on findings from the behavioral sciences developed from (say) causal analysis, correlation analysis, and probability theory. The second approach is to rely on "folk psychology": intersubjective knowledge people have about each other in the sense that: "I know it, you know it, I know you know it, and you know I know it." Folk psychology aims to understand others from the personal viewpoint; science does not. But it is such knowledge that gives people a head start in understanding other people, as opposed to understanding the behavior of, say, a bat.

Prediction on the Basis of Behavioral Science Findings

When it comes to predicting *voluntary* (intentional) action (as opposed to *involuntary*), the social sciences can draw on no universal laws from which actions can be predicted. It is easy to predict involuntary movement, like blinking (e.g., when someone suddenly waves a hand close to the eyes), but not intentional action, like winking. Of course, we may establish certain statistical regularities about future actions. From past experience, an observer may predict that a certain person will buy the *New York Times* on Sunday or that a certain person will pick up the phone if it is ringing and be the first to speak. While we may use statistical regularities to predict actions, we also use behavioral science findings. But we do not have anything resembling laws as per the natural sciences. Whenever so-called causal laws are found, they usually acquire whatever credibility they possess by cohering with rational behavior.

All lawlike generalizations about likely consumer actions must be taken with "an expanding grain of ceteris paribus." If marketing managers are better predictors of consumer behavior than statistical generalizations, it is because they keep continually up to date on what is happening in the environment. What the social sciences are able to do, however, is provide *sensitizing concepts* that can be converted into rules, as when we use the "reciprocity principle" to predict that those receiving a favor will feel obliged to repay. Sensitizing concepts sensitize marketing management to what is likely to be important in a situation. Marketers are now aware of concepts such as "expectations" and generalizations like the assertion that consumers commonly look to others to see what is the correct thing to do so that, for example, the most popular brand is seen as the best one to buy.

Some sensitizing concepts have been drawn from "folk psychology" (e.g., "You scratch my back and I'll scratch yours" expresses the principle of reciprocity) or have come to be a part of folk psychology—witness the incorporation into folk psychology of many Freudian concepts. Freudian concepts have entered the culture in crude and bastardized ways, as in terms such as "Freudian slip," or "the subconscious," all of which are now embedded in popular culture. The sayings and proverbs of ordinary language reflect a good deal of the wisdom of generations and constitute much of folk psychology. They can encapsulate what is held to be true about the culture, as in such (English) phrases as "It's not what you know, it's who you know," or "too clever by half."

Folk Psychology

We use and need folk psychology to understand the consumer and interpret consumer research findings. If one's knowledge of other people were confined to what psychologists have so far established, one would show no deep understanding of others and stumble badly in social relations. Those with Asperger syndrome, who can be highly intelligent, cannot make up for social skill deficiencies by reading psychology books.[5] It is folk psychology that helps people understand and get on with others and gives them confidence in saying how normal people would behave in various circumstances. It is this folk psychology that can make us critical of films and novels on the ground that "No one would behave like that under the circumstances. "The failure of a play, film, or book to be endorsed by folk psychology can lead to its failure as not being true to life, unless it is meant to be pure fantasy about aliens.

There are three different views as to how folk psychology works (1) people simply assume *rationality* in others; (2) people have *folk theories* about the relationship between mental states (beliefs and feelings/desires/goals/wants) and actions; or (3) people undertake a *simulation* of another's situation as a way to understand that person and to predict his or her actions.

Folk psychology as rationality. People may simply assume that others act rationally and explain consumer action by showing the action to be an effective means for achieving goals. In economics, this is the dominant premise on which behavior is predicted. It is also dominant in philosophy. Thus there is Dennett's "intentional stance."[6] People take an intentional stance toward another person, animal, or system when they ascribe rationality to that person (or animal or system) in terms of wants and beliefs and, on the basis of these wants and beliefs, go on to predict behavior.

In the intentional stance (which Dennett regards simply as a useful heuristic), there is the assumption of *ideal rationality* on the part of the individual—but it is not clear what that is. There is, in fact, no agreement about the norms of rationality, except those embodied in formal logic and decision theory, while, as we have shown, emotion in practice enters into all decision-making. The tenets of rationality as exemplified in formal logic presuppose a certain level of education to be understood and practiced. As Velleman points out, decision theory tells us how to be rational in our preferences by telling us how to have preferences that make sense.[7] However, there are many ways of making sense that may be in conflict with decision theory. The injunction to "maximize your expected utility" amounts to nothing more than "obey the axioms of decision theory, and you will have maximized any measure of expected utility that might be yours."

It is because people exhibit flawed rationality that Cherniak suggests the adoption of the less stringent concept of *minimalist rationality,* though that concept remains vague.[8] Rationality (whether ideal or minimalist) may dictate when it might be profitable to feign emotion, but it is a limited tool when it comes to predicting the emotional responses of others, as the usual concept of rationality simply focuses on *efficient* means to meet goals. There are limitations to this view. In the first place, goals themselves need to be considered, as there can be irrational goals. In the second place, efficient means cannot be the only consideration, since it is rational to take account of social norms, while the beliefs about what are efficient means might be untrue. Finally, many things are done simply because they have symbolic value or expressive meaning, as in (say) contributing to a lost cause, and not because they are instrumental to some higher-level self-interest goal. People support many causes that they view as hopeless (e.g., banning the automobile) and write letters of complaint they know will be ignored. They are emotionally propelled to show support and to feel that they are doing something to bring about a more just world. Supporting a hopeless cause can be a form of catharsis. Symbolic expressions of sympathy are common. If we have sympathy toward another we feel for their difficulties and want to alleviate their plight, but failing this we want to express our solidarity in a symbolic way.

Although the assumption of ideal rationality dominates approaches to decision-making like game theory, we are all obliged to assume some rationality (however flawed).It is necessarily assumed also in the other two variants of folk psychology, namely, folk theories and simulation. This is because completely irrational behavior would not be understood. We only understand others by making the assumption that their actions are intelligible, even if not highly rational.

Folk psychology as composed of folk theories. Folk psychology has been defined as the "principles" used by ordinary people to understand, explain, or predict their own behavior and the mental state or behavior of others. This view, known as the theory-theory view, is still retained by those who regard folk psychology as a theory. As a theory, folk psychology consists of psychological concepts (like belief, desire, and emotion) and the rules and practices employed by ordinary people in trying to understanding human behavior.

Most cognitive psychologists and philosophers interested in folk psychology tend to support a theory-theory view, but they are not unanimous in the way they picture it. Some claim that folk psychology is *tacit knowledge:* like our knowledge of grammar, we apply the principles of folk psychology without conscious effort or without necessarily being able to explicate any principles. This view is rejected by Fodor, who claims that folk psychology constitutes a theory in that it can be shown to consist of lawlike generalizations that postulate unobservable entities (like beliefs, desires, and emotions) that play an explanatory role. Similarly, Churchland, while regarding folk psychology as something likely to be displaced by neuroscience, claims that folk psychology is nonetheless an empirical theory that can be tested.[9] Human action, on this view, is a function of mental states like belief, desire, and emotion and "causal" relationships among these mental states. However, because many, many beliefs and desires may be involved, it is not possible to lay down in advance which are the causal ones. Hence, it is argued, social science resorts to collective dispositional categories like attitude.[10]

Winch regards folk psychology theory as simply the implicit network of concepts operating within the culture that are used to understand and predict the behavior of self and others. In regarding human action as rule-following behavior, he claims that the concepts used by people to describe their actions reflect the rules being followed.[11] Thus if a consumer says he bought Brand X because it was the most familiar, it is in the concept of familiarity that the rule lies: "Other things remaining equal, I buy the brand that is most familiar." The actions of people in another culture need to be treated like texts in an alien language: to understand their meaning, one must grasp the underlying system of concepts. Language embodies the concepts embedded in a culture, and it is this fact that makes language translation a skill: the conceptual system of one culture is being reoriented toward that of another. Thus the German word *heimat* is loosely translated as "homeland" but to fully nuance this concept in English would demand a long explanation.

Winch (1958) rejects the whole idea of intentional actions being "caused" in the sense used in the natural sciences. Nonetheless, he believes that knowledge of rules can lead to good (but by no means perfect) prediction of behavior: "If O wants to predict how N is going to act, he must familiarize himself with the concepts in terms of which N is viewing the situation; having done this, he may, from his knowledge of N's character, be able to predict with great confidence what decision N is going to take" (p. 91). It should be noted that Winch in predicting N's actions takes account of the concepts being used in *relation to the realities of the situation and knowledge of N's character*. Winch's views can be regarded as an assault on the whole idea of "causal" thinking when it comes to intentional action. There is a danger of this going too far and confining social science to what people take themselves to be "up to" in their actions, so that understanding others amounts to no more than merely describing or redescribing action and its purpose. Hermeneutics (the "science" of interpretation) does not generally confine itself to the Winch view but seeks to understand action "from within" to see the full rationality of the action. Max Weber (1864–1947) went further and argued that explanations of human action must be adequate both at the level of meaning and of cause; that is, the social scientist must both find the reasons that justified the action and the cause. Searle *seems* to argue similarly in claiming reason explains action whenever the relation between reason and action is both logical and causal.[12] But his concept of "cause" here is not the "billiard-ball" view of cause. In human action, he argues, cause and effect work the way they do because the cause is a representation of the effect in the mind or the effect is a representation of the cause.

Orthodox social psychology has an interest in folk psychology and studies it under the general label of *social cognition*. It claims people make inferences not just about the reasons or causes of behavior but also about another's personality. We agree that knowledge of a person's character in the circumstances can be important for prediction. But in folk psychology, it is commonly argued that certain traits seem "to go together." This gives rise to a tendency to ascribe another's actions to a character trait rather than circumstances.

Those who reject the theory-theory view of folk psychology point to situations where such a view is inadequate. Thus Goldman says that the Kahneman and Tversky (1982) experiment using the characters of Mr. Crane and Mr. Tees is inexplicable in the theory-theory view.[13] Others argue against theory-theory on the ground that no such theory has so far been set out, though this argument does not affect the Winch view of folk psychology as simply being a network of concepts brought together to form conceptual truths (e.g., "A person with high credibility and attractiveness will have more influence in persuading others than those of less credibility").

Folk psychology as simulation. The theory-theory view is not endorsed by those who promote folk psychology as *simulation*. Those advocating the simulation approach argue that we understand and predict the behavior of others not by any resort to folk psychological theory but by engaging in mental simulation. Folk psychology, on this view, is mainly based on our capacity to employ our normal decision-making capability in a simulation mode. One "inputs" a set of "pretend" beliefs, desires, and emotions into one's practical reasoning system and simply sees what decision emerges. This sort of simulation is used in experimental work. Thus we have the Kahneman and Tversky study, or the study of Schmitt and Leclerc, who asked their subjects to imagine that they had visited a restaurant where a delay occurred while (1) waiting for the table, (2) waiting for the meal, or (3) waiting for the check.[14] Not surprisingly, the service was judged more negatively when the delay occurred at the beginning or at the end of the restaurant visit. The subjects used folk psychology to predict behavior. Given the situation and the instructions, the prediction was more likely to be based on a simulation of the situation than on any set of principles. There are limitations, of course, to trying to establish lawlike generalizations from experimental simulations. Luce, Bettman, and Payne, whose studies rely extensively in experimental simulations, point out that a major limitation is that negative emotion is difficult to manipulate and measure within a controlled, laboratory setting.[15] Participants in the experiments are not threatened with actual, material consequences that might follow from real-world decisions, though participants may feel real threats to their reputation or self-esteem as decision-makers. These authors acknowledge that the overall levels of reported emotion exhibited in their experiments tended to be moderate and often below the midpoint of the relevant scales, even in the highest emotion conditions, and make no claim that obtained levels of emotion mimic the intensity of truly consequential, real-world decisions. Thus it would have been difficult prior to the terrorist attacks of September 11, 2001, to fully capture our emotional reactions to such an event.

A different view of simulation is verstehen, interpreted as empathetic understanding ("putting oneself in the other's shoes"). We try to imagine how things would appear from the other's point of view and predict on this basis. It was Dilthey (1833–1911) who made a sharp distinction between *causal explanation* as applied to the physical sciences and verstehen as applied to the humanities: "Nature we explain: psyche life we understand." Verstehen as empathetic understanding is closely identified with Max Weber, who saw it as being achieved through imaginatively reenacting the thoughts and mental states of those studied.

Unfortunately, verstehen today has no universally accepted standard interpretation. Taylor takes verstehen to be the whole set of intersubjective meanings within a culture, to be grasped *not* by empathy but through some hermeneutical (interpretive) approach. But no interpretive approach is free of problems. Quine talks of their being no "unvarnished news" of the world, to stress that interpretations of social facts are essentially interpretations of interpretations![16]

The original verstehen view of simulation is common, in that we assume others are like ourselves in relevant respects and infer from this their likely actions, after allowing for obvious differences. This is the view of simulation in the Kahneman and Tversky experiment involving Mr. Crane and Mr. Tees. Gordon argues that letting oneself stand in for another like this is simply *reasoning by analogy*, whereas in real simulation there is no implicit inference of any sort from oneself to the other. We simply project one's own responses given the situation, and this we do automatically. Gordon accepts that predictions of behavior often rest on the beliefs, desires, and emotions we believe to be at work in another's thinking.[17] He also accepts that beliefs, desires, and emotions, and other mental states, enter into explanations of action. But he raises the question: How do we recognize atypical situations to which to apply any generalizations we might have? He argues that we apply generalizations in the context of a simulation. In simulation we "pretend" another's state of mind, and with our mind in that pretend condition, we are able to understand the other and use that understanding to predict behavior.

Gordon would question Weber's view of verstehen, as he denies that to simulate another is *simply* to "put yourself in the other's place." Although he agrees that simulating may require imaginatively putting oneself in the other's place, he points out that, with likeminded others in close spatiotemporal proximity, we typically get by with "just projecting" without any adjustment at all for spatial or temporal differences. The term *projecting* is key for Gordon. People search the environment for emotionally relevant features to understand another's action and project their own beliefs about the environment onto the other person. Gordon claims that whenever we are made aware of others as others, we automatically project onto them our own beliefs about the situation / environment.

The first objection to the simulation view is that simulation inevitably deploys theory. Goldman (1995) gets around this criticism by distinguishing between theory-driven and process-driven simulation. While simulation can be theory-driven (common in computer simulations of consumer behavior), the form of simulation that describes folk psychology is the process-driven version. Unlike theory-driven simulation, process-driven simulation is simulation simply guided by a person's normal mental (thinking) processes, which just "run off" by themselves without theory guidance.

The second objection to the simulation view is that theoretical mental concepts are needed to decide what "pretend" beliefs, and so on, are to be taken as appropriate inputs. Goldman replies that the focus in folk psychology is on the environment and that there is role-*taking* rather than role-*playing*—in role-taking, I simply see the action I would take, given the other person's *perceptual inputs*. Role-taking is associated with symbolic interactionism in social psychology, where actions are analyzed as the outcome of "taking the role of the other" rather than adopting ready-made (scripted) roles (role-playing). For example, we are not given motives but look to the environment to discover the motive for the action.

Goldie (2000) rejects Gordon's claim about projecting one's own response, given the situation, and then making adjustments if necessary. We should think in terms of the subject's (not our) likely response, given the relevant information. This means we also need to know something about the character of the subject or players. In spite of the Goldie criticism, simple role-taking can be very effective in predicting the actions of competitors. May shows how at the beginning of World War II the German intelligence officer Ulrich Liss stood in for the Allied commanders as the German general staff played out various invasion plans.[18] He predicted that the Allies would rush their best forces into Belgium; place weak forces to guard the Ardennes approaches; be fatally slow to redirect their forces to counter the main German attack. He was right on all three. However, some might argue, a la Goldie, that he was also likely to be taking into account what he knew about the characters of the key Allied commanders.

A third objection is that simulation takes no account of the fact that some of the things that influence actions are not in consciousness at the time the action is taken, like the brand's position on the store shelf, though it influences choice (position effect has been well demonstrated). Gordon turns this objection into a benefit by arguing that it is the virtue of simulation that it fails to predict phenomena that our common-sense belief-desire-action psychology would fail to predict. However, prediction of action still needs to take into account such behavioral science findings.

Cognitive psychologists tend to be supportive of the theory-theory view of folk psychology because it fits their paradigm of internally represented knowledge structures, typically a body of rules or propositions. But Goldman (1995) points out that the knowledge-*rich* procedures in cognitive psychology's information-processing approach do not constitute the only paradigm, since cognitive science also posits knowledge-*poor* procedures, as when the mental processes posited are simply heuristics (rules of thumb). The simulation approach fits this knowledge-poor paradigm very well. Hence cognitive psychology supports both the theory-theory view and the simulation view.

The question of the nature of folk psychology cannot be resolved by a priori reasoning. There is a need for empirical investigation, and development psychologists have taken a lead in this, though the evidence so far is equivocal. Thus Gopnick and Wellman (1995) show that children over the age of five answer action questions in terms of wants and beliefs, not in terms of fears, fantasies, pains, and sensations, as we would expect if the simulation approach was valid. And Perner and Howes conclude, from their studies, that the developmental evidence suggests that it is unlikely that children come to understand mental concepts like wants and beliefs by means of simulation but that these concepts are acquired by "the formation of the prerequisite mental representations."[19] On the other hand, Harris argues that children *improve* their grasp of folk psychology by means of a simulation process.[20] While agreeing that we routinely make attributions to others of beliefs, desires, emotions, and other mental concepts, Harris argues that this does not imply any use of theory about the relationships between mental states themselves and mental states and action. While he also agrees that simulation could not anticipate that "position effect" would influence the consumer's brand choice, he claims that this is because this influence is not governed by the decision-making process but arises through the right visual field exerting an unconscious dominance over the motor system.

When experts disagree, there is likely to be some truth to each of the claims. We do sometimes use social science findings and concepts to understand others, and we always assume some rationality. And sometimes we do act as if we are using some version of theory-theory (folk psychological theory) to predict what others might do. We also sometimes engage in simulation to understand and predict behavior. Understanding the consumer can only be enriched by using all the approaches. However, for the purpose of predicting emotional responses, we suspect the simulation method has more to offer.

Gordon's play-pretend method of simulation is promising. In predicting behavior, we need to specify whether we are predicting:

1. Our own actions
2. Another person's future actions or group action
3. Immediate action or action in the very distant future

It is easiest to predict our own immediate actions (e.g., I will close the computer down at the end of this paragraph) and hardest to predict the future actions of a specific individual or group. What complicates prediction are future changes of circumstances, since we need knowledge of both the people themselves and the circumstance.

For Gordon, predicting emotional responses is much the same as predicting actions.[21] The best approach to predicting someone's actions is not by trying to invoke "laws," as suggested by the deductive-nomological model (that is, deductions from lawlike generalizations, as per Hempel),[22] for no such laws exist. The best approach lies in simulating the practical reasoning of those whose actions are to be predicted. Gordon refers to this method as the play-pretend method of prediction and recommends it also for predicting emotional responses. Play-pretend should be distinguished from mere empathy as it is popularly conceived. Empathy is used to suggest some inner radar to sense what others feel. Unless actor and subject are tokens of each other, empathy is not the answer. Gordon's point here is important (if we accept it) for marketing, since it is often argued that "being able to read" what the market wants means empathizing with customers. Gordon comes down firmly on the side of mental simulation.

In predicting emotional responses, the aim is to select the emotional response that gives the best fit to the likely wants and beliefs, given the situation. When action is intentional, beliefs identify appropriate means to achieve goals. Within the play-pretend method, Gordon speaks of "hypothetico-practical" reasoning for predicting action and "hypothetico-emotional" reasoning for predicting emotional responses; these are counterparts to the hypothetico-deductive method of the natural sciences. In all three cases, we set up a hypothesis for testing. All this assumes, of course, that we are not trying to predict the actions of the neurotic or the insane! Even if we are not, this method gives no cast-iron guarantee, as we can never fully know the emotional memories of another. There are no guarantees in predicting emotional responses; but this is also true of other fields of human behavior.

If Gordon's play-pretend method is distinguished from empathy as popularly conceived, Goldie (2000) still regards it as a version of empathy. Goldie views empathy as a process whereby a person imagines the thoughts, feelings, and emotions of another person. He claims that empathy, as he views it, goes beyond simply putting oneself in the other's shoes (the popular view of empathy) since it must take account of the character of the person whose behavior is being predicted. To empathize successfully, he argues, one must not only take on board the current thoughts and feelings of the other person but also his or her characteristics, such as the disposition to be hardheaded, kind, or whatever. On this basis, those trying to predict the behavior of Mr. Crane and Mr. Tees were simply putting themselves in the shoes of the two men but, without knowing anything about their characters, could not undertake empathy as Goldie views it.

Changing versus Influencing Emotions

Getting people into an emotional state is easier than *changing* their emotional state. In arousing an emotional state, we identify and activate the conditions that trigger it, whereas if the aim is to change or neutralize an emotional state, there is a need to negate the conditions that generate it. This is done typically by changing perspectives through a reinterpretation of whatever triggered the emotion. Mark Antony's funeral oration for the dead Caesar in Shakespeare's play *Julius Caesar* is an example. He is speaking to a crowd that is ambivalent, with fear of monarchical absolutism in tension with the love for Caesar. The accusation of the murderers and the assertion that Caesar was ambitious are repeated, each time with greater irony, as the phrase is juxtaposed with Caesar's deeds: "Did this in Caesar seem ambitious? When that the poor have cried, Caesar hath wept." Meaning is inverted to be its contrary via sardonic repetition: "Yet Brutus says he was ambitious; and Brutus is an honorable man." By the end the crowd is in a frenzy against Brutus.

Just talking about changing perspectives through the reinterpretation of whatever triggered the emotion simply names the strategy; success lies in the tactics. There is, for example, a need first to train service staff to recognize the emotion and its source and then to set out specific ways by which perspectives might be changed. This means first building up a data bank of incidents that can and do occur in which customers become emotional. This constitutes the basis for a training in how to handle emotional issues with customers. Without such training, staff inevitably become defensive and indulge in either fighting or fleeing. The most natural reaction to an insult is an angry response, which can simply result in the loss of customers. And an angry response will be what occurs without training using simulated situations.

Emotional Persuasion versus Rational Appeals

If the aim is to influence the consumer by rational means, the focus is on getting the consumer to reconsider in a rational way his or her beliefs about the desirability, efficiency, feasibility, and viability of the proposed action. If we wish to make counterarguments to a rational *argument*, we question assumptions and inferences. Whenever people get into an emotional state, it would seem that getting them to question their beliefs also might be the way to go. But commonly emotions are not changed by purely rational arguments. Changing consumer emotions to influence decisions typically requires marketers to focus on the appraisal and on changing the interpretation or perspective that lies behind it. Although belief-dependent emotions can be changed by rationally setting out the evidence, the more general need is to induce the consumer to *interpret* the emotion-arousing situation in a different way, reassessing its significance.

"Spin doctoring" is the art of affixing an interpretation or perspective to a fluid or unpromising political situation. Similarly, in consumer marketing the aim is to change interpretations or perspectives in line with brand appeal. Facts are not contested, only the way they are viewed or interpreted. Values remain in place but value judgments are changed through induced reinterpretation. A buyer who is angry at not receiving his order to time and specification is not likely to be pacified by being told that getting angry is not the best way to behave or being told why delivery as promised was not feasible. Instead the salesperson sympathizes, pointing out that the last thing her firm would want to do would be to antagonize a valued customer: an unfortunate mistake has been made that will be remedied at once. Acknowledging the wrong done, showing regret, and offering a generous solution induces the principle of reciprocity. The conditions tied to the emotional display are reinterpreted against background efforts to make amends, which soothes the buyer's injured feelings. All blows to the ego need assuaging, as people are more emotionally affected by blows to self-esteem than by any corresponding boosts.

In advertising there are those who favor "rational" appeals (tangible product benefits and features) and those who claim that advertising should be used to build an emotional bond between the consumer and the brand. But all brand choices have emotional overtones. It is all a matter of degree. In fact, consumers will seek to justify their purchase by providing rational or pseudo-rational grounds for their choices. Advertising with emotional content, however, is more creative than rational appeals and is more difficult to conceive, whereas—contrary to popular wisdom—emotional appeals have been used to sell brands in *all* consumer product categories, including cars, electronics, fast food, and even baked beans!

Emotional Fit among the Components of Emotion

Changing emotional states is largely a matter of bringing about a reinterpretation of the situation and its significance (i.e., changing appraisals/evaluations). This means focusing not necessarily on aspects of the situation that are objectively the most important but on what is most important for the target audience. Thus attempts to dissuade teenagers from smoking may fail if the focus is on health consequences in middle age; a more persuasive emphasis would be on *immediate* undesirable social consequences, such as bad breath, coughing, and "smelly" clothes, as well as the immediately felt lack of fitness.

Making changes favoring the seller may involve changing beliefs if these are not in line with the seller's goals. As already pointed out, the insurance advertiser may arouse fear, but the target audience may seek another insurance company's services and not the firm making the emotional appeal. Emotions are influenced by *normative* beliefs which are responsive to appeals that highlight behavior that is socially endorsed within one's social milieu. We are thus saying that people can be *talked into* an emotional state and talked into a *more intense* emotional state but also *talked out of* an emotional state.

Nozick speaks of a correct "fit" occurring among the components of an emotion when beliefs are true, evaluations correct, and feelings are proportionate to the evaluations.[23] When such a fit is lacking (because of false beliefs, wrong evaluations/appraisals, or disproportionate feelings) the emotion is defective. Any sense of defective emotions is what emotional persuasions seek to remedy. In remedying "defective" consumer emotions, there is a need to identify whether the beliefs are false, the evaluations are wrong, or the feelings are disproportionate to the evaluations.

An example of training people to achieve the right emotional fit is illustrated by the Hochschild study.[24] Hochschild makes a distinction between *emotion work* and *emotional labor*. Emotion work is the exertion involved in ensuring that private feelings are not revealed but instead are in tune with what is socially appropriate; for example, looking pleased about an unwanted present. Emotional labor, on the other hand, covers the way an *organizational role* exerts control over emotional displays as a result of pressure to follow prescribed standards of behavior; for example, appearing to enjoy all encounters with passengers while giving cabin service. The expressed feelings are those prescribed by management to enhance customer satisfaction. The salary of flight attendants could be said to include the buying of this emotional performance, and achieving this emotional performance is "emotional labor." Emotional labor occurs in face-to-face service occupations like that of flight attendant, store clerk, doctor, lawyer, and so on. Each of these roles carries different emotional obligations; a doctor has to seem understanding, for example, while a waitress has to seem attentive. Hochschild found that complying with the prescribed "feeling rules" need not be merely superficial, as some attendants performed according to the emotional script with feelings that cohered to the role. However, for those employees whose feelings were in conflict with their expressed feelings, the emotional labor was heavy.

Hochschild talks of *self-estrangement* as a dysfunctional side effect of heavy emotional labor when true feelings are marginalized. Yet for some, it is all an act with which they gladly go along. When the organizational role imposes heavy emotional labor and private feelings are out of line with expressed emotion, then true emotions, like aggression, tend to leak through and come to the surface. Hochschild's emotional labor side effects remain a danger that may seldom arise for many service providers who have the "right" service perspective and have practiced skills in dealing with various encounters, such as how to disagree without being disagreeable. Service staff who demonstrate concern, openness, and helpfulness will typically get a favorable response, given that most people respond in accordance with the principle of reciprocity. Where self-estrangement does occur, it may simply reflect lack of training or the selection of people unsuited for the job—something that applies to most jobs. It is easy to exaggerate the problem. Clients are usually aware that the service provider is playing a role, with satisfaction coming from knowing that the service provider is making the effort to play the role in a way that meets expectations. Service workers fear conflict or social embarrassment when a role is not played well, and this facilitates a fusion of role, private feelings, and expressed emotions. There is no reason why service providers should not be providers of a pleasant service experience, though it is true that consumers today are generally dissatisfied with service staff, which is a result of poor selection and training.

Anticipated poor service puts people off buying, while experiences of poor service can linger like a bad taste in the mouth for years afterward. Some firms feel obliged to materially compensate for poor service. One New York City department store, for example, on two occasions, mixed up pieces of furniture in an order for one of us and felt all it needed to do was send a little gift. Things need to be more personal than that to overcome the frustration and exasperation of having to get back to the store and send back the goods and being deprived in the meantime of the product. Barlow and Maul (2000) put heavy emphasis on developing emotional and not just technical competencies among service staff because of the urgent need to educate for the emotional challenges staff will face. In summary, they talk about providing staff with the needed (1) skills, (2) authority/power, (3) self-confidence, and (4) support. Training is key, particularly since, as these authors say, brief customer encounters can be scripted to a high degree without losing authenticity.

Although the study on the training of flight attendants by Hochschild occurred before Nozick wrote on "emotional fit," it can be used to illustrate the concept. First, whatever *false beliefs* the attendants had about their role, these false beliefs were overthrown by an emphasis on treating passengers as "guests in one's house." This analogy had emotional resonance and provided an attractive perspective for which the rules of behavior were already known. Setting out the attendants' role was basic, since being clear about that role brought with it a different set of emotions. As Parkinson says, many of the effects of culture on emotion are mediated by institutional roles.[25] Attendants were taught that *evaluations* to fit the role were to be based on the perspective of the passenger and that perspective was to provide the criterion for *any* evaluation. Here, Gordon's play-pretend simulation model was the appropriate one to follow for the attendants. Finally, the *feelings* to fit the role were brought about by training the attendants in "low private self-consciousness" so that they paid little attention to their own feelings. All was achieved by a process-driven simulation (see earlier) to help understand the passenger's wants at any particular time.

Epistemic Emotions

To return to what was said in chapter 3 about epistemic and factive emotions—in the case of epistemic emotions, like "fear," there is a need to decide whether the focus should be on the epistemic reason (ER) or the attitudinal reason (AR). The epistemic reasons are more open to persuasion. Unfortunately, a change in epistemic reasons may have little impact on the intensity of the AR. Thus people who fear flying may be persuaded to believe that there is less risk attached to it than crossing the road, but this does not remove all their fear. Nonetheless, changing epistemic reasons does have influence. If the aim is to enhance fear, the strategy is to stress the extreme likelihood of X—say, drug dependency if drugs are taken—and how the occurrence of X is outside a person's control. On the other hand, to reduce (say) fear (e.g., of hair loss), the strategy would stress:

- the unlikelihood of X (hair loss). (This is frequently adopted by medical practitioners who have patients who think they are going bald because they notice more hair in their brush after brushing.)
- that the occurrence of X (hair loss) can be prevented (if certain medical treatments are followed with a focus on medical advances in the area).

Figure 5.1.   Changing perspectives and emotions with a terrifying metamorphosis: the cigarette package becomes the coffin. Courtesy Crown Copyright.

Factive Emotions

In the case of the factive emotions, the focus is on getting the consumer to *reinterpret* the facts, just as showing an action to be socially appropriate (e.g., President Reagan wearing a hearing aid) eliminates the embarrassment connected with it. Language is all-important in shifting perspectives. If those who oppose Britain adopting the euro use the slogan *Save the Pound,* it is because this offers a more emotive perspective than simply saying that Britain should not adopt the euro. The language of real estate agents is famous for its choice of words, whereby an ugly row house becomes "genuine Victorian."

Language is a tool that is used to adjust perceptions. The metaphor in particular is powerful in persuasion, as it can be selected for its emotional resonance. As Klein says, metaphor structures our thinking and conditions our sympathies and emotional reactions.[26] To restructure thinking is to alter perspectives. Metaphors, in affecting what we see and how we interpret, influence not only our thinking but our emotional reactions. The Republicans call the inheritance tax the *death tax;* repeated often enough, it will come to be perceived as such by increasing numbers of Americans. Phrases like "trickle-down effect" are invented to make an ideology more palatable. Metaphors are commonly used to transform the image of something otherwise likely to seem too unpleasant; for example, "bathroom tissue" for toilet roll. Language can reposition in the mind some concept that earlier language had made problematic; thus Gandhi relabeled the Untouchables of India harijans (children of God). This example illustrates how changing descriptive terms can be a civilizing influence as an old and insulting lexicon—for example, *moron, mongol, spastic, cripple*—is jettisoned and replaced. Unfortunately, there must ultimately be a change in attitudes; otherwise the old connotations return and attach themselves to the new lexicon.

Value-laden phrases always resonate. In the novel *Lavengro,* by the Victorian novelist George Borrow, a gypsy leader persuades the (nongypsy) hero against suicide by recounting the glories of the natural world while repeating the phrase "Life is sweet brother, who would wish to die?" If someone within my social milieu describes the car I am about to buy as "flash" and "vulgar," this reduces the likelihood of my buying it, since the derisive imagery sticks, clinging to consciousness even though I may wish to erase it. The need for approval and fear of censure from those within our social milieu are major forces if they reflect social norms.

Moods are fertile ground for developing emotions that converge; a depressed mood makes a person much more susceptible to anger, and a happy mood is helpful in getting people to buy. To change a mood does not differ from changing other emotions, unless the particular mood is part of a manic-depressive personality. The aim is still to change interpretations. One person's mood can be caught by another.[27] In line with the general principle of reciprocity, we respond in the same emotional currency to the emotions of those with whom we are interacting but, in successful relationships, there are likely to be complementary patterns of emotional exchanges, so that negative emotional outbursts are followed by the other party providing reassurance.[28]

Advertising can help get people into a better mood by a focus on fun and liveliness. In changing a depressed mood, the aim is to get people to reinterpret the quality of their life (e.g., directing them to the bright side) or to reduce the significance of feelings experienced by providing counterstimulation (e.g., providing something amusing for those feeling bored). Hollywood dealt with fears of war by the device of humor; in Charlie Chaplin's *Great Dictator*, Hitler plays with an enormous globe, performing an elegant pas de deux with it to classical music, until it pops. To increase the self-esteem and the status of teachers, one ad featured the teachers of famous people being praised by their eminent alumni. Personal recognition is important for self-esteem, as major hotels have long known.

Influencing Buying Actions

We have talked about changing an emotional state, but what about changing buying action through emotional appeals? Edward Bernays, the father of public relations, who until his death a few years ago at the age of 103 continued to practice his craft in New York, influenced buying by tying his campaigns to fit changing values. When the emancipation of women was becoming an important value, he promoted cigarettes as a symbol of liberation and claimed that the taboo against women smoking simply symbolized male oppression.[29]

Symbolization is what a product stands for—what it signifies. Appeals to values via appropriate symbolism are important when there is ambiguity surrounding which brand to buy, in a market where brands are seen as simply tokens of each other. Symbolization may be a deliberate strategy, but some symbolism will be independent of the communicator's goals. Women smoking came to symbolize (signify, stand for) a moral position and a symbol of increasing solidarity among those seeking to remove the barriers to achieving equality with men. In advocating this change in perspective, Bernays managed within a few weeks to change the rules that prohibited women from smoking in the smoking rooms of Broadway theaters!

As de Sousa says, in an emotional argument, the strategy is not logical inference but getting the audience to share a perspective or conjure up a certain experience.[30] This is what *radical* reinterpretation is all about. Suppose there was a movement to declare that designer labels contrive to extract a premium price ("paying for the name") while (unbelievably) manipulating the buyer into acting as a billboard to advertise the seller's product. This would conjure up an experience of being conned and would induce a different perspective from the one buyers currently hold. Getting consumers just to reinterpret the facts, however, does not sufficiently capture the idea of emotional persuasion, which, to

Figure 5.2.   Associating Revlon's "Charlie" with a powerful symbol of female liberation. Courtesy Revlon, New York, NY.

be successful, aims at generating a new experience. Emotion in advertising must try to show the product in a certain light in order to induce certain emotional experiences involving the product. Bernays managed to get large numbers of women to experience a sense of exhilaration, of being liberated, every time they smoked a cigarette in public.

The problem is to find the set of values, paradigm scenarios, or experiences that have wide appeal among the target audience. One way to do this is to look at the changing values of a culture or subculture in contrast to traditional values and beliefs. If an advertiser looks at those values within the target segment, the advertiser in effect asks: "what values and beliefs tie members of the segment to their social groups? These are basic to the design of an emotional strategy.

Every culture is a storehouse of myths, which—though of questionable accuracy—suggest the origins of the culture's preference for certain beliefs and values and in the process reaffirm a set of preferences. The myths articulate cultural values and beliefs, and effective persuasion commonly draws from this storehouse, as Ronald Reagan constantly did. While another age might have politicians telling stories from Greek literature, Reagan was aware that he needed stories that would resonate with his audience because they were familiar and pertinent, derived from a shared media culture. Advocates of the permissive society in the 1960s changed perspectives by appeals to individual "rights," invoking this founding social principle to counteract another, namely, social puritanism. Feelings became sacrosanct, and freedom for self-fulfillment the superordinate value, embodied in such words as "liberation" or "freedom" and attack on ritual of any sort. Every culture has mythical heroes who are its role models, personifying the values of the culture. Emotional advertising exploits these culturally shared values by linking them to the brand. The most well known but somewhat shopworn example is the cowboy in the ad for Marlboro cigarettes. This ad links the cigarette to the American cultural values portrayed in countless movies. In general, the imagery involves the fantasy of being in control of our lives, a vision of rugged independence and a simple life without bureaucracy, where the bad and the good are easily distinguished and "real" men exhibit an independence and strength in manly pursuits. The theme projected of the cowboy, usually with his faithful horse, is not one of aloneness (this would suggest social ostracism) but of independence, a declaration of individuality that is welcome to those who are feeling dependence on others for emotional, intellectual, and material sustenance. The ad does not say directly that the user will be in control of his or her life or have rugged independence by smoking Marlboros, though some of this will linger in fantasy and action; more directly, the ad is saying that those supporting the values projected in the ad will find these values embodied in the Marlboro brand. It is displaying what values are symbolized by using the brand. The Marlboro ad has been used throughout the world with only minor changes (e.g., a white horse in China, a black cowboy in Nigeria), which suggests that these values have fairly universal appeal. But the association with America helps, since America for many throughout the world is still a land where dreams can be fulfilled: a longing that is reflected in the concept of displaced meaning (see chapter 2).

Meaning has been poured into the sign of the cowboy by countless films over many decades, each generation giving the genre a new treatment but preserving some of the original meaning: freedom; the rural, nonsuburban, and nonindustrial; and survival through physical qualities like physical strength, self-reliance, and aggression in response to danger. None of these attractive values comes across in antismoking or antidrug advertising, where the stress is on self-protection. But the meaning of any symbol is never fixed. New meanings are given to old symbols, as with the successive reworkings of the cowboy figure and the Western genre of film. The cowboy today is read by many as the totem of reaction and political incorrectness. In the 1960s the film *Soldier Blue* appropriated anti-Vietnam war protest to the western; the Indians now became the good victims as the bad U.S. cavalry slaughtered them. But the meanings of ads are not always transparent or even legible, and there will be many aberrant interpretations. Some now perceive the Marlboro cowboy as an icon of angry, oppressed white maleness.

This raises the whole question of idiosyncratic interpretations. Interpretations of a text are tied to the text's associations, and some of these associations can be unique to the interpreter. But it is important to distinguish between those associations and those that are common to all the ad's interpreters. Unless there is commonality of interpretation, there can be no common language. Academic interpretations of ads can often be just too profound to capture what impacts the audience. Thus Freudian interpretations may be claimed as the influencing interpretations, as they constitute the unconscious meaning to the target audience. It is not always easy to accept that such depth and complexity really characterizes the ad audience's interpretations. There is also the question of the validity of the Freudian system. In any case, once again, there may be a danger of overintellectualizing consumer behavior.

Goldman and Papson point out that, in markets packed with many undifferentiated products, brands need to attach to themselves signs that carry an additional element of value, just as Nike effectively harnessed the power of sports celebrities.[31] Advertisers scour the landscape, identifying cultural images—particularly celebrities, lifestyles, and subcultures—that have value for their target audiences. Some of these icons are old and relate back to the values of another century. It was the icon hunger of modern culture that Andy Warhol sought to satirize in his portrait of Marilyn Monroe. Goldman and Papson (1996) claim that the more intensely advertisers compete for the most valuable images, the faster these images "cease to sizzle." Appropriated images lose some of their valued meaning by constant illicit associations, just as a brand image can be diluted by the wrong sort of brand extensions.

The production of cultural images is a constant activity: sometimes they are new and sometimes they are resurrections and makeovers of old ones; for example, the British government's espousal of the phrase "Cool Britannia" in the attempted rebranding of Britain. Which of these images will catch the public imagination is usually a guess. Out of the imagistic cacophony of history, pop culture, and the like, advertising selects relevant symbolic images that the advertiser believes will resonate with the prevailing public mood. Typically, what we mean by "advertising creativity" is the ability to identify belief systems, values, and moods and find the right symbols to express them. Guinness, for example, in a famous multimedia campaign, focused on the public fascination with science fiction and cultlike programs. The aim of the Guinness campaign was to recruit youthful cohorts to an older generation's (acquired) taste by an appeal to quixotic individualism that lay outside traditional demographic and class-based appeals. The actor Rutger Hauer appeared in a sequence of bizarre ads set in a strange parallel universe to our own in which nothing was quite the same; the ads featured a dolphin as the main motif, with its suggestions of mysterious intelligence, and the slogan "It's not easy being a dolphin."

Symbolism is important as there is always some ambiguity (and therefore uncertainty) surrounding which brand to buy when buying for the first time. Beliefs cannot reach the truth here. This can make the brand's symbolism decisive. With ambiguity, symbols and slogans that capture relevant values evoke appropriate scenarios that attach to the brand.

A *symbolic marketing strategy* is one that focuses on altering behavior not through any change in substance like the product or distribution channels but by changing the symbols attached to the brand. Symbolic strategies may not change product reality but may radically change consumer actions as a result of fresh perceptions.

Many traditional brands of personal products are in danger of dying because new generations are not being attracted. This signals the need for novelty or an imagistic reinvention for new generations, which means identifying the key symbols of that generation and attaching them to the brand. Thus Brylcreem, the hair gel, found its image revival in being attached to the image of a popular Manchester United soccer team member.

In advertising and propaganda, appeals to group affiliation are pervasive. To try and change attitudes directly is apt to be interpreted as an attack. If feasible, it is better to associate the target consumer with a group that holds the persuader's views and allows group influence to come into play. Cults represent an extreme example of this, projecting to the neophyte the idea of the sharing of affections within a loving family. Cults fill the void left by churches, offering involvement and personal relationships that for many are missing in today's world. Effective persuasion does not rest on stick or carrot but results from an offer of solidarity, of sharing or affiliation, which the audience accepts or rejects. Rejection is perceived as hurtful to the persuader simply because persuasion itself is an offer of sharing. The offer of solidarity is helped by participation, as participation holds out the promise of a partnership leading naturally to mutual concessions in line with the principle of reciprocity.

Pratkanis and Aronson use the term "granfalloon" to refer to the technique of forming people into groups using the most trivial criteria and, in the process, getting them to see themselves as a group with something in common.[32] Tajfel was the first to discuss how labeling some set of people as having something in common has the effect of getting them to act as if they were good friends.[33] Having a sense of belonging to a group is a source of security and satisfaction. Advertisers may claim that buyers of a certain sportscar have a commonality in lifestyle, and audiences are predisposed to believe such claims, as it helps them to make sense of their lives and enhances their sense of self-esteem, affiliation/solidarity with others, and identity. Segmentation of markets (e.g., heavy versus light users) is sometimes carried out on the assumption that the granfalloon effect can be generated by advertising.

As Pratkanis and Aronson say, there can be granfaloons based on designer labels and lifestyles. But they regard televangelists as the masters of the technique. The viewer is asked to join the family of believers, with the implicit promise of a satisfying self-identity as one of "God's chosen people," obtained by watching the program, joining the club, and donating to "God's work." What the granfalloon effect does is give members a sense of being a social group rather than just a collection of people. Those who are not members of the group are consigned to being members of "out-groups." Out-groups are constantly being manufactured by in-groups to gain better self-definition. Militant German nudists refer derisively to nonnudists as "textiles," establishing them as a symbol of clothing and, as a consequence, the enemy. The creation of an enemy to hate, an antagonistic social image through which to achieve self-definition, has been fundamental to the work of demagogues throughout history, forming raw bigotry from the light earth of mild existing prejudice. Similarly, psychographic segmentation is segmentation of the market based on groups likely to respond to lifestyle advertising appeals, with the product and its packaging being given a certain "personality" to fit the lifestyle image. Whenever a seller or advertiser can achieve a sense of "oneness" with the target audience, a sense of common unity can be created.

In all attempts to influence buying actions through emotional appeals, it is useful to be on the same emotional wavelength as the target audience. Goldie (2000) argues this comes about through emotional engagement and empathy. Emotional engagement consists of:

- *Contagion.* Associating with the target audience, since the emotions exhibited can be contagious. Thus everyone clapping or laughing serves to suggest some social consensus, which becomes a cue for others to imitate: it is the thing to do to signify that one belongs. Anything that makes for similarity with the characters (like circumstances, age, or background) increases emotional contagion. One advertisement that tries to exploit contagion shows the product being demonstrated with the words "I'm impressed" appearing on the screen.
- *Identification.* When one person identifies with another, that person's sense of her own identity merges to some extent with the identity of the other, just as happens between mother and child. One form of identification in advertising is with someone's frustration arising from some interrupted plan. Thus in one ad we see the hostess's entertainment plans being interrupted when she sees that the wine glasses are "spotty." The audience identifies with the situation and the character's disappointment and then glee when Cascade (a dishwasher detergent) remedies the situation. It is not so much that we identify with the fictional characters in the TV commercial as that we assimilate the situation, coming to see it both from the point of view of its characters and from the outside as well. Without a capacity for identification and situation assimilation, no theater would be possible.
- *Emotional sharing.* When people are moved by the same scene or episode, the sharedness of the emotion enhances the depth of the emotional response. When people have a sense of emotional sharing, the underlying emotions are likely to become cognitively impenetrable—that is, not influenced by beliefs or reasoning.

Some Key Assertions for Marketing

1. If marketing management seeks to change consumer behavior by the most rational means, there is a need first to establish that both marketing management and target audience share the same set of relevant assumptions. The focus then lies in demonstrating to the target audience why the object being promoted coheres with their goals and is more efficient, feasible, and viable than displaced rivals.
2. If marketing management seeks to tap the emotions, the first job is to decide whether the situation is such that emotions need to be aroused/inten-

sified or to be neutralized or changed (e.g., from anger to embarrassment at making a complaint). If marketing management seeks to arouse emotions, the focus is on getting the message to resonate with the concerns of the target audience. If it seeks to neutralize or change the emotional state of the target audience, there is a need to change the perspective that lies behind the initial negative appraisal or to change beliefs through inducing a reinterpretation of the causal conditions. The facts are not contested but only the way they are interpreted, while typically there is an attempt to alter not the target audience's values but only value judgments that rest on how the situation is described. Thus situations that are proclaimed as most adhering to the norms of the target audience's social milieu can change value judgments.

3. If marketing management is to examine the emotional state of its target audience as a basis for changing it, there is a need to look at whether (1) beliefs are true, (2) evaluations are false, or (3) feelings are disproportionate to evaluations. Such knowledge points to possible strategies for change.

4. If marketing management is concerned with epistemic emotions, epistemic reasons are usually more open to change than attitudinal ones, and seeking a change in the latter through reinterpretation is likely to be key.

5. If marketing management is concerned with factive emotions, everything depends on getting a reinterpretation of the "facts" so as to change perspective. In this, metaphor can be a powerful aid.

6. If marketing management is to exploit symbols in promotion, it may adopt a symbolic marketing strategy, where marketing changes behavior not through any change in the product or its price or its distribution but in the symbols attached to the brand. Reality remains unchanged, only the symbolization changes. One focus in symbolic marketing is to declare what the brand stands for, providing that the target audience identifies with the same values. Similarly, in symbolic marketing the brand may symbolize a prized group affiliation.

7. If marketing management aims to treat some market segment as a group with shared interest, it might be possible to stimulate this sense by getting the group to see themselves as possessing something in common. The granfalloon effect is apt to work, because people are easily self-persuaded that they are part of a group with interests in common.

8. If marketing management seeks emotional engagement with its target audience, it needs to consider the generating mechanisms of contagion, identification, and emotional sharing.

6

Branding and Emotion

Brand Image

In marketing we are interested in how things are perceived, in contrast to how things really are from an objective point of view. The process of perception involves interpreting sensations and making inferences, which, in turn, are influenced by past experiences and expectations. When consumers do not have the product in front of them, they must rely on memory if they are to describe it or, more specifically, they must rely on the representations or image they have of the product in their minds. Consumers, like people generally, approach the physical world through their representations of it, and a brand image is one such representation. Brand image is a synthesis of impressions: a summation that can take the form of a gut emotional reaction or a mental flash of recognition, which typically reflects attitudes toward the brand and its perceived benefits.

Brand names were adopted to distinguish the manufacturer's product from that of rivals so that satisfied customers knew what to ask for. However, it became apparent that a brand name could be used to convey all sorts of sales-generating associations, and with this came talk about branding. We can distinguish between the meaning of the brand name itself and the meaning of the product lying behind the brand name. The meaning of the brand name itself is (1) what the brand name denotes in terms of product and (2) the brand image, or the ideas associated with the brand name in the consumer's mind. On the other hand, the meaning of the physical product itself is its significance for the consumer—what it implies or leads the customer to expect. While the meaning of a brand name is the product it denotes and the ideas it connotes, the meaning of the product can be both these things and any other things the consumer connects with it. Several comments can be made:

- The brand image, as a set of ideas conjured up by the brand name, can be very vague and even, on occasions, not adequate to determine a reference. In other words, it can be analogous to a mental image of "gold" that never gets beyond an image of a yellow metal that is precious, which is a poor guide to actually identifying gold.[1] Not all brand images have force to affect brand choice. There is a need to generate a memorable image, preferably revolving around the competitive or critical advantage of the brand.
- The different facets of a brand image may have no coordinating core, just as the image of someone we know may evoke ideas of voice, dress, walk, eyes, and hair with no coherent picture. The image of a brand can be fragmented, not constituting a coherent whole in the mind of the consumer. Yet the consumer needs to have a grasp of the brand as a unitary whole that serves the functions for which the product is bought.
- Although the memory of a product is an image, this image may be derived from actual experience of the real product. The emotional aspects of that experience will dominate the image; hence the importance of ensuring that all experiences with a brand are highly positive.

A brand image can speak to the imagination in a way that drowns out whatever speaks for substance. This is because it can symbolize a promise to meet or exceed expectations while, at the same time, stressing what values the brand stands for. An old established brand with a fine image is like a habitual buy; it suggests less risk in buying and lots of credibility. The image of a successful brand is a promise of performance in the functions for which it is being bought. The promise need not be in terms of superior performance in the core-use function but in terms of enhancing self-identity or other intangible benefit. And not only products have brand images; celebrities do. Mick Jagger has registered his name as a trademark embracing 20 products. This goes beyond mere licensing deals, allowing celebrities to exploit their names in building businesses. If we accept that possessions project a social identity and assert something about the buyers themselves, signaling where buyers stand and what values they are attracted to, the concept of a celebrity being marketed as a brand is not surprising.

The Power of Names

To illustrate the power of names, Montaigne (1533–1592) tells the story of a dissolute young man seducing a woman. On discovering she was called Mary, the name of the mother of Jesus, it struck such awe into him that he sent the woman away and in that instance converted to a life of virtue! The power arose from what the name symbolized. Tocqueville in the nineteenth century claimed that Americans sought symbols of personal identity for visibility and status in a society lacking a formal class hierarchy. Diamonds are not just gems but symbols of wealth. Whatever the case may be, brand images can evoke emotional bonding with the consumer, creating trust and arousing loyalty. Brand choice is seldom just a matter of evaluating the objective attributes of each brand. As with religion, there is also the matter of trust, and a favorable brand image inspires trust.

Trust in a brand is assessed by asking how much customers think they can trust the brand to fulfill the functions of interest—always? most of the time? some of the time? almost never? But the most basic question of all relates to loyalty: which buyers buy which brands and do so because they both trust the brand and have an emotional attachment to it? With what degree of commitment? For what functions? A loyal customer is not only devoted to the brand but sticks with the brand when it is at a competitive disadvantage, because there is faith that things will improve over the long term. In this sense, loyalty is a normative goal for brand managers rather than something routinely attainable. In fact, the consumer can be loyal to a cluster of brands. While this reduces the sentiment of consumers for any one brand, it does not necessarily lead to a reduction in trust for a brand.

Barlow and Maul claim (rightly) that the most important aspect of customers' experience is emotional, rather than "satisfaction" as measured in surveys of consumer satisfaction. They point out that such surveys do not provide the breadth or depth of information needed to assess performance or guide the company.[2] Satisfaction simply suggests "no serious complaints" rather than an emotionally pleasing experience, which needs to be the goal if loyalty is to be achieved. Surveys need to capture something more akin to the emotional meaning or experiential significance the customer associates with the brand.

As Barlow and Maul point out, many companies use satisfaction surveys to gather compliments and, since around 80% of respondents in satisfaction surveys tick the highest and next highest satisfaction rating, these surveys are misleading if they are used to gauge the degree of emotional engagement the customer has with the company. They are certainly no guide to the commitment that goes with loyalty. This is not to suggest that such surveys or questionnaires are useless; just making it known they are being undertaken will affect staff behavior to some extent.

Barlow and Maul hold that high levels of positive emotional involvement with a firm or brand drive customer loyalty more than judgments of quality do, and they argue that a customer focus requires that an organization implement what they term the five Cs of intimacy:

1. *Communication:* not just questioning after the fact but proactive questioning about expectations
2. *Caring:* implies valuing another individual for who he or she is
3. *Commitment:* means the company/service provider taking responsibility for creating the right emotional climate and a feeling of "we-ness"
4. *Comfort:* means reaching out to establish rapport with the other person, being emotionally in tune with the other person, creating a feeling of compatibility, and then helping all we can
5. *Conflict resolution:* creates trust so conflict is constructive and not destructive

Complaints always have the potential for stirring up conflict, and Barlow and Maul make this their consulting specialty. They point out that effective complaint handling makes a major difference to customer retention rates, even after product failure. Given the cost of obtaining new customers, this is important. It is loyal customers who are more likely to complain about poor service; others commonly simply walk away. Most people hate to complain. Loyal customers hesitate because they see it as affecting their relationship to suppliers; others hesitate because they want to avoid conflict and would prefer to just switch brands. While a bad experience with any good or service resides in memory longer than a good experience, conflict over that bad experience strongly reinforces the tendency of negative emotions to linger on, with constant mental postmortems. Barlow and Maul point to the general tendency to defend against attack by complaining customers. In contrast, they recommend always thanking the customer for letting them know about the problem. Afterward the firm should (1) make a major effort to understand the customer's point of view and feelings; (2) empower front-line staffs to settle the great bulk of complaints; and (3) write, if need be, pointing out how the firm understands how the customer must feel. We agree with Barlow and Maul that it is the customer's specific appraisal of some specific transaction that influences repurchase intention rather than long-term reflection, and it is this transaction that bequeaths its emotional print and is most readily available in the customer's mind.

Cognitive Storing and Brand Image

Brand image can evoke emotive imagery and beliefs about the likely performance of the brand and sums up thoughts, associations, feelings, and expectations about the brand itself. Cognitive psychologists have shown an interest in mental images, particularly since Kosslyn's seminal work.[3] From around 1915 until the late 1960s, imagery and mental representation generally were felt not to be fruitful topics for psychologists. It is now accepted that people do employ quasi-pictorial representations and use such representations in cognitive processing (thinking). Some psychologists modify this in claiming that what we really recall are *propositions,* that is, representations in the mind of beliefs and assertions. It is claimed that when consumers think of a brand what they recall are beliefs and claims about the brand and it is these that are used in cognitive processing. The evidence suggests that both images and propositional representations may be recalled. It seems that the relative speed with which the two types of information (images or propositions) are processed determines which type of information dominates in consumer thinking about (brand) image.

Brand images contain information that serve as data structures in memory. A mental image consists of a quasi-pictorial entity known as the *surface representation,* which is derived from a deeper representation of information in long-term memory. Psychologists point out that this image is not a "picture in the head." Images lack many of the properties of pictures. Unlike a picture, images are composed of previously processed information and are interpreted not by the human eye but in the "mind's eye."

The more times a brand name is recalled, the more the information stored in images is decoded into belief statements about the brand. We sometimes, in fact, need recourse to images to obtain belief statements. Thus if asked whether a certain make of car is of a certain shape, most consumers will bring an image of the car to mind, as this will be needed to describe the car's shape. Similarly, asked about the contents of a room at home, we first recall an image of the room. The consumer may have a vivid mental representation of the house she is about to buy but if asked to count the steps up to the front door may not be able to do so. Images, too, are useful in thinking about the consequences of buying. The images of a house bring forward thoughts about, say, its maintenance. They can also bring to the surface latent wants and intensify desires. Generating favorable brand images is thus important.

Psychologists reject the idea of images being stored as single wholes as if in files from which they are retrieved. A single image is constructed from elemental parts. Images, as a consequence, vary with the context. They are not static but consist of parts that fade in and out, while only the vaguest image may be retained without sustained effort. The extent to which a brand image is sharp and detailed depends on how hard a person is prepared to try and fill in details. But what is not already in the memory cannot be recalled, in that one may recall the image of one's computer but cannot read the name on the casing unless this is currently in active memory. An image cannot reveal to the consumer what he or she does not already know. Forming a mental image of a house or any other product is radically different from seeing the house. The actual experience of seeing the house is the greater persuader of what is so.

A brand's image is a composite of imagery representations and propositional representations, though marketers are apt to highlight one or the other. This is done by stressing experiences arising from using/consuming the brand or stressing belief claims (propositions) about the brand; for example, claims about quality. Imagery is associated with trying to generate affect-driven choices, while propositional representations are associated with trying to generate belief-driven choices. Thus Coca-Cola ads suggest the experiences to be enjoyed, while ads for Tide make tangible benefit assertions. Sometimes an advertiser manages to do both.

The history of a brand's advertising affects its image. In recalling the most recent campaign, the image of the brand that comes to mind will be nuanced by the half-conscious associations of advertising long ago. The initial "fixing" of associations is critical, with a need to determine whether these associations have positive staying power or unintentionally fix the brand with affinities that rapidly date it. Advertisers may think this problem is simply a matter of when to change the images attached to a brand. This misses out on the need for the brand to project a consistent position on what the brand stands for. There is a menace in image discontinuities. A brand needs to develop its imagistic lineage: the remarkable example of the long-running Absolut vodka campaign attests to this, where the basic creative paradigm can be continually reused and refreshed so that all meanings and symbols remain consistent and reinforced through time. In fact, the image came first and then the product. Once the image was established, the recipe that became Absolut was devised. It is currently America's most popular imported vodka.

The Importance of Branding

What makes a sharp and favorable brand image important is that it is part of the awareness of a brand that is *recalled* before contemplating buying or part of that awareness that occurs when a brand is *recognized* in the store. All thinking is an act of simplification, and, in line with this, consumers review rival brands (if they review at all) through a looking-glass that reflects brand images. Branding is condensed meaning and instant recognition. It is a signaling device to telegraph meaning in cryptic form—a meaning built up and nuanced over the years by advertising. This is sometimes denied, with claims that "branding is dead—with everyone branding, it doesn't work any more." This is like saying that when everyone has a marketing orientation, it doesn't work any more! It is true that if only one firm in an industry undertook branding, it would have more of an impact (competitive advantage) than when every competitor does it. But branding, like good marketing, is a condition for success in noncommodity markets. This is so even if growth through global branding is proving more difficult than anticipated.

Consumers can have a loyalty to their local national brand. It is not surprising that the big multinationals are buying local brands. RJR Nabisco has had more success in Russia with a new brand called Peter 1 than it did with Camel and Winston. Even Coca-Cola finds that its best-selling brand in India is not its Coke but its Indian brand called Thums Up! More worrying is the danger of the balance being tipped from group conformity to more stress on individuality in buying. The more consumers believe that what they buy must cohere to their individual idiosyncratic values (however dimly perceived) and desired self-images, the more likely they are to move away from mass-market brands.

Many articles about marketing are implicitly based on the assumption of a "one best way," which necessitates denigrating all other ways. But there are many strategies that are equally effective in building brand success. There is only one precondition, and that is a focus on the customer. Good marketing demands that companies be customer oriented or customercentric. A study by Deloitte Consulting and Deloitte & Touche concludes that customercentric companies are 60% more profitable than those that are not and have lower operating costs. In this study, being customercentric involves "a systematic process which sets objectives for customer loyalty and retention, and then tracks performance towards these goals."[4] Brand image acts like a conjunctive rule (options to surpass minimum standards) in eliminating brands that do not have a favorable image. Brand image typically lies behind the implicit favorite model, with the evaluation process becoming a confirmation exercise.

Brand Image and Symbolization

A brand image must symbolize something positive if the consumer is to contemplate buying the product. In other words, sellers must try to make their brands *significant symbols*. A significant symbol means that the target audience perceives the symbolization that was intended by the seller. Sellers aim to symbolize in brand image a certain experience, because imagining that experience means anticipating and contemplating possession, which is a form of self-persuasion.

A brand image needs to be constantly reinforced, as images fade or are undermined by rival communications. Brand images are altered by new information (including communication from rival bands), and this new information may undermine the image. Brand images can be rather fragile, and media commentators can damage them. Thus when Marks and Spencer, the British retailer, suffered a decline in profits, commentators rushed in to argue that the firm's product line and store layouts were dated. This left many customers feeling that their liking of the company's product line was also dated. There is a danger of such commentary, if loud enough, being a self-fulfilling prophecy.

Investment in Brand Image and Brand Extensions

The development of a strong brand image is an investment. In 1988 Switzerland's Nestlé paid $4.5 billion for Rowntree, a British confectioner; this sum was six times Rowntree's reported asset value, and this is just one example among many.[5] Brand images are exploited in brand extensions, and this is one reason why brands with a strong positive image are so valuable. This is not to suggest that all brand extensions are successful. Brand extensions can dilute the parent brand image. Any brand that has high up-market appeal has to guard against diluting the parent image. While selling in lower-priced segments under the same brand name need not seriously compromise brand image (if the brand extension is top-of-the-line in the segment), some dilution is likely to occur. For example, Mercedes-Benz has extended its range of cars to include much cheaper models. Even if these models are the best in their price segment, the Mercedes brand image has been diluted, since the top-of-the-line buyer can no longer just say he has a Mercedes and leave it at that. It is easy for companies to forget how vulnerable and fragile is the veil of historic mystique and how easily the patina of luxury becomes worn. Some firms recognize this and make more of an effort to distance themselves from products produced for lower-priced segments. Thus Rolex created the cheaper Tudor brand, with which no association was permitted, though connections always leak out.

The brand value of Coca-Cola is calculated as $83,845 million; McDonald's at $26,231 million; Mercedes at $17,781 million; and so on.[6] So powerful are brand image traces that a name like Buggatti can be successfully resurrected after many years of apparent extinction. Similarly, we have the ancient but historically resonant brand of Hispano Suiza possibly being brought back from the grave. Protecting brand image thus becomes key. Tommy Hilfiger refuses to sell to WalMart, not just because of its distribution system but because it is a discount chain, which is in conflict with Hilfiger's upscale image. What separates Hilfiger from the thousands of companies that make polo shirts is the brand name that projects the brand image. Part of that brand image consists of the outlets where the product is sold. Consumers feel more confident about the status of products that are bought at high-class stores, because the store's reputation rubs off onto the product. Consumers *feel* different about something bought at Brooks Brothers than at some cheap men's outfitter.

Brands with a very positive brand image "resonate" emotionally with the consumer. This does not mean consumers instantly and clearly recall everything about the brand. It is more a feel that is a compound of associations, some dimly and some clearly captured. Brand image is typically tied to the likability heuristic, which acts as a signal saying: "Don't evaluate, act." Constraints on time and resources oblige consumers to use informational shortcuts to discover what they seek. Consumers economize on information, just as they do with other resources, gathering only enough information to feel confident about declaring a preference. Of necessity, consumers delegate a good deal of the gathering and evaluation of information to "credible" sources. Many rely on the ads they see on TV and elsewhere. Gerber et al. claim that the more people watch TV, the more they believe that TV reflects reality, and heavy viewers of TV act in ways consistent with the television "reality" they watch.[7] However, because heavy viewers behave in ways consistent with TV does not mean they cannot separate reality from TV creations but merely means that TV simplifies choice.

Consumers accept much information on faith, without independent verification. In such circumstances, trust in the brand image can be decisive. With trust, consumers suspend calculation and questioning. With trust, consumers no longer balance what they put in against the immediate dividend, for they believe that things will even out over the long term. The principle of reciprocity thus characterizes any trusting relationship. Trust ties to values and values to emotion. Trust plus sentiment equals loyalty. When consumers buy on the basis of brand image, they do so not only to save cognitive energy but because they typically appraise a brand first for emotional significance and only later (if at all) undertake cognitive assessment. The unconscious appraisal ("gut feeling") that occurs in the first microsecond may determine preference. As pointed out earlier, a brand image can speak to the imagination in a way that drowns out whatever speaks for substance.

Inputs

The inputs that bring about an initial gut reaction to a brand are as follows.

1. *Negative information.* More than positive information does, negative information about a brand influences consumer choice because it stirs the emotions more. Consumers are more conscious of what they hate than what they like.[8] Consumers gain a sense of self-definition more through oppositions—that they are against this or that—than through what they like. What people dislike points to out-groups who do not share their values. A negative image can instantly rule out a brand. Consumers exclude many products or brands unconsciously. If they did not, they might never come to a decision. If political parties are regarded as brands, the art of political salesmanship lies in focusing on stereotypical aspects of the rival brands, usually in slogan or sound bite, for example, "It isn't fair, it's Republican."

2. *The surrogate indicators used.* No one apprehends "reality" directly; all perception is selective. In practice, consumers use surrogate indicators—indices or proxies of, say, quality, prestige, and so on—because of a lack of expertise or time or an inability to do otherwise (e.g., check the effectiveness of nonprescription drugs). When consumers cannot apprehend all the crucial aspects of a product directly, they fall back on indicators, just as people may judge a person's intelligence from that person's appearance (good-looking people are consistently judged more intelligent than those with plain looks). The surrogate indicators used by the consumer may represent some tangible property—for example, leather seats in a car—or may symbolize something like prestige. Even when consumers do not need to rely on indicators, they may still do so. This is because consumers are cognitive misers, and it may be just too much trouble to search for and absorb the "real" facts. Consumers may accord great significance to indicators that, unbeknownst to them, are irrelevant for their purposes—for example, the weight of a vacuum cleaner—believing that a heavy weight is key to cleaning performance. Similarly, many use branded bottled water as a surrogate indicator of purity, though the evidence suggests that tap water is typically just as good in every respect, at least in modern industrialized countries.

The use of surrogate indicators means that two consumers with exactly the same choice criteria who face the same set of brands can end up choosing different brands because they use different indicators. This is no different from interviewers of job applicants who agree on what they are looking for but do not agree about which candidate best fulfills the criteria. Different interviewers will differ in their assessment of behavioral styles. One interviewer may associate talking fast with quick thinking, intelligence, and good judgment while another evaluates fast talk as mere glibness and places great importance on a deliberate style of talking, which is taken to be reflective and wise.

One surrogate indicator in buying is brand image. This is because brand image, as a surrogate indicator, can operate as a symbol of quality, prestige, reliability, and believability of claims. Brand images, as with corporate and national images, can become mentally entrenched, in that thought patterns that would highlight other attributes of a product begin to atrophy. Insofar as brand images become entrenched, evaluations of other brands never arise. Trust in a brand substitutes for deficiencies in information. Sellers must identify the indicators of quality, prestige, low risk, and so on used by the consumer to ensure that marketing sends the right signals.

3. *Symbolization.* Symbols, instead of pointing to something concrete, represent social meaning. Shopping is a way some consumers have of giving social meaning to their lives to replace the meaning once given by traditional religion.[9] In any case, the right symbolization for a brand is crucial. When the array of rival brands is ambiguous as to relative benefits, consumers use the symbolism invoked by the brand to decide. The manipulation of symbols is the standard approach of politicians to the winning of votes, but it is equally important in consumer marketing, as the right symbolism can equate with brand significance in the mind of the consumer.

The problem is to attach relevant and meaningful symbols to the brand. Sometimes this presents no difficulty, since some symbols are unambiguous. The military uniform of tight tunic, trousers, and peaked cap has been adopted as the symbol of power in all parts of the world. What something symbolizes may be conventional within the culture (e.g., a nation's flag) or fairly universal throughout most cultures (e.g., fire as symbolizing energy). However, the meaning or significance of any specific symbol to an individual may be unique, depending on social context and the individual's unique experience. Context can be very important with respect to meaning. Consider the idiom. This is a group of words whose meaning cannot be grasped by simply knowing the meaning of the individual words. Take the expression "sour grapes" as meaning a denial of the worth of what a person cannot himself attain. Similarly, there is variation in the symbolic meaning of something. The cigarette can symbolize the attainment of maturity to someone entering his or her teens but not to everyone. Symbols such as brand names have a plasticity and so are subject to multiple and even oppositional readings. There is in fact a semantic autonomy of language, in the sense that words, as symbols, have the ability to carry meanings independent of the communicator's goals. Members of the target audience may understand the literal meaning of the words used but interpret the words in a way that takes into account numerous contextual understandings.

Advertisers sometimes build vagueness and ambiguity into ads to allow each person to adopt an individual interpretation. The advertiser thus might choose words and phrases that can be interpreted in many sometimes contradictory ways, just as a politician may say he or she stands for justice without saying which side of some current burning issue represents that justice. This is common in advertising that addresses feminist concerns. An advertisement featuring the man working at home and the woman arriving in a business suit and carrying a bunch of flowers can be read either as a humorous role reversal or as an endorsement of feminism, so that neither feminists nor social conservatives are antagonized. But relying on ambiguity and vagueness is risky, as it is not certain how effective such ads are in building brand image. Advertising is more likely to be effective when directed at a target audience that is sufficiently homogeneous to respond to the same appeals. This may be difficult. Thus advertising that projects strong family values might alienate other groups or even single people—by reminding them that they live alone. The question thus arises as to whether it is possible to target different groups without also varying the advertising.

Brand names themselves symbolize something positive or negative. The name is particularly important when the brand is first launched (later every brand name gets its own unique connotations), as the unity and uniqueness of the name symbolizes the unity and uniqueness of the product. The same goes for a site name on the internet. The continuity of the same brand name symbolizes a stability in relationships with customers. Many product failures are accelerated by the inept choice of name: one museum of failed products includes "virucidal tissues" (this frightened people); "dry beer" (people could not visualize what it would be like); and "meals-for-one" (people did not want to be reminded that they were dining alone). Even the wrong benefits may be stressed; smokeless cigarettes were a failure because the only people who felt they benefited were nonsmokers. The meanings of words are sharpened in thinking. In the case of products, this can mean our associating a product with a specific function and being quite unable to view it otherwise. This is one of the reasons why repositioning a product in another segment of the market might fail; the consumer may have difficulty recoding the product's function. It takes imagination to see alternative uses for a product.

Brand names can come to be viewed as codified symbols of status, prestige, reliability and quality or, for some consumers, just the opposite. As we have noted already, it is common today to talk about brand names becoming less important because the consumer is becoming more "informed." This is a restatement of the claim that if the consumer *really* knew, say, that the premium brand and the low-priced brand were equally "good," the premium brand would not command a higher price. There are several erroneous assumptions being made. The first is that consumers are concerned purely with utilitarian functions and not with symbolic meaning. In buying designer clothing, the consumer feels that such clothing symbolizes status, commands respect in others, and lessens the risk of wearing something that is derided by one's social milieu. The second assumption is that the brands on the market today will be roughly those of tomorrow. But products and brands are leaving and entering the market all the time, so the context of decision-making changes, and with it the utility of the old information. Third, there is the economists' fantasy of the highly rational consumer weighing up the pros and cons only of tangible (functional) benefits. This is generally far from the truth. Consumers in certain product categories may simply check how they feel about a product with the focus on aesthetics and symbolic meaning. The emotions are very much tied to symbolic meanings and aesthetics. As Campbell says:

> It should be obvious, however, that the gratification obtained from
> the use of a product cannot be separated from the images and ideas
> with which it is linked, in the way, for example that eating caviar
> or drinking champagne is popularly associated with luxurious
> living . . . for consumer behavior is just as much a matter of emo-
> tion and feeling as it is of cognition, as the centrality of issues of lik-
> ing and disliking clearly reveal.[10]

Marder's research (or at least his company's) indicates that in terms of market impact, the brand name, in general, is more important than an additional feature or some general advertising promise. Two of Marder's "principles" are:[11]

- *Name principle.* A name is worth money. For durables, a good name may permit charging as much as 20% more for a brand, on the average; in some cases as much as 50% more. It can also be of comparable value for consumables, but more rarely.
- *Promises principle.* For consumables, only specific features are likely to matter. General promises won't. For durables, both specific features and general promises are of major importance.

When a name symbolizes something "good" or of value, some of it rubs off on the brand. This is why there are fights over names. For example, for 25 years a fight in the European Community, led by the French and Belgians, has been directed at stopping British manufacturers (who sell without problems in the United States) from using the term "milk chocolate," because their products so named contain up to 5% vegetable fat, as well as cocoa butter. There was insistence that the British label their chocolate *"chocolate containing vegetable fats."* Does anyone doubt that such a label would affect the sales of British chocolates, making British brands sound second-rate? Names count as much as appearance on occasions. Brand names can symbolize the values of the times. Thus names relating to cars in the mid–twentieth century, like Coupe de Ville and Imperial, suggest power and status, while today names like Sterling and Infiniti suggest durability.[12] Opium, the name of a perfume, is a clever way of both evoking and denying the modern drug culture.

Corporate Image

It is not just brands that are imbued with an image; there is the corporate image. Corporate identity is composed of name plus logo, and identity enters into corporate image. Gregory views corporate image as the combined impact on observers of all the planned and unplanned visual and verbal effects generated by the corporation or outside influences.[13] This is better than saying that corporate image "reflects the core of values that define it," since we are concerned with buyer perceptions and not with corporate intentions. The corporate image of American Express (whereby members feel they are being taken care of) allows it to charge a relatively large annual sum for the American Express Card.

A favorable corporate image is important for reasons that affect profitability. Global corporations may face a growing animosity, with local citizens viewing them as lacking local loyalty, and no country likes to feel that its industry is beholden to foreigners. Coca-Cola's contamination problem in Belgium and France in 1999 was exacerbated by the belief that the company sold something that symbolized the hedonism of American culture while rotting the teeth of children!

Calkins of Calkins and Holden, an advertising agency, claimed in the 1920s that the collective success of a firm's brands depended on the firm's ability to achieve an overall, constant image for the company: a consistency reflected not only in corporate actions but in its stationery, like letterheads and business cards; literature, like catalogs; transportation, like trucks and business cars; packing, like cartons and labels; architecture, like exterior building and interior lobby design; signs, like directories; and sales materials, like uniforms and giveaways.[14] This becomes more important if the company uses the corporate name on each of its brands.

A corporation extends its visibility and reputational capital by promoting a uniform, recognizable, distinctive, and emotionally pleasing image that projects what the firm stands for. Calkins argued that all the firm's products, its packaging, and its distribution must cohere with an overall image. He even recommended trading off the higher quality associated with longevity for a more attractive image. The design of the product itself may be irrelevant to its technical functions but highly relevant to its image of "being in the swing of things." Calkins was an early pioneer in advocating "psychological obsolescence." There is a danger, of course, of the corporation not living up to the basic values it proclaims, which makes consumers both angry and cynical about it.

Marchand, a historian who writes on advertising, identifies Bruce Barton as the true pioneer of "institutional" (corporate) advertising.[15] Starting around 1900, Barton worked for giant corporations like AT&T, General Motors, and General Electric to shore up their image as highly likable, benevolent neighbors, and caring employers, to deflect attention from their monopoly profits, and to ward off the threat of government regulation. The appeal was to traditional American values; for example, showing the company founder raising himself by his bootstraps to philanthropic wealth. Barton's formula was to portray the corporation as a family embracing employees and customers, "making the nation into a neighborhood." The whole approach was directed at achieving emotional resonance with the public.

Gregory, who runs his own company specializing in corporate image, views image advertising as the promotion of ideas. He credits David Ogilvy with responsibility for more successful corporate campaigns than anyone else.[16] Gregory claims that a major reason for the growth in corporate image advertising is the growth in the number of mergers, acquisitions, divestitures, and takeovers that render current images obsolete or give rise to the need to consolidate several divisional logos, and so on, into one new corporate image. Corporate promotion of image will depend on objectives that Gregory classifies into seven categories: (1) a more favorable market position; (2) redefining the corporation after its merger with another; (3) preselling prospective customers; (4) influencing the financial market; (5) declaring where the company stands on some issue; (6) helping out in a crisis situation; and (7) enhancing the firm's reputation with employees and local community.

In developing a new name, Gregory recommends that a company start by listing the attributes a new name should convey; for example, the terms *independent, confident, lean, disciplined,* and so on. This is what commonly happens, but we suggest it might be better to start with finding out about the current image and what values the company believes it stands for so as to calculate the gap between what is and what should be. Thus Sainsbury's, the British supermarket chain, found that it had an image of being authoritarian and conservative and assuming a moral superiority out of step with the times. As the marketing director said: "The emotional attributes of our brand became increasingly old-fashioned."[17] After this historical review, the firm can move on to how the values it aims to stand for might be symbolized and implemented throughout the company. Sainsbury's acknowledges that implementation involves a far-reaching program of cultural change. Afterward there is then a need to test whether the target group's perceptions are what the company intended. This may not be so, because what the company claims to stand for may sound insincere and silly; for example, BP Amoco's claim to be a "force for good in everything we do." Consumers dismiss such statements as advertising puffery. There must be some coherence between what is done and what is claimed.

This problem is discussed by Klein.[18] In selling to the youth market, firms like Benetton, Nike, Calvin Klein, and so on seek to associate their brands with moral causes. This can and has come back to haunt them. In the process of declaring what they stand for (high ethical values), they implicitly set high standards for themselves. This has led to "activists" holding them to account for international sweatshops, polluting the environment, disappearance of jobs, and corporate censorship. Action, to these listeners, speaks louder than words. Wearing a brand is a public declaration of acceptance or affiliation, with the company suggesting also an identification with the values publicly espoused (if any). When a company's actions appear to negate these values, consumers can feel a sense not only of disappointment but betrayal.

Ford sought to change consumer perceptions of poor quality by dogmatic assertion in its advertising that "Quality is Job 1." Citicorp sought to establish a corporate image through a slogan that resonated with traditional American values: "Citicorp. Because Americans want to succeed, not just survive." While Citicorp is concerned with beating its new nonbank competitors, like Sears Financial Services, Du Pont (like Dow Chemical) is concerned to throw off its war image as being a "merchant of death." As a consequence, its advertising focuses on issues of public concern like breast cancer and automotive safety, selecting features of the product that connect with public concern to show that the company is making a positive contribution. Du Pont builds a good deal of emotion into its image advertising, for example, showing the courageous disabled veteran Bill Denby, who had lost both legs in Vietnam, being able to play basketball because of prosthetic legs made by Du Pont. Some companies enhance corporate image by advocacy in public issues, as in W. R. Grace's attack on capital gains taxes or Mobil Oil's advocacy of mass transit. Gregory argues that product advertising is more effective when it is coupled with corporate image advertising. Companies that have impressive subsidiaries, like United Technologies with Otis and Pratt and Whitney, should exploit the positive images of the subsidiaries to build familiarity with the parent company as this helps its impact on the financial community.

Corporate image can be key in marketing offerings that are "inscrutable," that is, whose quality cannot be evaluated by the consumer. In such cases, the reputation of the manufacturer or service provider stands as proxy (surrogate indicator) for the quality of the offering itself. A company's *reputational capital* is part of its image, and a reputation for trustworthiness, reliability, and quality makes its promises about a new product credible. The same argument could be used for the value of a positive brand image. It facilitates brand extensions; the trust is carried over to the new product. Corporate image can be a great help in a crisis, as Johnson & Johnson found when dealing with the Tylenol scare, where someone put poison into Tylenol containers. When consumers found that Johnson & Johnson were the owners of Tylenol and the company acted as their reputation would lead people to expect, damage was minimal. On the other hand, as Gregory illustrates, Union Carbide had no great image in India at the time of the Bhopal disaster, which caused all sorts of problems.

Yet corporate images can fade and become no longer fashionable. This could happen with Branson and his Virgin group of companies. While once having novelty appeal with the values of being antiestablishment, it is now too established to have that kind of attraction to new consumers entering its markets. Branson and his brand name, Virgin, now have less appeal. The name does not seem to have helped sell Virgin Cola, Virgin Express (a low-cost airline), or Virgin clothes or cosmetics. In any case, a company is perceived as part of some industry, and if that industry's reputation is damaged, then some of that rubs off onto each member of the industry. Thus pharmaceutical manufacturers are in danger of losing their image of being a caring, sharing industry in their apparent determination to stop the production and sale of cheaper AIDS drugs and life-saving drugs to the poor and destitute of the Third World, particularly Africa (*The Economist,* March 10, 2001). Financial service companies, banks, and financial institutions of all types have a major image problem because of their reputation for rip-offs and their general exploitation of customer ignorance. In June 2001, the Financial Services Authority, a watchdog agency in Britain, was damning in its criticism of financial services companies for promising too much, promoting opaque products to exploit consumer ignorance, and taking every opportunity to confuse customers for financial gain. The emotional toll in anxiety, distress, and loss of confidence was described as immeasurable. Similar criticism could be made everywhere in the world and of other industries. Every company that seeks to be ethical (and ethical violations do recoil on reputational capital) should always ask itself one simple question when in ethical doubt: if what we are doing were fully revealed to our customers and the public at large, would we feel embarrassed or ashamed? If a company replies "yes," it should think again about the ethics of what it is doing.

National Image

A nation itself is a brand, a compound of contemporary and historical associations that has relevance for the marketing of its products. Not surprisingly, nations are sensitive about their image, if for no other reason than that the national image can promote or inhibit trade. It can also produce sympathy and help when needed. The poor image of Chechnya as a country where foreign businessmen are kidnapped and brutally murdered has diluted the support it has received from the international community in the conflict with Russia. An attractive image gives the country a hearing, while a credible image in a product category, as Japan has in cars, reduces doubts and uncertainty about buying. A company may adopt a brand name simply because it sounds as if the product was produced in a country considered more likely to produce it well. Thus the German-sounding name *Haier* is used by a Chinese state-owned company that sells household appliances to the West. It is not uncommon to subtly mislead the consumer about the origin of, say, a fashion product made in the Far East by using a label that has instructions in French and English! The American originators of Häagen-Dazs adopted the name because it suggested Scandinavian origin.

A national image is not just for external consumption, as it can be used to infuse a nation with a sense of pride that helps unite it. The promotion of a national image can help generate a sense of solidarity with others. In some cases this leads to extreme nationalism and chauvinism. Yet appeals to nationalism can be effective. There is the success of Hyundai's Buy Korea Fund, which in a short time became the nation's largest unit trust fund, with investors being mainly ordinary citizens. The slogan, based on a nationalist appeal, resonated with the public in spite of the Government's expressed suspicions about the fund.[19]

Although it is meaningful to talk about a nation's image, a nation has a far wider set of images than any brand. If the concept of image demands a picture in the mind, then, to someone in Europe, the United States may simply conjure up the image of Hollywood or Times Square or Coca-Cola or McDonald's. What images come to mind depend on the context, as there is no sense of a composite, overall image. A nation cannot simplistically be viewed as a product writ large. In thinking about any country, consumers will (1) hold some position along a continuum from like to dislike and (2) in respect to buying a specific product, will have some sense of that nation's reputational capital for producing whatever they seek from such a product. The imagery part of brand image is tied to affect-driven choices, and reputational capital is tied to belief-driven choices.

The likability heuristic is far more likely to operate in respect to brand image than to the image of a nation, as it is easier to give a unity and uniqueness to a brand image that suggests the unity and uniqueness of the product. This is not to suggest that a nation's brand image can never activate the likability heuristic. There are consumers throughout the world who buy American goods simply because they want to feel they are buying part of America. This relates to McCracken's concept of "displaced meaning," already mentioned in chapter 2.[20] The concept of displaced meaning, or dream longings, explains the behavior of buying American as buying a piece of one's dream world (and America is a dream world for perhaps most of the human race).

The reputational capital of a nation in relation to a product category is likely to be more important than pure imagery in the buying of technical products. In other words, such buying is more likely to be belief driven than affect driven. However, some brand advertising has been very adept at attaching highly favorable images of the country of origin to the brand. For example, an episodic (serial) "soap opera" advertising campaign in Britain that went from 1991 to 1998 brilliantly exploited distinct images of the relaxed French lifestyle and countryside to promote the Renault Clio car.[21] The ads evoked a strong nostalgia for British audiences. The Clio's yearly sales in Britain went from 21,000 to 58,000 cars. This example shows how researching the attributes associated with a nation by the target audience *and* tacking on the most appropriate attractive images of the nation can be effective in overcoming negative views of other attributes of the country.

A brochure entitled *Debate: A Global Brand for Germany*, produced by Wolff Olins, a firm of design and image consultants, points out that although brands historically are associated with products and corporations, "the techniques of branding are essentially applicable to every area of mass communications." The brochure argues that political leaders, in order to inspire people, need to become "brand managers" of their parties and preferably of the nation. The brochure recommends that "Diversity and Unity" be the central idea for the new brand of the German nation. (Interestingly, the eighteenth-century scholar Francis Hutcheson promoted the idea of beauty being unity in diversity.) The phrase "Diversity and Unity" connects to the idea that Germany is now in a position to relax and be more human, with an expanded image that incorporates more than industrial achievement but shows Germany as an exciting and surprising country where different peoples can live and work together. The brochure acknowledges that for any branding to be successful, there is a need to be truthful, that is, for it to have at its core a unique idea that corresponds to what the organization really stands for.

Jarvis, a political scientist, points out that conflicting images of a nation and its intentions give rise to disagreements in other countries about how to treat that nation.[22] He claims that an important instrument of statecraft is being able to affect other countries' images of one's own country and thus their beliefs. Every country tries to project a desired image, and this means trying to estimate how significant countries will see a country and interpret what it is doing. While the Wolff Olins brochure on Germany stresses the need to be truthful, Jarvis acknowledges that many countries want to project a misleading image and put across information that would be provided by a country that actually did fit that image. But target audiences are more impressed by information that the government cannot manipulate for purposes of deception. Thus the information that Germany does not give citizenship to those of "non-German blood" even if born in Germany (now about to change), and that even those of "German blood" returning from German communities settled in Russia are treated as foreigners, is incongruent with the "Diversity and Unity" theme.

Jarvis emphasizes how the establishment of a desired image for a nation can be defeated by perceptual predispositions of those in other nations, since their expectations and needs strongly influence what they "see." In fact, under conditions of high ambiguity, people turn inward to preconceived images of each other. The image that a nation seeks to project is only one of the factors that influence the perceiver's image. In fact, the perceiver may dismiss all attempts at image-building and just assume that every nation behaves similarly in similar circumstances. There are many factors that contribute to national image that are beyond the control of a nation's image-makers; for example, a country's geography and history. Jarvis makes a distinction between "signals"— for example, a statement of intentions—and "indices," which are perceived as carrying inherent evidence that the image projected is correct because it (1) is linked to the nation's self-interest; (2) is beyond the nation's power to control; and (3) involves very high cost. These indices are important for all brand images.

Developing Meaningful Symbolism

How do we develop meaningful symbolism to enhance an image, whether of a corporation or nation? We discuss three methods, as follows. (There is considerable conceptual overlap among the three methods; their differences are mainly in emphasis.)

Resonance Model and Brand Image

One way of developing meaningful symbolism is Schwartz's *resonance model*.[23] He argues that the best ads are those that resonate with the target audience, and these are those that tap, with respect to the product, the relevant *experiential feelings* of the target audiences. It is the same with journalism: the most persuasive journalism is that which links up with the raw nerves of the readers, on the basis of their experiential feelings. The feelings of interest are *emotional* and are specifically those that transmit a *value* to the experience, giving a like/dislike tone to the experience. ("They laughed when I sat down at the piano. But when I started to play . . . ") Thus when in West Berlin President Kennedy said: "Ich bin ein Berliner," this statement of shared identification with the residents resonated far more than saying in English that he had sympathy for their plight.

Schwartz's resonance model echoes the neo-Gibsonian school of cognitive psychology, which rejects the computer metaphor with its information-processing approach in favor of the "resonance" metaphor, where the mind is viewed as analogous to a tuning fork, which spontaneously responds to particular stimulus configurations without any intervening processing stages.[24] While there would be little support for viewing the resonance metaphor as a substitute for the computer metaphor, Damasio's concept (see chapter 1) of positive and negative somatic markers does support the concept of resonance. But resonance with an absence of imagery/representation is another matter.

The Schwartz model claims that the most effective persuasion is that which strikes an emotional chord, which in practice means eliciting an emotionally persuasive message *from* the target audience itself rather than trying to implant one. The message that resonates is that which speaks to values/needs/wants/desires and not that which just sounds good. But how do we obtain an emotive persuasive message from the target audience? He recommends finding out what feelings are generated in relation to the activities associated with the product. What feelings are evoked when consumers buy and drive a sportscar? Such feelings provide a sense of ease or dis-ease. In dramatic advertising these feelings are acted out and, in the process, resonate with the target audience, as the ad "touches a nerve" or "gets close to home." Schwartz criticizes what he calls the transportation idea (one-way flow) of communication, as communication is a coproductive activity. Once having identified the feelings that are associated with the product in various contexts, advertising is used to evoke them or bring them out of the target audience. The ads incite the audience to recall the experiential feelings associated with the product. This is what is meant by the "message resonating": it resonates in feeling toward the product or brand.

Dramatic advertising (1) targets the feelings of the audience; (2) is concrete, vivid, and image-provoking; and (3) deals with a subject matter close to home. Schwartz created the so-called daisy ad in the Lyndon Johnson versus Barry Goldwater presidential campaign: the ad contrasting a very vulnerable small girl symbolizing the future, with a male voice giving a nuclear countdown. But Schwartz recognizes that a new product cannot exploit people's emotional memories of buying and using it. In such cases, he suggests "planting" relevant experiences in advertising. Think in terms of what pleasant experiences, what celebrities, what cultural images can be meaningfully attached to the product. This is, in effect, *transformational advertising*, which associates the possessing, using, or consuming a product with certain values and emotional experiences that are highly desirable.

An advertisement for Calvin Klein jeans is one example. A book insert in *Vanity Fair* magazine, the ad chronicled a slice of the life of a pop group. It has been analyzed elsewhere as follows.[25]

If the advertisement exemplifies the sensual, nonconformity life style, how does this rub off on to the product? There are the following links:

- Ad for Calvin Klein jeans → pop group
- Pop group ↔ sensual, non-conforming life style.

Therefore:

Sensual, nonconforming lifestyle → Calvin Klein jeans.

The arrows point to the associations. Single arrows indicate what is *denoted;* double arrows indicate what is meant to be *exemplified.* Whenever anything *A* refers to something *B*, *A denotes B*. On the other hand, *A exemplifies B* when *A* both refers to *B* and is an instance of *B*. Specifically, the advertiser would like the prospective buyer to view Calvin Klein jeans as not only denoting but also exemplifying the sensual, nonconforming lifestyle. In other words:

Sensual, nonconforming lifestyle ↔ Calvin Klein jeans.

The Calvin Klein advertisement communicates its message nonverbally and in a way that would be outrageously vulgar if expressed in words, while no words could capture all the nuances of the advertisement. Advertising does not have the same freedom as movies and TV soap operas to openly deride social conventions—though, as with the Calvin Klein ad, it may ostentatiously flirt with the boundaries of good taste without actually breaching them, attempting to seem at the "cutting edge" without antagonizing the rest of society.

Although the term *transformational advertising* is of recent origin, it goes back to Harry Dexter Kitson in the 1920s, who argued that advertising should stress the *emotional* experiences of owning and using the product. For this to be done, an ad should tie into the values of the audience and evoke the type of experiences (the paradigm scenarios) that led to the values in the first place. There are difficulties here. In the first place, consumer values may be ranked, but the ranking may elude the advertiser. In addition, the type of experience evoked may not be adequate, either because it is not that meaningful to the target audience or because it evokes an entirely different set of associations or images from those intended. There will always be aberrant interpretations, as not everyone is privy to the same "code." In growing up in a culture consumers do absorb certain codes for interpreting the behavior. These "codes" help interpret behavior in various contexts, as codes tie types of context with types of communication.

People may remember an ad but not the brand advertised. This is the danger with all emotional advertising, where the emotional elements are the ones imprinted in memory. The numerous sports celebrities in sneaker ads confuse consumers about which celebrity wore what shoes. And by constantly changing the cultural images attached to a brand, advertisers may attach an associaton of "pleasantness" without providing the brand with a continuing memorable image, so the target audience has no sense of what the brand stands for. Something important is lost as a consequence. This is a familiar problem for those attempting to "freshen up" the image of an old brand. The advertising agency that recommends radical surgery can do lasting damage. In disconnecting the brand from its historical identity, there is a loss of sentiment attached to the brand from past buying and advertising.

When Schwartz talks of using "dramatic" advertising, he talks of the emotion embedded in the verbal, auditory, and sight scripts used in an ad.

Verbal script. Any communication carries not only a message but also a tone. Words shape that tone by influencing feelings, mood, and perspective. Words that carry an emotional overtone color consumer attitudes and the meaning given to words. When advertisers select words and pictures, they in effect invite the target audience to conceptualize, analyze, and appraise the product, or cause or person, in a particular way, that is, in line with the descriptive words used. There are some words that are essentially feeling words, like *annoyed, burdened, crushed, distraught, exasperated, fearful, hurt, pressured, sympathetic, tired, worried,* and so on. There are words that have highly positive connotations, like *progress, new, safe, security, low calorie, fat free,* and words with negative connotations like *old-fashioned, artificial, non−user friendly, gas-guzzler,* and so on. These words never entirely lose their power. But words are more important in a general sense, since words exercise a restriction on thought. If consumers do not have a word for something, they might not even notice it since we mainly note things for which we do have a name.

Paralanguage is important in molding the tone of spoken words. Paralanguage is the set of extra linguistic factors that accompany the spoken word: for example, (1) *voice quality*—since voice qualities, like pitch and rhythm, communicate much about the emotional state of the person who is speaking, and (2) *vocalizations*—like laughing and crying, yelling or whispering, yawning—since these modify utterances in a way that directly influences interpretation. Paralanguage can negate any attempt to attribute a fixed ideological meaning and can aid ambiguity when this is desirable.

Auditory script. The use of music (even that used when customers are on hold) should cohere with the intended brand or corporate image projected, as music, like visual factors, influences brand feelings. Music and sound effects arouse emotions. Music resonates with emotional memories. Hence the popularity of the pop music of the 1960s in advertising. Even though much of the target market may not have been alive in the sixties, there is a collective memory that exists independent of direct personal experience that provides a storehouse of usable symbolism. Recalling the sounds that trigger emotional memories of using the product (e.g., the sound of opening a can of beer) predisposes a target audience to think favorably about the advertised brand.

Sight script. The aesthetics of the design, the movements, the angle camera shots, the colors, and the props are all part of the emotional drama of any ad. Pictures evoke feelings, and visual metaphors can be more effective than verbal ones. This is perhaps why pictorial metaphors are increasingly being used in advertising; for example, showing a dog being "tuned" up like a car after taking "doggie vitamins" or, in a car security ad, showing roaming hyenas instead of actual car thieves.

Sight scripts and the Internet. We might include under sight scripts being able to see the other person physically. When people see each other, they are more inclined to like and trust each other and to cooperate more readily. This is because just listening to what people say is only one way to assess attractiveness and credibility. Talking over the phone can be a tense experience for many, because they cannot see and hence adjust fully to both verbal and nonverbal communication. The great advantage in face-to-face selling (and in face-to-face conversation in general), is the ability of the participants to react instantly to questions, confusions, and misstatements. This means there is far more likelihood of each participant resonating with the needs of the other.

The lack of face-to-face contact becomes acute with the development of consumer sales over the Internet (business-to-business sales are somewhat different). And the promise of Internet sales, for many writers, is high. As Lester Thurow says, in talking about the potential of the Internet to eliminate the need to go to the local store, the Internet not only eliminates the expense of location, inventories, and large numbers of workers to serve customers but enables the small firm to compete head-to-head with the retailing giants.[26] Even universities fear being left behind, as the Internet promises to transform education. They have been signing agreements with Unext.com and Learning Network Inc. to create course materials for the Internet. But the approach has to be made interactive. There is a need to make the computer seem human, so users interacting with the computer will be unable to tell whether there is a face behind the screen or just machine parts. It is argued the Internet is ideal for allowing marketers to integrate and coordinate all their dealings with customers into one medium to both better customize the offering and personalize the execution, the twin goals of service excellence. A provider of a service may provide one but fail the other, just as a doctor may customize his or her service but fails to personalize the execution. Nonetheless, there is always something lost as we move away from face-to-face selling.

While acknowledging the advantages of the Internet in terms of wide selection, convenience, speed, and information, Underhill feels stores still have the advantage for many in offering sensory contact, immediate gratification, and social interaction.[27] It might also be added that most purchases cannot be expressed as a digital code, while distributing physical goods and dealing with returns can be prohibitively expensive.[28] Once a website is established, it is not just a matter of waiting for customers to come along. There is a need to reach out to prospective customers with tailored messages that resonate with those logging on.

Angela Mollard, a journalist, has written about the importance of normal shopping for her; after describing the experience of buying a particular piece of clothing, she writes:

> The joy of a perfect purchase is the reason why High Street shopping will never be usurped by the Internet—for women at least. Shopping is not just a process of re-stocking your sock drawer: it's a sensual, soul-enhancing experience akin to scaling a mountain or listening to a beautiful aria. No such pleasure is afforded by a two-dimensional picture on your computer screen. Likewise, where's the exhilaration in tapping out your credit card number, then pushing the enter key? You don't even get the goods upfront, let alone a glossy, ribboned-tied [sic] bag. It's not that I'm a techno-phobe. I use the net for everything from checking flights to researching the pieces I

write. But shopping is so much more than just a financial transaction. (*Daily Mail*, January 27, 2000, p. 38)

For many consumers there is the problem also of risk and of having to hang around waiting for delivery. The following is an extract from a buying protocol recorded during the buying of a ground positioning system over the Internet. After expressing worry about quality and reliability, the buyer says:

> I am afraid to send my credit card details over the net, [and] besides, I don't know if the company I am buying from really exists and if they are solid. I really don't feel like buying it through the computer, but the difference in price is substantial. Another problem is that I prefer to see and feel the products before I buy them. It allows me to feel the quality and somehow the resistance. The unit I am looking for must feel heavy and with a resistant body. Also, should it feel kind of sticky, I wouldn't like to lose it because it slipped from my hand. I don't like waiting days to receive the product. I prefer to give the money and receive the goods; otherwise I feel vulnerable. . . . I also didn't like the idea of giving my address and other personal information. And besides, the idea of paying and not receiving is making me nervous. I have no receipt from them, nothing in hard copy. But a lot of people are buying this way, so I think I might not have any problem.[29]

Stage-setting, and the atmosphere it creates, is also critical to purchase and cannot be fabricated in the same way online. Thus *The Economist* (June 17, 2000, p. 94) describes a visit to Christian Dior's boutique: "Exquisite handbags hang like modern art in classic, silvered rooms. The floors have been imported from a castle in Scotland. Elegant assistants talk lovingly about the handstiching and les petites mains that still work in the shop." As the article says, in such an atmosphere, paying $1000 for a Dior handbag seems, well, rather a bargain. But would it on the Internet?

Finally, as Brown and Duguid say, the fulsome predictions about the future of the Internet fail to take into account the most dominant human characteristic: sociability.[30] Few employers would hire someone on the basis of an interview conducted by e-mail or finance a startup without actually meeting the principals. For Brown and Duguid, communication amounts to more than just sending text messages over the net but involves the trust generated through dealing with others face-to-face, where you can observe all the nonverbal communication that accompanies speech. Physical propinquity is important, as people together learn from watching and talking to their colleagues, while distance learning cannot replace the experience of people coming together to acquire knowledge through discussion. What shopping malls need to do to counter the Internet is to focus on shopping as an "experience," or a total pleasure package. The real Internet revolution so far is in business-to-business communication, allowing firms to interact much more efficiently with suppliers, employees, and customers.

We are all familiar with the massive failure of dot.coms recently and some of the reasons lie in the preceding discussion. But one gain for the consumer is websites that use programs to identify the lowest prices of everything from cars to flowers. There is an *emotional* compulsion not to pay more than need be. The new shopping robots (known as "bots") search hundreds of websites, which puts pressure on retailers to meet or beat the price of their competitors.[31] Surveys confirm that men spend twice as much as women on Internet purchases, which shows perhaps that the computer is still not friendly enough. It also reflects the claim that women are more wedded to face-to-face communication. Evans and Wurster see success in Internet marketing as tied to:

1. How many customers the business can access and how many products it can offer
2. Affiliation toward the consumer
3. Richness in the depth and detail of information that the business gives to or collects from the customer.[32]

Building these three may require making alliances with rivals.

Self-persuasion via Self-imagining

Another way to create a positive brand image is through stimulating self-persuasion via self-imagining.[33] The effectiveness of self-persuasion was demonstrated in World War II by Kurt Lewin in the United States trying to get housewives to serve offal and pregnant women to drink more milk.[34] Group discussion (participation), role playing, and getting people to imagine a certain course of action were all used. Lewin focused on participation. But a marketing focus lies in getting prospective customers to imagine possessing and using the product. Getting prospects to imagine, in an emotional way, what something would be like to have and experience is a method of self-persuasion. As consumers imagine or fantasize about possessing and using, for example, a brand of sneakers, feelings are aroused as they talk themselves into buying. *Whereas transformational advertising plays on associations, self-persuasion focuses directly on getting the target audience to use its imagination.*

Self-persuasion via self-imagining is well understood by religions and cults, who recognize that getting their cadres involved in active evangelism is important because in persuading others, they persuade themselves. Many promotional questionnaires sent through the mail aim at inducing the receiver to think about the product in a way that self-persuades. One car dealer, offering a prize, sent prospects a mailing that asked them to mark which famous buildings, and so on, best reflected the car's attributes. In other words, the questions directed attention to attributes that favored the brand by drawing attention to what it had to offer.

A good deal of "slice-of-life" advertising (essentially a miniature drama that involves some incident to demonstrate the use of the product) gets the target audience to vicariously experience the feelings of the characters in the ad and in this way talk themselves into identifying with the brand. The slice of life ad tells a story, and stories are always an effective way to persuade. Myths are a culture's dialogue with itself and the way the culture transmits its core values—even if the myth (as in the case of the Greek myths) does no more than show what happens when such values are forsaken. Myths are stories, and Jesus Christ chose storytelling as the vehicle of his message.

Enhancing Self-esteem or Ideal Self-image

The third approach to developing a favorable brand image is to position the brand as a way of enhancing self-image and self-esteem. A good deal of advertising is concerned with helping the target audience form a conception of the advertised brand as being one that people like themselves would or should prefer because it coheres with their preferred self-image or boosts their sense of self-esteem. In promising consumers that the product will help them live up to some ideal or promote a higher sense of self-esteem, advertising stimulates the imagination, the daydream, the fantasy that this can all be made possible or at least facilitated by using the product. Psychographic segmentation recognizes the importance of this and aims at segments oriented to differences in values and lifestyles that reflect differences in self-image and self-esteem. Psychographic segmentation is most likely to be adopted when there is little differentiation among the brands in the market. The problem arises as to whether similar values and lifestyle will lead to similar standards of judgment in making buying decisions.

Some Key Assertions for Marketing

1. If the marketing of a brand is to be successful, then brand image is a key ingredient to success. Conclusive evidence as to a brand's relative superiority for its purposes is rarely available, and when falling back on trust, brand image plays a decisive role.

2. If marketing is to build up a brand image, there are two components:
   (1) imagery representations and (2) propositional representations (beliefs).
   Brand image is a summation of impressions involving imagery and beliefs.
   Where ads put the most stress on imagery (e.g., experiencing the product),
   the orientation is toward generating affect-driven choices, because imagery
   can trigger self-persuasion and the adoption of the likability heuristic to
   say: *Don't evaluate, act.* A stress on belief claims (propositions) is usually
   an orientation toward generating belief-driven choices to make the brand
   the logical purchase. Brand images are not analogous to files retrieved
   from memory but are constructed during recall, so context influences the
   particular image constructed. Since new information about a brand can affect its image, no brand image is entirely fixed. The imagery and beliefs
   constituting a brand image, however, typically symbolize a promise to meet
   or exceed customer expectations, while an established positive image suggests less risk in buying. Brand image enters into the awareness of the
   brand that is recalled before contemplating buying when a brand is recognized in the store and so can be used as a shortcut for determining emotional significance in choosing what brand to buy. Brand image can act as a
   conjunctive rule in reducing options to a manageable set, while a highly
   positive image generates trust, in which calculation and questioning are
   minimized.
3. If marketing management is concerned to build an enduring brand image,
   the initial fixing of associations can be critical, in that they may unintentionally fix the brand with affinities that rapidly date it. Negative information
   about a brand has more influence in consumer choice than some nominally
   equivalent positive information. Brand image can be a codified symbol of
   quality, prestige, reliability, and believability of claims and so operate as a
   surrogate indicator of these attributes being present without further investigation. Thus the aim is to attach to the brand meaningful symbols that project what the brand stands for. This is easier to do when the market segment and its target customer group are defined so as to be fairly
   homogeneous in relevant wants and beliefs.
4. If marketing management believes that corporate image rubs off onto its
   brands, then corporate image cannot be neglected. Brand advertising can
   be more effective when coupled with effective corporate image advertising.
   Corporate identity (name plus logo) is the visual part of corporate image,
   which consists of the summary evaluation that target audiences have of the
   company. Corporate image reflects the firm's reputational capital (e.g., GE's
   corporate image) and can be a decisive factor in determining which brand
   to buy. A corporation extends its visibility and reputational power by promoting a uniform, recognizable, distinctive, and pleasing image that projects what the firm stands for and wants the target audience to believe
   about it.
5. If a company aims to be ethical, it should avoid all conduct that would
   cause it shame and embarrassment if revealed to its customers and the
   public at large.
6. If the company belongs to a nation that has reputational capital in the product category within which the brand falls, that part of the nation's image

(constituting its reputation in the product category) can be exploited in marketing abroad, particularly for products where belief-driven buying (typically in terms of technical and economic criteria) operates. However, on occasion, the imagery part of the nation's image can be exploited to generate affect-driven choices.

7. If marketing management seeks to develop meaningful symbolism to enhance brand or corporate image, it should consider (1) the resonance model; (2) self-persuasion via self-imagining; and (3) symbols to enhance self-esteem. The resonance model claims that the most effective ads are those that resonate with the target audience in tapping the relevant experiential feelings. The messages that resonate best are those that come from the target audience itself; after marketing management finds out what feelings are generated in the activities associated with buying, using or, consuming the product, the ads are designed to recall. This assumes that the product is already out there and that the ad can capture the emotion in the verbal, auditory, and sight scripts. But because a new product cannot exploit emotional memories of buying and using the product, the advertiser may need to resort to "planting" the relevant, meaningful experiences in early advertising. The self-persuasion via self-imagining approach focuses on getting the target audience to imagine, in an emotional way, what something would be like to have and to use or experience (what it would *really* be like to have and to experience) so that self-persuasion can occur. The approach of enhancing self-esteem focuses on getting the target audience to conceive of the brand as one that people like themselves would or should prefer because it coheres with some ideal self-image of themselves.

7

Emotion in Building Brand Equity

Brand Equity

Branding has little significance unless it is perceived as offering assurances to those who buy the brand. The assurances offered may have nothing to do with the core function of the product and may be mainly social, as when the brand symbolizes social acceptance and status. Although market exchange follows the cost-benefit principle, in that both consumer and seller weigh costs against benefits, benefits for the consumer are not confined to tangible benefits. Every brand in fact has a *product* component and an *equity* component, though the boundary between them is apt to be fuzzy.

Product Component

The product component embraces the observable attributes of the functions of the product, as well as attributes accepted on trust. The following list of possible attributes relates to earlier discussions:

- *Functions:* core-use function (e.g., nutritional); ancillary-use functions (e.g., dietary); convenience-in-use function (e.g., ease in opening package); integrative functions leading to a better integration of self and self with community; economic/sacrifice functions; and the adaptive function in reducing unnecessary risk and uncertainty in buying.
- *Enjoyments:* taste (e.g., refreshing); feel (e.g., feels pleasant); aroma (e.g., smells fresh); aesthetic appeal (e.g., looks appetizing); sound (e.g., soothing); and just general liking.

We need to know the attributes of the whole offering and the *experiential* benefits these attributes offer to the target audience(s). We seek tangible benefits and emotional benefits (as illustrated in chapter 1).

Equity Component

Brand equity (if positive) is the additional value put on a brand by its customers over and above the brand's objective performance vis-à-vis its rivals. Aaker defines brand equity as the set of assets, such as brand-name awareness, loyal customers, perceived quality, and other associations, that are linked to the brand image that add or subtract value to or from the product being offered.[1] Positive brand equity arises from customers' *perceptions* of better value, symbolized by the brand name, trademark, and logo. The "better value" may not be in terms of perceptions of performance in the core function but in terms of, say, potential snob appeal. As Marder says, buying a brand amounts to sending a message to the world, saying *This is the type of person I am.*[2] Such social meaning is important in buying major items, like automobiles. Even a counterfeit Rolex is priced higher than the same watch without the name, though buyers know the watch is not authentic.

The equity component looms large in fragrances and designer clothes, while the product component dominates when a brand is a commodity product. Within a commodity market, brands are tokens of each other and so can be sold by description. But what should be a purely commodity market may be changed by manufacturers adding some differentiation. It was in the 1930s that Jack Beddington, head of promotion at Shell, employed distinguished artists and cartoonists of the day to design posters to affix cultural images to what would otherwise have been just a pure commodity product. There are three hundred brands of bottled water in the United States, objectively the same, but this has not meant that buyers regard them as mere tokens of each other. In consumer tests of fragrances and beers, where brand names are absent, preference rankings bear little resemblance to relative prices or to rankings when brand names are given.

Brand Persona. The term *persona* (from the Greek word for a mask worn by an actor in a play) was used by Jung (1875–1961), the Swiss psychiatrist, to refer to the social role a person plays in life. The persona acts like a mask behind which one hides as one plays a role in line with the persona. In the same way, brands can be said to have a persona, defined as the public face a brand projects. Marketing seeks to control this persona, trying to ensure that it becomes the face marketing wants to project.

Consistency of persona symbolizes certainty and a commitment to whatever the image suggests. Inconsistency is a cause of confused brand image. Lack of consistency can arise through advertising, as when advertisers constantly switch associations and the values they support. If the band persona that is adopted fits the preferred self-image of the target audience, buying the brand reinforces the consumer's own persona. Advertising should highlight the persona of a brand in a way that fits the assumed self-image of the target audience. One car ad in Britain showed a slick "City" type with a south London accent, a parody of the "1980s man," listing the virtues of the car he is driving. We have the impression that he is pitching for the car. Suddenly he stops and becomes dismissive—"not my kind of thing." Then a long-haired, more casually dressed, gentler type gets in the car and drives it away. Advertisements rarely make social value contrasts so explicit, as they do not want to offend people who might otherwise buy.

Brands speak an imagistic language. The desired persona of a brand is the image presented to the public by the firm. On the other hand, *brand image* is the actual image the public has of the brand, which includes the consumer's own view of the brand's persona. The persona of a brand is sharpened by the addition of a logo, the package, a picture, the shape of the product, or some associated character. Characters are *personifications* of symbols that sharpen brand image. Thus it is difficult to imagine Kentucky Fried Chicken without Colonel Sanders, Quaker Oats without the Quaker, McDonald's without Ronald McDonald, Green Giant without the Giant, or Pillsbury without the Dough Boy. A logo is a visual symbol of the brand; visual representations are more likely to resonate emotionally. On occasions, the logo and the character are the same. For many years, the logo of the Jaguar car itself echoed the design, resembling a large crouching cat (the character). Sometimes the brand name or company name—for example, Apple—suggests the logo. The logo is a way of differentiating a brand in a market composed of otherwise undifferentiated products.[3]

Brand Personality. The concept of *personality* in psychology has several meanings: (1) a person's character; (2) a set of behavioral traits; (3) the conscious self; and (4) a person's social mask. Brand personality as a social mask would be the same as brand persona. However, when the term *brand personality* is used in marketing, it typically refers to a set of character and/or behavioral traits. Brand personality is typically identified by asking consumers to describe the brand as if it were a person ("If the Mercedes were a person, how would you describe that person, or how would you write its obituary, or if it were a movie, what would it be about?"). The personality of a brand is a key element of brand image.

David Ogilvy believed in *creating* a personality for a brand rather than focusing on trivial product differences, creating, for example, the mysterious "man with the eye patch" as the personality of the Hathaway shirt. Many regard brand personality as a major way to get a brand to stand above, and distinguish itself from, its rivals. Brand personality, like brand persona, can be sharpened by the addition of a logo or the addition of commercial "characters," for example, the bubbly, apple-cheeked Campbell Kids (promoting Campbell soups).

The brand name helps shape perceptions of brand image. On the other hand, a brand's logo can evoke one of the clearest sensations possible about a brand. Even in the early nineteenth century, there were logos. A particularly well known one was Hercules slaying the Hydra, to show the strength of Swaim's Panacea. (Claimed to be a panacea for all health ills, it included the poison of sublimate of mercury!) One survey claimed that 55% of brand or company logos shown to consumers evoked very different reactions from when consumers were just shown the brand or company names alone.[4] Of 24 logos tested, 17 evoked more positive responses than the brand names alone. Thus, in the case of the Buick car, the score for trustworthiness and quality (on a scale from 1 to 100) increased by 16 percentage points when consumers saw the full-color Buick logo instead of the name alone. In six cases, however, the logos scored less than did the brand or company name when shown alone.

A slogan, like a logo, can sharpen a brand's image by drawing attention to unique benefits—for example the Marlboro cigarettes slogan "Filter, flavor, flip-top box" and Miller Lite's "Tastes great, less filling"; can be a promise, like a Florida Bank's slogan: "We treat all customers the same. Different" or Continental Airline's "Our priorities are simple. They're yours"; or can be a reminder, like a New York lottery slogan: "You've gotta be in it to win it." The shorter slogans tend to be the better: for example, General Foods' "Good to the last drop" or Nike's "Just do it." Perhaps the most famous slogan of all is "Diamonds are a girl's best friend." Like metaphors, slogans are ways of shifting perspectives. But some slogans prove to be dysfunctional. The slogan "Safety First" helped ensure that the Conservatives in Britain lost the general election in 1929, as the slogan encapsulated all that the electorate disliked about them. On the other hand, the slogan "Time for a Change Anyway," used by the Republicans in the United States immediately after World War II, resonated with many. While slogans are fairly fixed, ads can be varied to prevent them from wearout. One way is by choosing an advertising theme that is capable of endless permutations. An example, already noted, is the theme used for Absolut vodka, where the product's shape and name appear in many attention-getting guises.

Brand Image as a Social Construct

As a brand image is socially constructed, advertising tries to influence that social construction to bring about a convergence of meaning between seller and buyer. While a brand image is the typical impressions and associations *conjured* up by the brand in the mind of the consumer, brand images are not stored in the mind as facsimile images: there are no permanently held pictures of anything. The brand images conjured up are not fixed images retrieved as "files" in memory. They are reconstructions, and this explains why different contexts (image of a convertible in the middle of winter as opposed to early summer) conjure up different images.

A brand image is not fixed, in that:

1. It is updated when significant new information comes along that is relevant. The meanings of all words grow as knowledge grows, and meanings can change fundamentally as things change. Thus, in medicine, the names of diseases date back a long time but sense-meaning or connotations change with the advances of knowledge. The symptoms of Huntington's chorea were specified in 1872, but it was only in the 1990s that its genetic causes were discovered. Before the eighteenth century, the term *democracy* was associated with mob rule or worse, while it is now such a positive term of approval that Americans and EU countries think the whole world should adopt it! Similarly, images of brands mature and change. If the change is for the worse, the aim is to reverse the decline, just as the "frumpy" image of Avon is presently being upgraded by the opening of glamorous new spas.
2. Different facets of an image are emphasized depending on context, just as context will affect the image that comes to mind of the ex-president Bill Clinton.
3. The value attached to a brand (brand equity) erodes if left unattended. The earliest affected are the better educated, who keep abreast of such things; the poorly educated are more likely to stick to habitual buying patterns. But, as with religion, it is the strength of the loyalty that is apt to vary rather than the direction of the desire; consumers may

weaken in their preference for a brand but are less likely to weaken toward the product class. In other words, consumers tend to switch to other brands within the segment rather than move out of the segment altogether. Loyalty toward a brand is usually less stable than "loyalty" to the segment. While many consumers buy within several segments of the market for different use-occasions, it is difficult to get the consumer to give up on a segment for a *very* different segment of the market; similarly, when abandoning one religion, people tend to move to one close in doctrine.

4. Part of brand image is what the brand symbolizes: what it stands for, its social meaning over and above its objective properties. This can also change.

Packaging

Packaging is another way to sharpen brand image. It can even explain the success of a brand, as in the success of the selling of L'Eggs pantyhose in egglike plastic containers. As Hine says, every package and anything on a package is capable of triggering feelings such as excitement, as well as beliefs about the brand and its trustworthiness, because when we look at a package, we see a personality and a set of values.[5] The packaging of motel chains and fast food chains are their buildings. This allows companies more control over brand image by ensuring that the "package" has a coherence, symbolizing the values being promoted. In any case, packaging adds to brand image and competitive advantage (which is often a constellation of things) in any of the following functions.

Protection. The traditional function of packaging is to protect the product against dirt, damage, theft, mishandling and deterioration. Uneeda biscuits, introduced in the last century in the United States, established their position in the market with their protective/preservation system: a double-sealed package to preserve the taste.

Promotion. Packages link up with emotions and values. Attractive packaging increases product appeal and distinguishes a brand from competitors. The package that is most aesthetically appealing is one that is commonly bought. Packaging can have the same function as point-of-purchase displays in triggering a sale. Packaging may actually endear consumers to a product while the product is actually being used, thus functioning as an advertisement whenever the consumer looks at it at home. Sometimes protective outer packs may be made to unfold into an attractive display or dispenser for the retailer. All attractions are emotionally appealing. Promotional packages can thus be regarded as billboards in miniature. The elements of packaging are:

- *Package design*. Good design has intrinsic appeal that is essentially aesthetic. What helped Marlboro to raise its profile was a new and original design—the top that flipped open—which added little functionally but had wide intrinsic appeal while cohering with the positioning of the cigarette as one for the tough rugged man. If consumers on average spend only about one-sixteenth of a second looking at a package before moving on, good aesthetics ensures that further attention is pleasurable. If good aesthetics are part of the package, packages can function as (ephemeral) domestic furnishings. In this sense the package is part of the social identification of the buyer. Hine claims that there is no field of design that deals more effectively with the emotions as packaging does. He quotes Loewy's redesign of the Gestetner duplicating machine, which, while in no way affecting technical function, dramatically changed the way users *felt* about the machine. This could also be said about Apple's iMac computer. It has been selling well. Most PCs have tended to project a masculine image, facilitated by a dull commonality in design. The iMac projects an image of simplicity with a design that can be displayed around the home. Aesthetic packaging can be key when the product is a gift and can allow higher pricing! A distinctive package design is crucial to merchandising at the point of sale. Louis Cheskin found in the 1930s that the design of the package had an impact on perceptions of the taste of crackers, perceptions of the richness of beers, and so on. The sales of Absolut vodka are tied to its well-advertised package. Manufacturers study the use of the package right through to disposal, in that, for example, facial tissues have to fit different color schemes and decors in bathrooms.
- *Content*. A package may mislead as to its contents. A can of stewed steak should not be mistaken for dog food, while a hair cream or shaving cream in a tube should not be confused with toothpaste. It is not uncommon for the consumer to be misled by packaging into imagining something emotionally unpleasant.
- *Promotion, packaging, and brand image*. A well-designed package can transform a lifeless image into that of something exciting and tempting to try. A brand that lacks robustness and vivacity fails to energize the consumer into buying. A package with emotional appeal attracts interest (sustained attention). Even the size of the container affects image in fragrances, in that large containers connote cheapness. The package always needs to cohere with the image being sought. A package projecting an image of quality and softness must not be perceived as cheap and hard. Packaging is important in generating credibility. Thus, the carton of one organic oat drink shows a windmill logo with a

country scene (always attractive to urban dwellers), aesthetically symbolizing health and purity, and backs its credibility by pointing out the drink was developed in a university laboratory (though without using genetic modification) and that only "contract farms" operated as suppliers.

Visibility. A striking package draws attention to itself. This is essentially a promotional role but is given separate billing here because of its importance.

Convenience (including ease in disposability). Brands like Kleenex, with its pop-up feature, were made successful by the convenience offered by the package. Just enlarging the cellophane window had a significant effect on sales of Mueller's macaroni and spaghetti. Murphy's Oil Soap dramatically increased sales when it exchanged its traditional cylindrical glass bottle for a larger size with a handle, making the product easier to use. Packaging always imposes some demands on the user, but these should be minimal. Lack of convenience in packaging is emotionally frustrating. Yet functions do sometimes conflict, as when the demand that aspirin bottles be tamper proof conflicts with the desire to provide an *intuitive* way to get access to the tablets. Similarly, the original Coca-Cola bottle, though graceful in design, took up too much space on shelves and did not have the convenience of the pull-top can. However, because of the symbolism attached to it, the bottle may still make a comeback. Since World War II, the demand for convenience in the use of products has been one of the major movements affecting marketers (the others are fashion and health). Some products, like hair sprays, were only made possible by developments in convenient packaging, namely, the aerosol. The convenience of the package may in fact determine the use to which a product is put, just as tub brands of margarine are largely used for spreading, while wrapped margarine is largely used for cooking.

Provision of information. Packaging provides information on contents, instructions on use, and (if necessary) information required by law. The *convenient* provision of information is important. Instructions are often hard to read without a magnifying glass and are often frequently vague and ambiguous. Older consumers long for bigger typefaces. This is important when we remember that many buying decisions are based on what is written on the package, and this has led some manufacturers to adopt flat bottles to obtain more space for clearer information. Too often instruction manuals are poorly written. This can be emotionally frustrating. With regard to computer software instruction manuals, a mini-industry has grown up in providing alternatives to the manufacturers' manuals, which users find incomprehensible. This should not be. Instructions need to be tested for understanding with the target customer group. Lack of instruction clarity leads to errors and is a reason for nonrepeat of purchase. Instructions are part of the total offering. All too often there is a failure to recognize the problems of interpretation and the supreme need for clear drafting to prevent emotional frustration.

Symbolism. A package not only may protect, promote by its design, be visible, be convenient, and provide useful information but also can be used to symbolize a set of values—for example, honesty, quality, friendliness, integrity, trust, value-for-money, or a way of life. A package can symbolize a product's strength and durability and endow a product with gender through its styling. A package is an implicit promise statement. What does McDonald's symbolize by having its container for French fries always slightly overloaded? McDonald's stands for more than hamburgers: it symbolizes, in the United States, value-for-money and social awareness, evoking a feeling of warmth toward the firm and its product. If brand loyalty is sought, the firm must deliver on the values it symbolizes. If it does not, and it is an icon, like McDonald's, it will not escape damage from detractors. In a recent libel case involving McDonald's, two critics had published a pamphlet with chapter headings like McRipoff, McGarbage, McGreedy, and McMurder. If a product symbolizes America and its values, it is not surprising that it has both friends and enemies abroad. Only this could explain the periodic ransacking of McDonald's establishments by international protesters.

Color. Hine (1995) regards color as the most potent tool for emotional expression in packaging and shows that shadings make an enormous emotional difference in the way we feel. Some companies aim to be associated with just one color: for example, IBM with blue, Coca-Cola with red. The chosen color fits the positioning of the product in the market. Some colors are warm and some are cold; some heavy; some cheap (like yellow); some happy; some sober, and so on. In cigarettes, white packaging suggests low tar, while red packaging suggests a strong flavor. As Hine points out, we experience colors in packaging from three points of view:

1. *The autonomic physiological reaction.* This is emotional, as when blue makes one feel that little bit more calm.
2. *The cultural.* Colors come to symbolize general qualities in all cultures. In the West, these qualities are: white—delicacy; black—mourning or business; red—strength, vitality, excitement, danger; yellow—youth, hope, and cheer; blue—harmony, honesty, and calmness; green—the outdoors and country life; brown—friendliness, trust, and reliability.
3. *Expectations.* Different colors come to be associated with certain product categories. yellow packaging for margarine echoes the coloring found in the product itself. Pink is feminine, and gray is masculine,

with one men's fragrance specifically calling itself Gray Flannel, while blue is not something associated with food products. On the other hand, certain colors are deemed wrong for the occasion; green is considered unlucky in a wedding dress but is otherwise associated with anything natural, while in the United States red, but not maroon, goes with low prices.

Private label (store brands) in certain grocery categories are equal in quality to the national brands and considerably cheaper. This has led to a fundamental shift in consumer perceptions of private label versus national brands. It has been helped by private labels adopting attractive packaging that is far removed from the "generics" of thirty years ago.

Brand Continuity of Identity

When a brand is invested with a good deal of goodwill and symbolizes something that consumers trust, then, in making changes, there is a need to ensure a *continuity of identity:* the present identity needs to link both with the past and the anticipated future. Consumers accept the new only when they have made sense of it in terms of the old. Drastic changes in the product or packaging can be perceived as a discontinuity of identity and can be emotionally alienating. Similarly, changes of name undermine continuity when, as typically happens, an acquiring firm insists that its corporate identity be extended to the acquired company. There can be a loss both in terms of the goodwill attached to the original name and because people seek continuity. The new Loomis, Fargo does not connect with Wells Fargo.

The repositioning of the brand from one market segment to another can cause problems with continuity of identity, since consumers have to recategorize the brand as suited to another purpose. But the major danger in repositioning is the loss of existing buyers and the failure to attract the new target buyers as additional customers. This is not uncommon when magazines are repositioned. The latest is *Harper's Bazaar.* As reported in the *New York Times* (June 1, 2001), after a new editor-in-chief tried to move the magazine in a younger direction, the anticipated increase in sales was not realized, and sales actually decreased. As is usual, the editor-in-chief was replaced; she acknowledged that the changes in the magazine "may have come as a shock to some readers." Line extensions are less of a problem. As Marder says, provided you can get the line extension into the stores (sometimes a big *if*), a good line extension is likely to do more for a firm than repositioning one of its brands in the market.[6]

There is a need to balance the preservation of a core identity with the need for continuous makeovers. It is not surprising that products associated with religion, like church bells and coffins, do not tend to change. (One firm of bell-makers in England has made exactly the same bells for four hundred years!) One way of easing the tension between the desire for the familiar and the desire for a product to be updated is through making sure the changed product, the changed packaging, and so on have links with the old so that the brand, though forever changing, is forever the same. The continuity of slogans, logos, and brand names helps give this consistency. A change in logo signals a discontinuity, which can be discomforting. This happened when British Airways abandoned its British identification in the tailfins of its planes and decorated them with various examples of "ethnic" art from around the world. What made this risible was that the new tailfins did not cohere with anything else, like the British nationality of the air crew, the continuing formality, and the "nanny-knows-best" way of handling passengers. If changes like this are made there needs to be systemic change so that the whole system coheres. Another example is Levi's attempt to enter the fashion jean market. Unfortunately, Levi's did not understand that "cachet sells jeans, not functionality."[7] While outside the United States Levi's are regarded as the people who invented jeans and their product as a slice of modern America, in the United States itself, the problem was for Levi's to avoid destroying the appeal of their heritage in seeking to be fashionable, hip, and sexy. Perhaps the answer would have been to acquire a company with core competencies in the fashion segment while the Levi's name stayed with what the company did best.

Any organization must be flexible enough to respond to changing conditions yet constant enough to maintain a distinct identity. What can give substance to the continuity of identity is a set of *enduring practices:* for example, how the company reaches out to its customers in dealing with complaints; deals with ethical issues; is known to treat its employees; and so on. Continuity is not just a matter of showing the symbols of the past. There is a poster outside the sales office of the *QE2* of an earlier age with the slogan: "Cunard: Advancing Civilization," which now reminds its audience more of past arrogance than greatness.

Brand choice is not just a matter of evaluating objective factors but also a matter of trust. Brand image can provide that trust. Yet there can be trust without loyalty. Consumers may trust a brand but no longer buy it because it seems old-fashioned or out-of-date in some way. This relates to the constant demand for novelty. What is wrong may simply be the dated or lifeless image of the packaging. For some brands that have been going for a long time, like Kellogg's cornflakes and Heinz ketchup, packaging has been constantly updated while the product has remained the same. The Campbell Soup Company, after 102 years, is altering its soup labels. It has decided to update its classic red-and-white Campbell's soup label, immortalized in Andy Warhol's silkscreens. The new label is updated with modern graphic elements, showing a photo of the soup in a bowl and helping shoppers choose soup more conveniently. Five colored banners have been added to the new labels: "classic"; "fun favorites"; "special selections"; "great for cooking"; and "98% fat free." Continuity is maintained by the use of red and white and Campbell's unique script typography, which are the elements consumers most associate with Campbell's.

There are good reasons for ensuring a continuity of identity: not only past investments in promotion and the goodwill that results in the brand's high familiarity but the good sense of having one and only one essential persona/personality that continues to enter into promotion. Sensibly, Volkswagen has included elements of continuity in the design of the new Beetle so the feel of the Beetle is preserved. Other car firms like BMW and Renault stress their continuity by employing the metaphor of evolution. Ads for both companies exploit the popular misconception of evolution being always a progressive step so that the latest version is an improvement on the last. As one of the ad agencies said: "The advertisement is intended to convey the idea of development allied to heritage."

Continuity of identity is needed even when changes in direction are required because current strategies are not working. Laura Ashley, the clothing and furnishings manufacturer, is a case in point. Unless there is continuity to exploit Laura Ashley's reputational capital, the firm might as well be starting off from scratch. If a brand is to have a continuity of identity, there must be a *narrative of connectedness* linking the various changes in the life of the brand, and this connectedness must to publicized and shown in the packaging and elsewhere. Laura Ashley is tied to images of Victorian schoolrooms and country vicarage tea parties, manifested in soft, shaped dresses decorated with "country" patterns. Updating does not mean necessarily surrendering ancestry. On the other hand, the new story must be in harmony with the facts today. Burberry, another fashion/clothing company, has seemingly been successful in updating the Burberry brand; we say "seemingly" because the new in-your-face Burberry may alienate many former customers.

Nations seek a continuity of identity so that citizens will have a sense of who they are and how that has evolved. Citizens need a sense of cultural sharing. This is why multiculturalism and multiethnicity can be perceived as threatening rather than enriching.[8] After all, multiculturalism can be a barrier to assimilation: with the tendency for the European nations to break up into smaller units (e.g., Scottish, Welsh, and English rather than British), loyalties move to smaller and smaller groups with all their entrenched interests. Intellectual critics of the British monarchy often fail to see what many ordinary people feel in their bones: that it provides a reassuring symbol of continuity amid the uncertainties of change.

Building Brand Equity

Every company seeks market power. Failing a monopoly position, a company must do something to beat its rivals. In other words, it must seek a competitive advantage or, better still, a critical advantage, in that such an advantage is both unique to the company and of central importance to the function for which the product is bought. In seeking such an advantage, the company may:

1. Choose segments of the market where the critical factors for market success match, relatively better than competition, the firm's key skills and demonstrated capabilities
2. Analyze rival firms for relative strengths and weaknesses to identify where they can be beaten
3. Question the basic rules of the competitive game to see if violating the implicit rules of competition could yield an advantage. As a way of securing an advantage, this is the least obvious; yet this was the main route to success for the newspaper magnate Rupert Murdoch. As *The Economist* (July 3, 1999, p. 92) said: "It was Mr. Murdoch's contempt for the established order that created News Corp.—his ability to walk into a market, flout the rules and do the things that nobody else had thought of doing. He did it in Britain, when he bust the newspaper unions and turned a failing newspaper group into a hugely profitable one; he did it in America, when he created a fourth broadcasting network, which everybody said was impossible; he did it again in Britain, where the television establishment sneered at pay-TV and he created BskyB, once the most profitable television company in Europe." Violating the rules means a lot of emotional upsets and conflicts and a willingness to go against business norms.
4. Seek new and novel applications for the firm's existing products
5. Identify latent wants and try to meet them. This ties to innovation, which is the major engine for progress in living standards. A good deal of innovation today is done by firms entering into technology-sharing contracts with competitors to spread the risk. Customization of products is now possible, so firms that are good at this have an advantage. But this is not feasible for most products. Although it is claimed that the computer makes it possible to mass-produce individ-

ually designed products, as in the case of bicycles, what happens is that the consumer is able to choose from a wider number of possible *combinations* of parts that are predesigned (mass production of parts but diversity in assembly). This is unlikely to satisfy a "want" in *all* its technically feasible particulars.

6. Use Michael Porter's value chain, his basic tool for analyzing a firm's activities and how they interact, as a basis for identifying a competitive advantage (though in practice the technique is *only* suited to discovering a competitive *cost* advantage rather than some other type of advantage)[9]

7. Build more brand equity into existing brands (considered hereafter)

Robinette et al. spell out the Hallmark's strategy for increasing brand equity.[10] Their model for doing this they regard as a model for "emotion marketing." They claim that this model, when applied, is a practical method of incorporating both rational and emotional components to generate a more complete value proposition for the customer. The model has five components, namely, what they term *equity, experience, energy, product,* and *money.* The emotional Es are equity, experience, and energy, while money and product are claimed to be the rational components. The authors argue for the need to get all five in line with customer expectations, but they also argue that the rational elements (product and money) are easily copied, so the firm needs to use equity, experience and energy to get an advantage. We will review each in turn.

- *Equity.* For these authors brand "equity" is best based on emotion, as reflected in trust. They point out that there is no reserve of trust to draw on with the first-time buyer. Yet trust is basic to loyalty, even if trust is not a sufficient condition for that loyalty. We can trust a brand without being a loyal buyer of it. These authors stress building up a strong brand on the grounds that a strong brand helps (1) acquire new customers, (2) retain current customers and win back defections, (3) establish positive word-of-mouth referrals, and (4) establish a barrier for competition.

- *Experience.* For these authors, this has everything to do with exploiting the occasions when consumers and companies exchange sensory stimuli, information, and emotion. Such exchange occasions (which can occur in one encounter) are classified as (1) transactional exchanges— when goods and services are bought, delivered and paid for; (2) informational exchanges—when "rational" data are exchanged; and (3) emotional exchanges. The goal is to ensure that all these exchanges constitute a pleasant experience that is hassle free.

- *Energy.* The focus here is on saving time and energy: making things easier, convenient, and personalized.
- *Product.* A quality product, it is argued, is taken for granted today, while ancillary functions, features, and style offer only a temporary advantage. The rational advantages of a product are likely to be quickly copied.
- *Money.* Under this heading come all aspects of price.

Robinette et al. view these five components as a framework for (1) evaluating a brand's value proposition compared with competition; (2) analyzing value for the different consumer segments; and (3) assessing an individual's motivation and helping to tailor a product to personal preference. This is a pretty tall order for a simple checklist. What must be contested is the basic division into rational (money and product) and emotional ("equity", experience, and energy), since anything that is of acute concern to the consumer can arouse the emotions, and all aspects of the product and of money exchanges can be of acute concern. Whatever use the categorization into five components has for Hallmark's purposes, it would be foolish to only look for emotional stimuli among the "equity", experience, and energy elements.

Robinette et al. quote with approval the claim that it is impossible to maintain a loyal customer base without loyal employees. This assumes that employees can only be effective with customers if they are loyal. This single-motivation view of employees is manifestly false, as employees have many reasons for doing a good job with customers. It is nonetheless true that loyalty does contribute to good service performance. But it is difficult to get loyalty among service staff who are badly paid and tend to be transient. Loyalty has to be earned. Even if staff are paid well, the result might simply be rented allegiance that does not project the needed spontaneity in giving service. McDonald's hires a million people a year in the United States, many of whom are in their teens with hopes going beyond serving hamburgers. As Schlosser shows, fast food chains aim to constrain rather than train employees, to ensure an assembly-line efficiency. Nonetheless, most of the teenagers he spoke to seemed to like the job and just gave it up when they did not.[11] Training and indoctrination and a culture that promotes solidarity are key factors in developing the right behaviors.

Earlier we defined *brand equity* (if positive) as the additional value put on a brand by its customers over and above the brand's objective performance vis-à-vis its rivals. But brand equity can erode. This is not always the result of competition. Contrary to conventional wisdom, new producers entering the market can actually increase the size of the market, because if they are specializing in different segments, they appeal to more consumers and add credibility to the basic product, far more than the solitary firm trying to appeal to the whole market. Because there will always be variation in consumer preferences, new market entrants catering to this variation will always arise, unless restricted by government. A monopoly, on the other hand, can become so complacent that consumers exit the market and reduce its total size. One is reminded of Adam Smith's remark in *Wealth of Nations* about the Church of England: "the clergy, reposing themselves upon their benefices, had neglected to keep up the fervour of faith and devotion of the great body of people; and having given themselves up to indolence, were incapable of making vigorous exertion in defence even of their own establishment."[12] The great growth in religion in eighteenth-century America did not arise from the demand side but from the supply side, namely, successful marketing campaigns by evangelical Protestant preachers like Finney and Whitfield. As Finke says, a supply-side shift explains what has since been claimed as a change in market demand.[13]

A positive brand image and positive brand equity go together. Brand equity is built through (1) building brand visibility, (2) liking (attractiveness), and (3) credibility, which we will now discuss.

Building Visibility

The first task is to establish brand visibility with the target audience. Without having high visibility, a brand cannot be part of the evoked set of options for that audience. Visibility is best achieved through emotional means of getting attention. Thus we have the success of the film *The Blair Witch Project,* which was produced on a shoestring budget. College interns were sent out to clubs, bookstores, trendy stores, and cafes to distribute fliers of the actors' faces, T-shirts, and comic books of the *Blair Witch* lore. Most important, the interns steered the target youth segment to the website, so those who logged on knew that the movie promised "an authentic scare at the movie theater that didn't feel cynical or prepackaged and manufactured in a factory but captured the uneasiness of a generation in uncertain times." But getting attention generally costs money. This is particularly so in political campaigns, since high expenditure equates with high repeated exposure, which equates, other things remaining equal, with more familiarity and consequent liking. Where the voting public is unable to evaluate the issues, the likability heuristic may operate. It is not surprising that Elizabeth Dole as well as others dropped from the presidential race, believing adequate funding to be necessary to success, since a necessary condition for success implies a sufficient reason for failure.

It is common today to talk about advertising evoking experiences in its target audience. But emotional advertising always generates an experience, and emotional experiences demand attention. Although there is talk about emotion interfering with reason, what is more likely is that emotional experiences can be so intense that they completely absorb one's attention. It is because emotional experiences distract that an emotional ad can remain in memory while the name of the product is forgotten.

The problem of gaining attention is partly responsible for the pervasive use of sex in advertising, since both males and females remember best the ads with an appeal to sex. It may also be because in a society where there is so much to divide people, there is a desperate search for the most (lowest?) common denominator that unites us. Getting attention is being made more difficult with the proliferation of television channels and the arrival of remote controls that allow the viewer to skip commercials. There is also the sheer monotony of the ads. An article in the *New York Times* said that Lipton became tired of the formula advertising being used to sell food products, namely, the attractive mother cooking dinner; the happy, good-looking children, and the good-natured father.[14] Lipton tried an offbeat approach, whose novelty (with its eccentric families composed of incongruous celebrities) seems to have captured the attention of its target audience. Other ways of getting attention can also be ingenious, as when Texas Instruments placed microchips in copies of *Business Week* or as in "scratch and smell" perfume ads in magazines. Such tactics help to fix the product in the mind through getting the consumer to actually carry out some action to do with the product that induces self-persuasion.

Unfortunately, the need to get attention is considered so paramount that much advertising today is exclusively concerned with it and has little else to recommend it, having given up on any attempt at persuasion other than that achieved by the repeated exposure effect, in that repeated exposure does lead to familiarity and perhaps liking. Often so-called creative ads are simply creative in getting attention. Alka-Seltzer's spicy meatball ad attracted a great deal of attention. The ad showed a man fluffing his lines while eating spaghetti; nonetheless, "despite its brilliance and popularity, the most famous commercial about making a commercial didn't work as people thought it was for spaghetti sauce and this did not help sales of Alka-Seltzer."[15] Of course, some advertising is simply designed to remind existing customers to buy or to arouse curiosity, though encouragement to action is still involved. Nonetheless, what is striking is the brilliance of attention-getting ads that have little inherent persuasive appeal. A persuasive appeal is important, since ads can attract considerable attention with images that are off-putting.

When it comes to employing emotion in advertising, the persuasive appeal is typically through *associationism;* this may be only one of the methods of making a persuasive appeal, but it involves emotion the most. One way brands acquire positive or negative associations is by coming together in time or space with things that have positive or negative connotations. This is because spatial and temporal contiguity influence perceptions. Whenever we connect a brand with a new set of associations, we are in effect placing that brand in a new context, and a new context demands a reconsideration of old meanings. The contiguous association of a brand with something desirable, whether a celebrity, say, or a lifestyle, can lead to some of the prized qualities infiltrating the brand: the desirable associations become attached to or fused with the brand image in the mind. The advertised brand can be associated with anything that appeals to the target audience that is likely to produce a halo effect, that is, the high rating of the associated object by the target audience is likely to carry over to a high rating of the brand. The association can be with anything that evokes positive feelings. Thus Schwartz's resonance model (discussed in chapter 6) falls under associationism, in that the aim is to associate the brand with the highly positive feelings generated by activities tied to the product. However, the following are the most common ways of establishing a positive association.

1. *Association with the values or valued images of the target audience.* Persuasive appeals here resort to the presentation of symbols of valued things that stand on their own as effective persuaders, just as a country's flag might do in battle. The target audience rallies around what the brand symbolizes. In associating the brand with values that it claims to stand for, the aim is for the consumer to view the brand as the embodiment of its symbolization. This way of using symbols to persuade is what Mayhew calls the rhetoric of presentation, where the display of symbols outweighs discursive argument.[16] Nike from its inception (when it appealed in advertising its running shoes to the values of the me-generation) has been extremely successful in this approach. This form of associationism could be related to the symbolism employed in "enhancing self-esteem and ideal self-image," as discussed in chapter 6, in that the symbolization associated with the brand adheres to the target audience's ideal self-image and the promotion of self-esteem.

2. *Link to a feeling of solidarity with others.* While persuasion that appeals to a feeling of solidarity with others incorporates a value appeal, the solidarity appeal is more usefully understood as an offer of *affiliation*. Mayhew claims that all persuasion presupposes that the persuader and the target audience share a common interest—not all interests in common, but the interest relevant to the appeal.[17] For Mayhew, an attempt to persuade is an *offer* of affiliation, and its acceptance is an *act* of affiliation. While shared interests may not currently form the basis for any "solidaristic" identification, they may become so through rhetorical appeals. This form of associationism is most common in

politics by recourse to promotions that stress what certain voters have in common and need to preserve.

3. *Association with position and prestige.* A persuasive appeal can be associated with prestige—Mayhew views this as drawing on the "influence of hierarchy." In general, those higher in the social hierarchy, celebrity hierarchy, or knowledge hierarchy have an advantage in persuasion. While there may be some questioning of an argument, compliance is often driven by a desire to identify with the prestige position. This is why all organizations concerned with persuasion look for high-status spokespersons who will endorse their position, since this will accord it something of their prestige. This form of associationism could be related to the symbolism employed in "self-persuasion via self-imagining" discussed in chapter 6, since the possibility of being associated with positions of prestige feeds the fantasy leading to self-persuasion. Whenever an ad associates a brand with a prestigious celebrity or a luxurious lifestyle or prestigious other brands, this is an appeal to the "influence of hierarchy."

The preceding discussion may give the impression that advertising is theory-driven. But the creative directors of advertising agencies do not necessarily have a systematic approach to devising persuasive appeals. Advertisers typically develop persuasive ads without any formal reference to consumer psychology. As Randall Rothenberg, a well-known advertising columnist for the *New York Times*, made clear, while the ad agencies may be constantly promoting quasi-scientific theory about how advertising works, most of what they do is based on intuition: the theory simply masks what they believe to be so from experience.[18] In other words, they have an implicit favorite model and apply it with a coating of rationalization.

The problem in getting audience attention arises because consumers expose themselves selectively to information. Attention is like a light that people switch on only to illuminate things that arouse them. Marketing wants its promotional message to be a *replicator*, that is, something (e.g., like our genes) that causes others to copy it. A good joke is a replicator. Richard Dawkins invented the term "meme" for replicators that are human ideas, such as jokes.[19] Dawkins reinterpreted Darwin's theory as the theory of replicators: the replicator that is best at getting itself replicated in a given environment will be the ultimate winner, as the others are worse at getting themselves replicated. It is not the fittest species variant that survives but the fittest gene variant. Analogously, a brand that is the best at getting itself replicated in a given market is on the road to beating competition. The best such brand is not necessarily the best in some objective sense. What helps replication is novelty. We would suggest that the major factor behind making a promotional message a replicator is the novelty of what is being promoted, since it is novelty that has most potential for getting the consumer to anticipate, contemplate, and fantasize about the product. Novelty can lie behind word-of-mouth promotion that initiates the replication, since it can suggest both centrality and uniqueness. Whenever marketing is putting over a story, it must be strange (novel) enough to invite attention but not so strange that the audience cannot make it part of their own thinking. Koehn points out that from the earliest days of Wedgwood there was the recognition of the "strong thirst for novelty," with Samuel Johnson grumbling that nowadays men were even "to be hanged in a new way."[20]

Blumer argues that people turn their attention to the media for four reasons: (1) surveillance—keeping track of the surrounding world; (2) curiosity; (3) diversion from day-to-day routines; and (4) to facilitate self-identity.[21] *All these reasons have an emotional basis.* If TV programs can be classified on the basis of the primary reason for viewing, it may be that a firm's ads can be made to cohere. In any case, TV needs to exaggerate movement and play on viewers' emotions to retain its audience. The selection of the right media is important, since it is easier today to have the right message but the wrong messenger. Only 20 years ago the three networks in the United States accounted for 90% of the peak audience, but now the media have split into hundreds of cable channels and thousands of magazines and entirely new media like the Internet.

Visibility is facilitated by brand name, logo, and slogan—and by having something distinctive to declare, preferably with a "criticalness" in its differentiation so as to facilitate positioning the brand in the mind of the consumer. As mentioned earlier, a *critical advantage* implies that the advantage is both unique to the firm and central to the function for which the product is being bought. Uniqueness alone is useless unless it has relevance to the wants of the consumer. Novelty implies uniqueness and, if effective, has a certain psychological centrality in creating emotional anticipation, attention, and contemplation.

There is a particular difficulty in getting visibility when entering a mature market. Incumbents have a prominence that any new entrant will find hard to match, while target consumers see the new product as coming from nowhere and so are less likely to perceive it distinctly. Häagen-Dazs entered the mature ice cream market in Europe through first establishing itself in up-market ice cream parlors, which gave it early visibility. No marketing campaign is a one-shot attempt at persuading. There is a need for repeated exposures to dramatize the brand and position it clearly. Positioning is positioning the brand vis-à-vis its rivals in the market and, hopefully, and most important of all, positioning it in the mind of the consumer. Positioning thus relates to key marketing questions:

- Why should the consumer buy from us?
- How are we going to compete?
- What do we want the brand to stand for in the consumer's mind?

A positioning statement captures the brand's points of difference with its rivals, both real and perceived. With any brand there are always alternative positioning possibilities. Thus Pampers might have been positioned as the first disposable diaper to be biodegradable, as the disposable diaper that prevents diaper rash, or as the disposable diaper that is softer and more absorbent than any other diaper. The best choice depends on what research reveals. Weight should be given to (1) what the positioning lends itself to; (2) what resonates emotionally with the target audience; (3) what enhances self-esteem; and (4) what facilitates self-persuasion. Good positioning makes creativity easier, as it offers a concrete guide.

Enhancing Liking (Attractiveness)

Brand Liking. Mere familiarity with a brand leads to liking, and high familiarity induces liking plus sentiment. This describes the repeated exposure effect.[22] Many brands are chosen simply because the consumer is most familiar with the brand so that the likability heuristic operates. If the initial encounter with a brand is positive, subsequent exposures add to liking, as the brand becomes an informational anchor to a certain way of life in an uncertain world. But brand attractiveness may not be a necessary condition for success. There can be high credibility without liking. Sales can be high without an attractive brand image, though this is probably rare. Nonetheless, this has probably been the case with Microsoft, whose monopoly position has evoked so much antagonism.

Advertising is not always helpful. A recent advertising campaign for the Fiat Punto suggests that all men are boring and thick and all women are "airheads." It was meant to get attention (it did) by what it thought to be humor. It merely annoyed people. Any dependence on the repeated exposure effect assumes that the firm has deeper pockets than rivals and that the ads are not distasteful or frustrating in the first place. It also assumes the avoidance of ads that are so indistinct that they could be used for any rival brand.

The repeated exposure effect is one explanation for the sadness people feel at the death of some public figure whom they have never met or the way one feels when a writer dies whose works have given one much pleasure. This is not to suggest that constant repeats of the same ad cannot be irritating but that the annoying effects of the repetition of the same ad *tend* to wear off, while the induced attraction remains. However, "wear-out" does occur if the ad becomes

Figure 7.1.   Reminder ad that resonates (repetition with variation category). Bottle shape is shown in the gum. Courtesy The Absolut Company and TBWA\CHIAT\DAY.

tedious to watch. Wear-out is alleviated by "repetition of the ad with variation," so the ad introduces some novelty as time goes on. But repetition with variation may not satisfy the thinking viewer, as it fails to counteract boredom.[23] Yet repetition of a claim over time often comes to be believed and accepted. One reason for this is because repetition induces a sense of permanency and security and because society's continuity, that is, emotional comfort, is involved. But acceptance also depends on existing beliefs and whether these cohere with what is being claimed. If they do not, change can take very much longer.

The soap opera TV ad introduces variation while sustaining and even increasing interest. Thus we have the success of episodic advertising campaigns like the one for Nestlé coffee where the viewer experiences "the magical, mystical moments of courtship, of possibility." Serials here become soap operas, allowing the characters to develop their own personalities with which the viewer can identify. Serials tell a story that builds on the previous one. This contrasts with the usual commercial, with everyone carrying out the same routine. Liking the product, the person or the cause has the potential to motivate supportive action, though this is not to suggest that such liking is either necessary or sufficient for purchase. Liking for a brand or company is built on all encounters, from the way callers are treated on the phone to the look, smile, and enthusiasm of those associated with selling or promoting the product, the speed of service, the convenience in obtaining and using the product, and whether follow-up and after-sales service occurs.

There is, as we already pointed out, a danger in confining advertising to pleasant images. Coca-Cola a few years ago seemed to accept that there was nothing tangible to say and decided just to entertain by employing Creative Artists, a Hollywood film agency. This did nothing to provide Coca-Cola with a definite persona to signal what the brand stands for. Although pleasant associations increase liking, brands become vulnerable by neglecting credibility factors. When an advertised brand is fused with many different images, there is the inherent danger of a confused image. As Stephen Brown says, the images attached to brands have become increasingly detached from their true referents, with way-out connotations being attached to products, resulting in a countervailing desire for "authenticity"—the value of something being true rather than untrue.[24] Thus the ads for the Saturn car emphasized the "authenticity" of the place where the car was made and the people who make and buy it.

Goldman and Papson talk about an "image bank," stocking free-floating, interchangeable currencies of sunsets, farm scenes, sea birds, and so on, with "referential density" (frames packed with references to multiple cultural images) coming to displace "narrative coherence," where the ad is tied in a coherent way to a product.[25] There is a lack of analytic bite about such a process, which enables advertisers to avoid thinking rigorously about the important questions of meaning.

Advertising is capable of generating a good deal of emotion and, as a consequence, quickly creating visibility and awareness of a brand. The question arises as to whether the emotions aroused are sufficient to build an attractive image over the long term. Benetton in its corporate image advertising felt it need not bother if it offended those outside its target audience, as if any target audience is entirely isolated from other groups. Oliviero Toscani was behind Benetton's notorious emotional advertising, which included priests kissing nuns, women with penises, a black Queen Elizabeth, and a poster of inmates on America's death row. The Benetton logo on one occasion was affixed to blown-up photographs of a man who had clearly just died of AIDS. In these ads Benetton was either declaring what it stands for as an appeal to target audience values or was simply inviting wide discussion of the issues the ads raised as a way of getting Benetton talked about. The provocative advertising put the brand on the map. The ads did indeed get considerable attention and publicity but in the process succeeded in offending gays, Jews, Catholics, and blacks—did Toscani think their opinion would have no effect on members of the target audience? Emotion about the ads was intense among consumers. Toscani claimed he was introducing "reality" to the world of advertising and dismissed complaints as simply "Anglo-Saxon neurosis," though such people constituted the largest customer base for Benetton.[26] When Sears pulled out of a deal to open eight hundred Benetton outlets in the Sears chain, Toscani became an ex-employee of Benetton. No talk about the ethics involved, only that the advertising was no longer a profitable proposition.

Personal Liking or Attractiveness. When it comes to finding a person attractive, similarity of background and/or liking arising from supportive interaction through time are the two dimensions most commonly cited in psychology. These two factors suggest that the key factor is a sense of *sharing* with the other person, whether through shared background or through interacting with them. Similarity of background suggests a sharing of values. People who come from a different culture or subculture can be perceived as threatening, and differences in cultural values between people can lead to a good deal of difficulties in communication. But commonality of background and supportive interaction over time are just aspects of needing to be emotionally in tune with another person so that all goes smoothly. The need to establish rapport before serious business occurs is the recognition that without small talk to create the right emotional climate, there will be no big talk later. Yet people do not find it easy to do this emotional fine-tuning, commonly because of a conflict between wanting to be liked and wanting to dominate the relationship. People *give off* as well as *give* information about themselves. They try to convey a certain impression of themselves to others, but the information they give off (mainly nonverbal) may make it impossible to sustain that impression. Feelings that are faked typically fail to be congruent with verbal behavior.

Bailey quotes two dimensions that relate to being emotionally in tune with others: relative power and solidarity.[27] With respect to relative power, one can come across as being superior, equal, or inferior, while attempts at solidarity can be perceived as hostile (rivalry), indifferent, or friendly (alliance-seeking). Being superior manifests itself in peremptory or condescending communications, while being inferior is conveyed by obsequiousness. Being emotionally in tune means focusing on projecting friendliness with no superior power plays. Thus World War II propagandists had to change the pronoun in poster slogans from "You" to "We" after people complained about the tone being patronizing.

Television, as a medium, suggests that speakers addressing themselves to the viewers should project themselves in a relaxed and friendly way, since they are like guests in the nation's living rooms. As Jamieson says, TV is essentially an intimate medium, so it is better to court the audience than harangue them.[28] She has proclaimed the "feminization" of rhetoric—the relaxed, intimate, self-disclosure style that persuades TV viewers. This fits the view of effective persuasive communications being an offer of affiliation. Her exemplar is Ronald Reagan, whom she sees as the *doyen* of "feminine rhetoricians." President Reagan recognized that TV *for speakers* was a medium of affection and not confrontation. It was Marshall McLuhan who described the singer Perry Como as the "low-pressure king of a high-pressure realm," and this is a good description of the art of TV projection if the audience is to be emotionally in tune with the speaker.

Cialdini quotes what he calls the six principles of *automatic influence* in face-to-face encounters such as direct selling.[29] We have touched on these earlier. They are commitment/consistency; reciprocation; social proof; authority; liking; and scarcity. Cialdini regards these as mechanisms that compliance follows as a sort of knee-jerk reaction. All relate to aspects of credibility and attractiveness. They can be described as follows:

1. *The commitment/consistency principle.* Commitment to a position induces behavior consistent with that commitment. Thus salespeople who make a commitment in writing to achieve certain sales goals are more likely to be motivated to achieve them. As one changes one's commitments, one's self-image can change. Cialdini argues that the commitments that are effective in changing a person's self-image and future behavior are commitments that are made in public, have not

been easy to make, and are actively advocated. All religious groups recognize these factors in true conversions. There is social pressure to be consistent in line with the commitments. In any case, people desire to be consistent, as consistency helps in upholding a favorable self-image. Being inconsistent makes us less attractive, consistency being the mark of sincerity and commitment. That people like to be consistent is one reason used to explain why seeking a little favor (e.g., asking a retailer to put up a poster) facilitates asking for a big favor later on (e.g., that it place an order), known in selling as the "foot-in-the-door technique."

2. *The reciprocity principle.* There is a social obligation to give, to receive, and to repay favors in kind. It makes people feel attractive to return favors, as it is a social norm to do so, and this is used to explain why "free" inspections or giving small gifts tend to facilitate a sale. It may even explain why, when a brand has earned buyers' trust, they reciprocate with loyalty. It can also be used to explain the effectiveness of what salespeople call the "door-in-the-face" technique, whereby a salesperson first asks a very big favor, which is expected to be refused. The salesperson then asks a much smaller favor, which is accepted. This happens because the very act of making it a small favor comes across as a sort of concession, which brings the norm of reciprocity into play. Also at work here is the *contrast effect* between the large original request and the minor final one. We are influenced by contrasts, which explains why being shown a house of poor value and then one of good value by a real estate agent makes the latter much more desirable. All small courtesies invite reciprocal acts, even if the small courtesy is simply a greeting or the provision of free coffee and doughnuts. All salespeople and service staff should be taught this simple fact.

3. *The social proof or social validation principle.* People commonly look to what others say and do to see what is correct. Cialdini argues that social proof is most powerful when people feel unfamiliar or unsure in a situation, as under this condition people feel obliged to look beyond themselves for evidence of what to believe and how to behave. In addition, though, a sharing of values and beliefs among those in the same social milieu makes for solidarity and mutual attractiveness. People like their judgments to be socially validated, and this explains the selling effectiveness of telling the buyer that rivals have all bought the product or that the buyer alone has yet to recognize the superiority of the seller's offering.

4. *The authority principle.* Cialdini points out that people in general have a deep-seated sense of duty to authority. We are trained from birth

that obedience to proper authority is right and disobedience is wrong. Distinctive uniforms like that of the police can help promote respect for authority. There are social rules as to what constitutes a credible authority, and the quoting of such authorities (e.g., a doctor on medical matters) can be an effective tactic in persuasion. Other things remaining equal, debate over facts ceases once the expert or person in authority has spoken. To question the opinion of those who are considered experts in an area is to deviate from one of the cultural "givens," so questioning appears unreasonable. People may be conditioned to follow all kinds of authority, like those of parents, teachers, and bosses, and not to question such authority, and this can on occasion impede the adoption of some innovation; this explains why advertisers seek the endorsements of authority figures.

5. *The scarcity principle.* Anything made to appear hard-to-get becomes more desirable. In fact, consumers often use the scarcity of an item to judge its worth. We are all familiar with what the banning of a book or the love choice of one's child can have in intensifying the desire. It seems we value even more things that have only recently become less available than things whose scarcity is a constant factor. This is what explains the frequent use of such appeals as "last few"; "last chance to buy"; and "only one per customer." Consumers may desire something simply because they cannot have it. Brehm, in an experiment, eliminated certain options and found they were then valued more highly.[30]

6. *The liking principle.* We like things that are familiar to us, and things or people become familiar through constant supportive interaction through time. The interaction must be supportive, as happens in cooperative endeavors, contact alone is not enough. We have already mentioned the repeated exposure effect as leading to increased liking of the ad or advertised product, but it should be remembered that the initial experience with the ad or product must not be distasteful. We tend to like those who are similar to us in background, opinions, and so on. As Cialdini says, many sales training programs urge trainees to "mirror and match" the customer's body posture, mood, and verbal style, as these have been shown to lead to positive results.

In selling or offering a service we might roughly sum up a buyer's wants with the following "five Is":

- *Image* (consumers want products and communications to be supportive of the image they wish to project)

- *Interpersonal relations* (consumers want products and communications to bolster their interpersonal relations)
- *Integrity* (consumers want to feel that whatever is done is supportive of their ideals)
- *Innovation risk avoidance* (consumers want to avoid unnecessary risk)
- *Investment payoff* (consumers seek a payoff from their efforts)

These five motivations link up with Cialdini's principles of an automatic influence and with the consumer choice criteria discussed earlier, as follows:

1. Consistency principle → image → choice criteria: integrative/intrinsic
2. Reciprocity principle → integrity → choice criteria: integrative.
3. Social validation principle → interpersonal relations → choice criteria: integrative/legalistic
4. Authority principle → innovation risk avoidance → choice criteria: adaptive
5. Scarcity principle → investment payoff → choice criteria: economic/technical/intrinsic

In practice, selling is an amalgam of persuasive skills and tactics—for example, learning how to disagree without being disagreeable. We could teach sales trainees all that is known about the interpersonal influence process, but this would not necessarily make someone a good salesperson, since selling, like all skills, needs to be practiced. On the other hand, knowing something about the psychology of selling does provide the foundations for developing an overall strategy, even if success is tied to skills in implementation. No doubt Al Gore had all the help possible to turn him into an attractive personality, but he was not the favored candidate because voters could not imagine sharing a social drink with him. Typical dysfunctional tactics are (1) to hog the conversation by talking too often and too long; (2) not seeing the need to speak with confidence; (3) relying on scripts, as it impedes natural flow and continuous eye contact; (4) not being relaxed; and (5) not voicing sentiments that resonate with the target audience. All these things inhibit being emotionally in sympathy with an audience.

We have made no direct reference to physical beauty. Yet good looks are what most people think of when referring to someone being "attractive." The attractiveness of physical beauty is a good illustration of the likability heuristic and of acting on instant appeal. As Etcoff points out, beauty is powerfully pleasing, and when we see someone beautiful, we typically stop evaluating, selecting, and criticizing so as to "simply revel in the sight for just a moment."[31] In other words, we act on the emotion of "gut" liking without cognitive evaluation. People are more likely to help the good-looking but less likely to ask them for help!

Enhancing Credibility

Consumers are satisfied with a promise if they feel confident that it will be honored. This in turn depends on the credibility of those making the promise. A lack of credibility means a lack of trust, an absence that implies more risk. The credibility of an information source is important, whether that source is an individual, product, or company. Credibility and believability are often used as synonyms, though a communication source can be believable without being credible, as credibility suggests *general* believability. Credibility goes with persuasion, and a credible claim is one that consumers believe will be honored. Usually a massive advertising campaign does provide some credibility, since it is perceived as the company "putting its money where its mouth is." The aim is always to avoid a "credibility gap": a disparity between what is being claimed and the facts on the ground.

Every promise in marketing, whether in an ad or on a package, has some company or human face behind it. For a person or an institution to have credibility, it must be perceived as trustworthy and as having the relevant expertise or capability needed to deliver on the promise. The way a sales or service person fields questions and the apparent sincerity of expressed views operate as indicators of credibility. Sincerity is assumed to go with trustworthiness and is the counterpart of authenticity in products.

In the literature on persuasion, persons with high credibility have more persuasive impact—that is, find an audience that is more predisposed to believe the claims they make. This is not so much an empirical proposition as a conceptual truth, since a source of high credibility must have more persuasive impact than a source of low credibility as a matter of definition. However, saying what is involved in establishing credibility is something different. A brand's reputation supports its credibility, while integrity is part of credibility, as it implies trustworthiness and honesty. Unethical conduct, poor service, exaggerated promises, poor quality, and tacky marketing hurt credibility. On the other hand, a high reputation increases trust, and trust is an essential element in credibility.

Although actual product performance is important, if a product does not have perceived credibility, it may never be bought in the first place. The seller's signals of product performance must cohere with what the consumer uses to judge the product as a "good" one: product, price, promotion, and distribution are all involved in sending out the right signals, as are the brand name, the logo, the slogan, the packaging, the stationery, and the employees encountered.

An image of high quality may demand up-market distribution outlets and a premium price. You only have to go into a store where the clothes are all massed together on racks to appreciate how such treatment devalues each of the brands involved.

Consumers seldom can simply look at a product and understand how well it will perform in the functions for which it is bought. Providing a sample (including, say, a free consultation or test drive) helps the prospect make a more informed decision while predisposing him or her toward the seller through the reciprocity principle. In fact, the absence of sampling can be a major reason for market failure.

The brain constructs its own model of reality that does not simply mirror the physical sensations that are received from the nerve endings. This is not to suggest that what the mind "sees" is very different from the objective facts (life otherwise would be impossible) but that the mind to some extent reshapes the facts. Perception is selective. To see may be to believe. But to already believe may result in one's seeing that which is already believed. Consumers cannot immediately apprehend that a computer will be reliable and durable or a cereal will be nutritious. Consumers consult others "in the know," and who is consulted is not easy for the seller to control. Or consumers may fall back on brand image, since the evidence before them can never be conclusive, and trust in a brand fills the gap.

Where celebrities are used, credibility is tied to perceived expertise and trustworthiness, which is projected by manner, tone of voice, and body posture. In general, celebrities need to:

1. Exemplify the values being promoted
2. Have an intimate, nonaggressive style
3. Have a background like that of the target audience so as to appear "just like us" while feeding the hope that there is a similar opportunity for someone of like background
4. Have achievements that mirror the longings of the target audience

Copying what a celebrity wears or consumes feeds the fantasy of being like that person in important respects while at the same time knowing that what one is doing is endorsed by one's social milieu. The most successful U.S. magazine in recent years, *In Style,* covers fashion, home furnishings, and beauty purely in relation to the celebrity. But using celebrities can backfire, since advertisers cannot guarantee they will not misbehave, like O. J. Simpson, and alienate former fans. The Bank of Scotland had to abandon its deal with Pat Robertson, the American TV celebrity evangelist, after it was claimed that he described Scotland as a "dark land" that had lost its morals and said something to the effect that in Scotland "you can't believe how strong the homosexuals are."

Person, a clinical psychiatrist, regards celebrities as icons that serve as "frames" on which the consumer builds her fantasies; they are imagined to have characteristics that the consumer hopes to incorporate.[32] Thus the Beatles combined the aspirations of the upwardly mobile with the energy and irreverence of youth. A celebrity who has become a celebrity through expertise in a field has the most credibility. One TV cook in Britain, through her recommendations while cooking, sent the sales of an aluminum pan skyrocketing from 200 to 90,000 per year in just four months; cleared Europe of its entire stock of liquid glucose in just two weeks; and sent sales of cranberries soaring by 30 percent, creating a national shortage.[33]

Credibility and attractiveness are not completely independent, since attractiveness casts a halo over credibility. In any case, the reputation of many a brand has more to do with its image than with performance. When a speaker in an ad relies on dogmatic assertion or assertive rhetoric, the appearance of *sincerity* is essential, as there may be little else to go on. To come across as insincere is to be judged by others as not presenting a "true" (authentic) self, which carries over into the belief that what is being asserted is also likely to be untrue.

Just as it is not what speakers say but how they say it that may impress, it is also not what a product is but how it is described, presented, and promoted that influences buying. For example, benefit segmentation is based on what the product or offering is expected to do for the buyer. But how such benefits are described, presented, and promoted is all-important, in that the seller needs to connect benefits to experiences that resonate emotionally. Demographic segmentation based on some combination of age, gender, educational level, regional location, occupation, social class, or family life cycle may be the first step from which to infer—at the very broadest level—the tangible benefits likely to be sought, but these categories can also give guidance on how a product is to be described, presented, and promoted. Psychographic segmentation reflecting lifestyle and values comes closer in suggesting what emotional appeals are likely to resonate with target audiences, being a particularly important approach when the product depends on brand image rather than anything more tangible. The problem to date, however, lies in devising a system that actually does define different value segments that are empirically sound and meaningful in terms of differentiating likely appeals.

Brand launch: Every marketing manager is interested in getting the product off the ground in a dramatic way. Gladwell exploits the analogy of the epidemic to show how quickly social trends can accelerate or reverse themselves as a result not of major happenings but of minor ones.[34] Epidemics have tip-

Figure 7.2.   An attractiveness appeal using a genial celebrity. Courtesy Liggett
Group Inc.

ping points—points at which they are subject to sudden change—and this is
analogous to a dramatic and sudden increase in the sales of a product. Gladwell sets out to answer the questions: Why is it that some ideas, behaviors, or
products initiate social epidemics and others don't? And what can we do to start
and control epidemics in the sales of new products?

Gladwell argues that there are three rules of epidemics that apply to the tipping point:

1. The law of the few: that tipping can be done through the influence of a few special kinds of people.
2. The stickiness factor: tipping can occur through changing the content of communication by making the message so memorable that it sticks in the mind and compels action.
3. The power of context: tipping can be brought about through minor changes in the context or environment.

Law of the few. Just as disease epidemics tip because of the behavior of a few carriers, so a few people can play a similar role in a dramatic change in a product's fortunes. Gladwell argues that effective word-of-mouth communication remains a mysterious process until we recognize that its success is tied to just three kinds of people, whom he calls *connectors, mavens,* and *salesmen.* Gladwell holds that word-of-mouth communication starts all social epidemics via tipping. These three roles may be combined in just one individual or they may be undertaken by separate individuals.

"Connectors" are that small number of people who are linked to all relevant others through just a few other persons, with others then being linked through these special few. As Gladwell says, his social circle, like the social circles of most of us, is not a circle but a pyramid, with the top of the pyramid being a single person who is responsible for the overwhelming majority of the relationships that constitute his life. Connectors are those who know lots of other people but, more particularly, know the kinds of people of interest to those hoping to start their own social epidemic. Connectors span different worlds and subcultures. This reflects their personality, which is a combination of curiosity, self-confidence, sociability, and energy. The closer knowledge of a product or an idea gets to a connector, the greater the opportunity for its rapid diffusion and adoption. For Gladwell, effective word-of-mouth communication is not simply a matter of me telling you about a new restaurant with great food, you telling a friend, that friend telling his friend, and so on. Truly effective word-of-mouth communication begins when someone tells a person who is a connector, because word-of-mouth epidemics are the work of connectors.

"Market mavens" is used in the marketing literature to describe those who possess and provide considerable information to others across a wide range of product categories. ("Maven" or "mavin" is a Yiddish word for an expert in everyday matters). Gladwell views market mavens as being people who have both the knowledge and social skills to start word-of-mouth epidemics and pass along information because they want to help. They belong to that small group of people who notice (say) when manufacturers and retailers are in some way indulging in sharp practice and protest about it and tell others about it. In this way, they keep deception in check. While mavens are the data banks who provide the message, connectors, as a sort of social glue, spread the message. However, the key persuaders are the "salesmen."

Salesmen have the skills to persuade when people are unconvinced by the unvarnished message itself. They are as critical in the tipping of word-of-mouth epidemics as the other two groups. This is because they:

- Are able to repackage the message, that is, reframe it to show the message in a different light so that the target audience adopts a different perspective in viewing it. Here Gladwell refers to the processes of diffusion and adoption (he conflates the two), pointing out that ideas that make perfect sense to early adopters do not necessarily make sense to the early majority, who have a different perspective. Connectors and mavens but, most of all, salesmen are the ones who make it possible to overcome the problem of different perspectives as they translate what may be highly technical or specialized knowledge into language others can understand. The innovators may be the ones who try something new, but mavens, connectors, and salesmen adopt it and make it palatable for mainstream people. In this way they make it *contagious*—by repackaging it, dropping extraneous detail, and exaggerating certain aspects so that the message comes to have deeper meaning. Gladwell accepts that an advertising campaign can serve this role.
- Have enthusiasm and charm. Gladwell stresses how little elements of nonverbal behavior make all the difference in persuasion and claims that the persuasive personality draws others into his or her own rhythms to dictate the terms of the interaction.
- Are able to overcome objections because of the number and quality of their answers.

The stickiness factor. The "law of the few" presupposes that the message itself is something that it is worthwhile to pass on. In discussing connectors, mavens, and salesmen, Gladwell assumes that the message has impact, or "stickiness," which means that the message sticks in memory. The aim is thus to make the message memorable. (This ties in with our stress on the importance of novelty). He argues that changes in the presentation and structuring of information can make a big difference in the impact it makes. Gladwell does not give any general principles for making a message memorable but simply cites examples; for example, making people "participants" in a process of self-persuasion when, say, peeling off the scent strip in a magazine. While contagiousness is a function of the messenger, "stickiness" is more an attribute of the message itself.

The power of context. This term refers to the influence of context on behavior. The primary urge to engage in a certain form of behavior may come from some feature of the environment. As Gladwell says, all epidemics are sensitive to conditions, circumstances, and the places in which they occur because people are sensitive to context. Gladwell's primary example is how the crime epidemic tipped in New York City. The epidemic was reversed/tipped by "zero tolerance," that is, recognizing the effect on crime of little things in the environment, like broken windows, or of ignoring of the jumping of turnstiles on the subway, as these things signal that no one cares.

The *Tipping Point* has had considerable sales success, which we might attribute to the stickiness factor (the message is memorable) and the salesman, Gladwell himself (he is a journalist whose illustrations and writing are very persuasive). But how original are the ideas, beyond a more persuasive framework? Does *The Tipping Point,* beyond being a good read, add anything substantive to marketing beyond what is presently contained in the persuasive communication literature, the adoption process literature, and the factors involved in the rate of diffusion of innovation?

The "law of the few" is concerned with communication/information source, and that is one component of the persuasive communication approach, pioneered at Yale in the late 1940s and 1950s by Carl Hovland, who viewed the effectiveness of persuasion as dependent on:

- The individual recipient's mental disposition and other characteristics
- The communication/information source
- The content and presentation of the message

Gladwell focuses mainly on the communication/information source. In psychology this translates into the credibility and attractiveness of the information source. If credibility consists of technical expertise and perceived trustworthiness, then this is what defines "market mavens," as discussed by Gladwell. If attractiveness consists of projecting a likable image and that appears open, as if revealing all, then Gladwell's "salesmen" can be defined as having attractiveness along with enough credibility to field questions or answer objections. Connectors have influence through having attractiveness (primarily) and credibility. What Gladwell contributes depends on the utility to marketers of the division into connectors, market mavens, and salesmen whose characteristics he describes in detail. But such characteristics are a matter of empirical inquiry.

Gladwell provides examples from which we are meant to generalize. If it seems useful to distinguish the three roles, the problem then lies in actually identifying people in the market who occupy each role or the individuals who play all three roles. What can be said is that the three roles of connector, maven, and salesmen could be found in a carefully selected celebrity.

The "stickiness factor" is considered in psychology and the consumer behavior literature under content/presentation of the message itself, where the factors considered are:

- The latitude of acceptance of a message (outside a certain latitude of acceptance, consumers reject the message)
- One-sided or two-sided presentation (a one-sided presentation appeals to the already converted; a two-sided presentation—yet leaning toward the persuader's position—is better when not speaking to the converted)
- Techniques of self-persuasion (e.g., getting consumers to imagine possessing and using the product)
- Liking and persuasion (likability in itself can be persuasive)
- The nonverbal channels of conveying a persuasive message (nonverbal channels must cohere with what is said, since the nonverbal message can be more influential than the verbal)
- Gender differences (women, for example, are more uncomfortable than men when they cannot see the other person, as in internet sales)

Gladwell provides no solid advice (merely examples) on how to make a message sticky and certainly covers little of the preceding.

In the persuasive communication approach, in relation to the individual receiver of the communication, some of the topics are the same as those covered in Gladwell's book, as follows:

- Getting attention
- Message repetition
- The cognitive, cultural, social, and emotional background of the target audience
- Inducing self-persuasion
- The need for the target audience to hold a relevant perspective, the role of rhetoric in changing perspectives through metaphor, and so on

Gladwell does talk about the role of connectors, mavens, and salesmen in changing perspectives, but his discussions of changing perspectives lack the depth found in the social psychology literature. He has little to say about the individual receivers of the message and treats them as if they were a homogeneous set. This is not surprising, as it is a weakness of all diffusion theory that it focuses on the rate of diffusion and fails to take account of what makes buyer A more fertile ground than buyer B for buying a product or idea.

It is on the "power of context" where what Gladwell has to say is important, since it is typically neglected in consumer behavior research. We need to be reminded of its importance. Whatever has been said about the originality of Gladwell's thesis, Gladwell's work has the main advantage of having a story that is user friendly and inspirational. In other words, its sales depend on the froth and not the meat.

A similar emphasis on word-of-mouth communication and getting visibility via novelty is Godin's *Unleashing the Ideavirus*.[35] Godin argues that those marketers succeed who manage to create a "buzz" with a new product to encourage word-of-mouth communication. (Our concept of novelty would provide this role.) The aim is to spark an idea that becomes fashionable and spreads like a virus (an echo of Gladwell here). Godin believes that companies are finding it more and more difficult to compete through real product advantages and so need to focus on what "symbolism marketing" can add to the product. As he says about Nike, it is the sizzle, not the fit. However, Godin finds himself falling back on traditional tactics when it comes to suggesting how the marketer is to start the virus (Gladwell would have helped here)—like free samples, sales promotion, public relations, product placement and sponsorship.

Some Key Assertions for Marketing

1. If marketing management is to increase brand equity, which (if positive) is the additional value put on a brand by its customers over and above the brand's objective performance vis-à-vis its rivals, every attempt should be made to project a consistent brand persona and brand personality. Brand persona is the image presented by the firm; brand image is the actual image the target audience has of the brand. The persona of a brand is sharpened by the addition of a logo and slogan. Both a slogan and a logo can draw attention to what the brand can do to enrich the buyer's life, and both can change perspectives. Brand personality refers to the set of character or behavioral traits that the target audience attributes to the brand. Brand image, brand persona, and brand personality can be helped to cohere by an appropriate brand name. Brand equity erodes if it is not nurtured.

2. If marketing management's brand involves packaging, this offers further potential for enhancing brand image and brand equity, since packaging can arouse feelings of excitement, favorable beliefs about the brand's trustworthiness and its persona, its personality, and the values for which it stands— and trigger a sale. A well-designed package can transform a lifeless image and conjure up a sense of novelty.

3. If marketing management is not to squander its investment in a brand, there is a need to ensure there is continuity of identity in any changes that are made. Consumers accept the new only when they have made sense of it in terms of the old; there must be enough links with the old so that, while things are forever changing, the brand is forever the same in a valued lifestyle.

4. If marketing management is to seek specific ways for building a positive brand image and subsequently higher brand equity, it should think in terms of enhancing (1) brand visibility and (2) brand attractiveness and credibility. Brand visibility can be raised through seeking to make the brand message a replicator so that, like a good joke, consumers pass on the information about it. Ways of doing this are through brand name, logo, and slogan but most of all through the brand having novelty and possessing a critical advantage. With respect to brand liking, if the brand has appeal, the repeated exposure effect increases familiarity, and typically familiarity comes with increased liking. In selling, mutual attractiveness (excluding the purely physical) is based on similarity of background and/or supportive interaction through time. This helps people to be emotionally in tune with each other so that friendliness is projected without a power play. With respect to brand credibility, this is achieved by ensuring that communications project the right degree of expertise and exude trustworthiness. In selling, credibility is typically inferred from how the salesperson fields questions.

A final comment might be as follows:

In the end, durable customer relations are only partly about clever technology, however imaginatively used. Mainly, they require relentless attention to detail: good products, prompt service, well-trained staff with the power to do a little extra when they judge it right to do so. No wonder firms that send you away with a smile on your face are so rare." (*The Economist,* July 14, 2001, p. 12)

Notes

PREFACE

1. John O'Shaughnessy and Nicholas O'Shaughnessy. (2000). "Treating the Nation as a Brand: Some Neglected Issues." *Journal of Macromarketing,* vol. 20, no. 1 (June): 56–64.

CHAPTER 1

1. Isen, Alice M. (1987). "Positive Affect, Cognitive processes and Social Behavior." In *Advances in Experimental Social Psychology.* In M. Zanna (ed.) Vol. 20. New York: Academic Press, 203–53.

2. Neville, R. C. (1981). *Reconstructions of Thinking.* Albany: State University of New York Press.

3. Horgan, John. (1996). *The End of Science.* New York: Addison-Wesley, p. 5.

4. Elster, Jon. (1999). *The Alchemies of the Mind.* Cambridge: Cambridge University Press, pp. 403–404.

5. Cockcroft, W. H. (1982). *Mathematics Counts.* London: HMSO, p. 7.

6. O'Shaughnessy, John. (1987). *Why People Buy.* New York: Oxford University Press.

7. Marder, Eric. (1987). *The Laws of Choice: Predicting Customer Behavior.* New York: Free Press.

8. Underhill, Paco. (1999). *Why We Buy: The Science of Shopping.* London: Orion Business Books.

9. Brittan, David. (1997). "Spending More and Enjoying It Less." *Technology Review* (July): 12–13.

10. Calder, Lendol. (1999). *Financing the American Dream: A Cultural History of Consumer Credit.* Princeton, NJ: Princeton University Press.

11. Reported in "Attention All Shoppers," *Time,* August 2, 1999, p. 36.

12. Hodge, Robert, and Gunther Kress. (1988). *Social Semiotics.* Ithaca, NY: Cornell University Press.

13. See, for example: Dittmar, Helga. (1992). *The Social Psychology of Material Possessions.* New York: St. Martin's Press.

14. Schiffer, Frederic. (1998). *Of Two Minds: The Revolutionary Science of Dual-Brain Psychology.* New York: Free Press.

15. Flanagan, Owen, (1996). *Self-Expressions: Mind, Morals, and the Meaning of Life.* New York: Oxford University Press.

16. Goffman, E. (1971). *The Presentation of Self in Everyday Life.* Harmondsworth, England: Penguin.

17. Gronow, Jukka. (1997). *The Sociology of Taste.* London: Routledge, p. 5.

18. Flanagan, Owen. (1996). *Self Expressions: Mind, Morals, and the Meaning of Life.* New York: Oxford University Press.

19. Wolf, K. (ed.). (1950). *The Sociology of George Simmel.* Chicago: Free Press.

20. Unger, R. M. (1984). *Passion: An Essay on Personality.* New York: Free Press.

21. Campbell, Colin. (1987). *The Romantic Ethic and the Spirit of Modern Consumerism.* Oxford: Blackwell.

22. Gronow, Jukka. (1997). *The Sociology of Taste.* London: Routledge.

23. Kagan, Jerome. (1999). *Three Seductive Ideas.* Cambridge: Harvard University Press.

24. Wright, Robert. (1994). *The Moral Animal.* New York: Pantheon Books.

25. Bell, David E. (1982). "Regret in Decision Making under Uncertainty." *Operations Research,* vol. 30, no. 5 (Sept.–Oct.): 961–981.
Bell, David E. (1985). "Disappointment in Decision Making under Uncertainty." *Operations Research,* vol. 33, no. 1 (Jan.–Feb.): 2–27.

26. Park, Denise C., and Angela Hall Gutchess. (1999). "Cognitive Aging and Everyday Life. In *Cognitive Aging,* edited by Denise Park and Norbert Schwarz. Philadelphia: Psychology Press, pp. 187–208.

27. Csikszentmihalyi, Mihaly. (1990). *Flow: The Psychology of Optimal Experience.* New York: Harper and Row.

28. Cook, Emma. (1999). "What's Getting up Your Nose?" *Independent on Sunday,* May 16, p. 22.

29. Roy Sheldon and Egmont Arens, quoted in: Ewen Stuart. (1988). *All Consuming Images.* New York: Basic Books, p. 49.

30. Fisher, Philip. (1999). *Wonder, The Rainbow, and the Aesthetics of Rare Experiences.* Cambridge: Harvard University Press.

31. Holbrook, Morris B., and Douglas V. Holloway. (1984). "Marketing Strategy and the Structure of Aggregate, Segment-specific, and Differential Preferences." *Journal of Marketing,* 48 (winter): 62–67; Holbrook, Morris B., and Stephen A. Bertges. (1981). "Perceptual Veridicality in Esthetic Communication." *Communication Research,* vol. 8, no. 4 (Oct.): 387–424; Holbrook, Morris B., and Robert B. Zirlin. (1985). "Artistic creation, Artworks and Aesthetic Appreciation: Some Philosophical Contributions to Nonprofit Marketing." In *Advances in Nonprofit Marketing.* Vol. 1. New

York: JAI Press, pp. 1–54; Holbrook, Morris B. (1986). "Aims, Concepts, and Methods for Representation of Individual Differences in Esthetic Responses to Design Features." *Journal of Consumer Research*, 13 (Dec.): 146–156; Holbrook, Morris B., and Punam Anand. (1990). "Effects of Temp and Situational Arousal on the Listener's Perceptual and Affective Responses to Music." *Psychology of Music*, 18: 150–162; Holbrook, Morris B. (1981). "Integrating Compositional and Decompositional Analyses to Represent the Intervening Role of Perceptions in Evaluative Judgments." *Journal of Marketing Research*, 28 (Feb.): 13–28; Holbrook, Morris B. (1987). "The Study of Signs in Consumer Esthetics: An Egocentric Review." In *Marketing and Semiotics*, edited by Jean Umiker-Sebeok. New York: Mouton de Gruyter, pp. 73–122.

32. Holbrook, Morris. (1999). Introduction to *Consumer Value*. New York: Routledge, pp. 1–28.

33. "A Revolution of One." (2001). *Economist*, April 14, p. 84.

34. Barlow, Janelle, and Dianna Maul. (2000). *Emotional Value*. San Francisco: Berrett-Koehler.

35. Ortony, A., G. L. Clore, and A. Collins. (1988). *The Cognitive Structure of Emotions*. New York: Cambridge University Press.

36. Goldie, Peter. (2000). *The Emotions: A Philosophical Exploration*. Oxford: Oxford University Press.

37. Griffitths, Paul. (1997). *What Emotions Really Are: The Problem of Psychological Categories*. Chicago: University of Chicago Press.

38. Zajonc, R. B. (1980). "Feeling and Thinking: Preferences Need No Inferences." *American Psychologist*, 35: 151–75.

39. Damasio, Antonio R. (1994). *Descartes' Error: Emotion, Reason and the Human Brain*. New York: Putnam.

40. LeDoux, Joseph. (1997). *The Emotional Brain*. New York: Weidenfeld.

41. Goleman, Daniel. (1998). *Working with Emotional Intelligence*. New York: Bantam Books, p. 52.

42. Lewinsohn, P. M., and C. S. Amenson. (1978). "Some Relations between Pleasant and Unpleasant Mood-Related Events and Depression." *Journal of Abnormal Psychology*, 87: 644–654.

43. Goleman, Daniel. (1998). *Working with Emotional Intelligence*. New York: Bantam Books, p. 56.

44. Thayer, Robert E. (1996). *The Origin of Everyday Moods*. New York: Oxford University Press.

45. Csikszentmihalyi, Mihaly. (2000). "The Cost and Benefits of Consuming." *Journal of Consumer Research*, 27 (Sept.): 267–272.

46. De Sousa, Ronald. (1990). *The Rationality of Emotion*. Cambridge: MIT Press.

CHAPTER 2

1. Elster, Jon. (1999). *Alchemies of the Mind: Rationality and the Emotions*. Cambridge: Cambridge University Press.

2. Frijda, Nico H. (1988). "The Laws of Emotion." *American Psychologist*, vol. 43, no. 5 (May): 348–358.

3. Rokeach, Milton. (1971). "The Measurement of Values and Value Systems." In *Social Psychology and Political Behavior,* edited by Gilbert Abcarian and John W. Soule. Columbus, OH: Charles E. Merrill, pp. 63–85.

4. Hyman, Herbert, and Charles E. Wright. (1979). *Education's Lasting Influence on Values.* Chicago: University of Chicago Press.

5. Leach, E. R. (1974). *Levi-Strauss.* London: Fontana.

6. Meredith, Geoffrey E., and Charles D. Schewe. (1999). "Market by Cohorts, Not Generations." *Marketing News,* February 1, pp. 3–4.

7. Meehan, Eugene J. (1969). *Value and Social Science.* Homewood, IL: Dorsey Press, pp. 27, 25.

8. De Sousa, Ronald. (1990). *The Rationality of Emotion.* Cambridge: MIT Press.

9. Skilleas, O. M. (2001). *Philosophy and Literature.* Edinburgh: Edinburgh University Press, p. 134.

10. Macdonald, Margaret. (1968). "Natural Law and Natural Rights." In *Readings in the Philosophy of the Social Sciences,* edited by May Brodbeck. New York: Macmillan, p. 732.

11. Sniderman, Paul M., Richard A. Brody, and Philip E. Tetlock. (1991). *Reasoning and Choice: Explorations in Political Psychology.* Cambridge: Cambridge University Press.

12. Kleinberg, Stanley S. (1991). *Sources of Power: How People Make Decisions.* Cambridge: MIT Press.

13. Nozick, Robert. (1989). *The Examined Life.* New York: Simon and Schuster.

14. Campbell, C. (1987). *The Romantic Ethic and the Spirit of Modern Consumerism.* Oxford: Blackwell.

15. Frankl, V. (1963). *Man's Search for Meaning.* New York: Simon and Schuster.

16. Mumford, Stephen. (2000). *Dispositions.* Oxford: Oxford University Press.

17. Carroll, Noel. (1990). *The Philosophy of Horror.* New York: Routledge.

18. Rozin, Paul, L. Millman, and C. Nemeroff. (1986). "Operation of the Laws of Sympathetic Magic in Disgust and Other Domains." *Journal of Personality and Social Psychology,* 50: 703–712.

19. Ewen, Stuart, (1988). *All-Consuming Images.* New York: Basic Books.

20. Porter, Roy. (1999). *The Greatest Benefit to Mankind: A Medical History of Humanity from Antiquity to the Present.* New York: HarperCollins.

21. Person, Ethel S. (1996). *The Force of Fantasy.* New York: HarperCollins.

22. Frank, Robert H. (1999). *Luxury Fever.* New York: Free Press.

23. Csikszentmihalyi, Mihaly. (2000). "The Cost and Benefits of Consuming." *Journal of Consumer Research,* 27 (Sept.): 267–272.

24. Bauman, Z. (1991). *Modernity and Ambivalence.* London: Cornell University Press.

25. McCracken, Grant. (1988). *Culture and Consumption.* Bloomington: Indiana University Press.

26. Baritz, Loren. (1989). *The Good Life: The Meaning of Succes for the American Middle Class.* New York: Knopf.

27. Kahneman, Daniel, Jack L. Knetsch, and R. H. Thaler. (1986). "Fairness and the Assumptions of Economics." In "The Behavioral Foundations of Economic Theory," edited by R. M. Hogarth and Melvin W. Reder, part 2. Special issue of *Journal of Business,* vol. 59, no. 4 (Oct).

28. Barlow, Janelle, and Dianna Maul. (2000). *Emotional Value.* San Francisco: Barrett-Koehler.

29. Rawls, John. (1980). "Kantian Constructivism in Ethics." Dewey Lectures. *Journal of Philosophy,* 77: 3–32.

30. Darwall, Stephen L. (1983). *Impartial Reason.* Ithaca, NY: Cornell University Press.

31. Quine, W. V. (1987). *Quiddities.* Cambridge, MA: Belknap Press.

32. Csikszentmihalyi, Mihaly. (1990). *Flow: The Psychology of Optimal Experience.* New York: Harper and Row.

33. Singer, J. L. (1973). *The Child's World of Make-Believe.* New York: Academic Press.

34. Carroll, Noel. (1990). *The Philosophy of Horror.* New York: Routledge.

35. Gosling, J. C. B. (1969). *Pleasure and Desire.* Oxford: Clarendon Press.

36. Ortony, Andrew, Gerald Clore, and Allan Collins. (1988). *The Cognitive Structure of Emotions.* Cambridge: Cambridge University Press.

37. See Clore, Gerald. (1994). "Why Emotions Vary in Intensity." In *The Nature of Emotion,* edited by Paul Ekman and Richard J. Davidson. New York: Oxford University Press.

38. Gordon, R. M. (1987). *The Structure of Emotions.* Cambridge: Cambridge University Press,

39. Laird, J. D. (1974). "Self-attribution and Emotion: The Effects of Expressive Behavior on the Quality of Emotional Experience." *Journal of Personality and Social Psychology,* 29: 475–486.

40. Ginsburg, G. P., and Melanie E. Harrington. "Bodily States and Context in Situated Lines of Action." In *The Emotions: Social, Cultural and Biological Dimensions,* edited by Rom Harre and W. Gerrod Parrott. London: Sage.

41. Elster, Jon. (1999). *Alchemies of the Mind: Rationality and the Emotions.* Cambridge: Cambridge University Press.

42. Elster, Jon. (1999). *Strong Feelings: Emotion, Addiction and Human Behavior.* Cambridge: Cambridge University Press.

43. Lyons, W. (1980). *Emotion.* Cambridge: Cambridge University Press.

44. Zajonc, Robert B. (1994). "Evidence for Nonconscious Emotions." In *The Nature of Emotion,* edited by Paul Ekman and Richard J. Davidson. New York: Oxford University Press, p. 293.

45. Bornstein, R. F. (1989). "Exposure and Affect: Overview and Meta-analysis of Research, 1968–1987." *Psychological Bulletin,* 106: 265–289.

46. Kunst-Wilson, W. R., and R. B. Zajonc. (1980). "Affective Discrimination of Stimuli that Cannot Be Recognized." *Science.* 207: 557–558.

47. Goldie, Peter. (2000). *The Emotions: A Philosophical Exploration.* Oxford: Oxford University Press.

48. Livingstone, Sonia. (1998). *Making Sense of Television: The Psychology of Audience Interpretation.* 2nd ed. New York: Routledge.

49. Frijda, N. H., P. Kuipers, and E. ter Schure. (1989). "Relations among Emotion, Appraisal, and Emotional Action Readiness." *Journal of Personality and Social Psychology,* 57: 212–228.

50. Ellsworth, Phoebe C. (1994). "Some Reasons to Expect Universal An-

tecedents of Emotion." In *The Nature of Emotion*, edited by Paul Ekman and Richard S. Davidson. New York: Oxford University Press.

51. Simon, H. A. (1960). *The Science of Management Decision*. New York: Harper and Row, p. 39.

52. Davitz, Joel R. (1969). *The Language of Emotion*. New York: Academic Press.

CHAPTER 3

1. Elster, Jon. (1999). *Alchemies of the Mind: Rationality and the Emotions*. Cambridge, England: Cambridge University Press.

2. Wollheim, Richard. (1999). *On the Emotions*. New Haven, CT: Yale University Press.

3. Searle, John. (1999). *Mind, Language and Society*. London: Weidenfeld and Nicolson.

4. Velleman, J. David. (2000). *The Possibility of Practical Reason*. New York: Clarendon Press.

5. Haack, Susan. (1998). *Manifesto of a Passionate Moderate*. Oxford: Blackwell, p. 9.

6. Goleman, Daniel. (1995). *Emotional Intelligence*. New York: Bantam Books.

7. Baudrillard, Jean. (1994). *Simulacra and Simulation*. Ann Arbor: University of Michigan Press.

8. Poster, Mark. (1988). *Jean Baudrillard: Selected Writings*. Palo Alto, CA: Stanford University Press.

9. Gordon, R. M. (1987). *The Structure of Emotions*. Cambridge: Cambridge University Press.

10. Lyons, W. (1980). *Emotion*. Cambridge: Cambridge University Press.

11. Goldie, Peter. (2000). *The Emotions: A Philosophical Exploration*. Oxford: Oxford University Press.

12. Sniderman, Paul M., Richard A. Brody, and Philip Tetlock. (1991). *Reasoning and Choice: Explorations in Political Psychology*. Cambridge: Cambridge University Press.

13. Tanner, John F., James B. Hunt, and David R. Eppright. (1991). "The Protection Motivation Model: A Normative Model of Fear Appeals." *Journal of Marketing*, 55 (July): pp. 36–45.

14. Lazarus, R. S. (1968). *Emotions and Adaptation*. New York: Oxford University Press.

15. Parrott, W. G., and J. Sabini. (1990). "Mood and Memory under Natural Conditions: Evidence for Mood Incongruent Recall." *Journal of Personality and Social Psychology*, 59: 321–336.

16. Watson, David, and Lee Anna Clark. (1994). "The Vicissitudes of Mood: A Schematic Model." In *The Nature of Emotion*, edited by Paul Ekman and Richard J. Davidson. New York: Oxford University Press, pp. 400–406.

17. See Hill, Ronald Paul, and James C. Ward. (1989). "Mood Manipulation in

Marketing Research: An Examination of Potential Confounding Effects." *Journal of Marketing Research*, 26 (Feb.): 97–104; Cantril, Hadley. (1942). *The Psychology of Social Movements*. New York: Wiley.

18. Williamson, Judith. (1978). *Decoding Advertisements*. London: Marion Boyars.

19. Taylor, G. (1985). *Pride, Shame and Guilt: Emotions of Self-adjustment*. Oxford: Clarendon Press.

20. Douglas, Mary. (1996). *Thought Styles*. London: Sage.

21. Cialdini, Robert B. (1993). *Influence: The Psychology of Persuasion*. New York: Morrow.

22. Williamson, Judith. (1978). *Decoding Advertisements*. London: Marion Boyars.

23. Veblen, T. (1965). *The Theory of the Leisure Class*. New York: Augustus Kelly.

24. "Campaign for British Knights to Escalate Sneaker Wars." *New York Times*, February 20, 1991.

25. Lal, Deepak. (1999). *Unintended Consequences: The Impact of Factor Endowments, Culture and Politics on Long-run Economic Performance*. Cambridge: MIT Press.

26. Cialdini. R. B. (1984). *Influence*. New York: Morrow.

27. Greenspan, P. S. (1995). *Practical Guilt: Moral Dilemmas, Emotions and Social Norms*. New York: Oxford University Press.

28. Carlsmith, J. M., and A. E. Gross. (1969). "Some Effects of Guilt on Compliance. *Journal of Personality and Social Psychology*, 11: 232–239.

29. Frankfurt, H. (1971). "Freedom of Will and the Concept of Person." In *Free Will* edited by Gary Watson. Oxford: Oxford University Press, pp. 81–95.

30. Pliner, P., H. Hart, J. Kohl, and D. Saati. (1974). "Compliance without Pressure: Some Further Data on the Foot-in-the-door Technique." *Journal of Experimental Social Psychology*, 10: 17–22.

31. Cialdini, R. B., and K. Ascani. (1976). "Test of a Concession Procedure for Including Verbal, Behavioral and Further Compliance with a Request to Give Blood." *Journal of Applied Psychology*, 61: 295–300.

32. Leavy, S. A. (1988). *In the Image of God*. New Haven, CT: Yale University Press.

33. Lewis, Thomas, Fari Amini, and Richard Lannon. (1999). *A General Theory of Love*. New York: Random House.

34. Unger, R. M. (1984). *Passion*. New York: Free Press.

35. Sniderman, Paul M., Richard A. Brody, and Philip E. Tetlock. (1991). *Reasoning and Choice: Explorations in Political Psychology*. Cambridge: Cambridge University Press.

36. Rogers, R. W. (1983). "Cognitive and Physiological Processes in Fear Appeals and Attitude Change: A Revised Theory of Protection Motivation." In *Psychophysiology: A Source Book*, edited by J. T. Cacioppo and R. E. Petty. New York: Guilford Press, pp. 153–176.

37. Leventhal, H. (1970). "Findings and Theory in the Study of Fear Communications." In *Advances in Experimental Social Psychology*, edited by L. Berkowitz. Vol. 5. New York: Academic Press, pp. 119–181.

38. Tversky, A., and D. Kahneman. (1986). "Rational Choice and the Framing of Decision." In "The Behavioral Foundations of Economic Theory," edited by R. M. Hogarth and Melvin W. Reder, part 2. Special issue of *Journal of Business*, vol. 59, no. 4 (Oct.).

CHAPTER 4

1. Frijda, Nico H. (1988). "The Laws of Emotion." *American Psychologist*, vol. 43, no. 5 (May): 348–358.

2. De Sousa, Ronald. (1990). *The Rationality of Emotion*. Cambridge: MIT Press.

3. See: Sniderman, Paul M., Richard A. Brody, and Philip E. Tetlock. (1991). *Reasoning and Choice: Explorations in Political Psychology*. Cambridge: Cambridge University Press.

4. Solomon, R. C. (1984). "Emotion and Choice." In *What Is an Emotion?* edited by Cheshire Calhoun and R. C. Solomon. New York: Oxford University Press, pp. 305–327.

5. Darwall, S. (1983). *Impartial Reason*. Ithaca, NY: Cornell University Press.

6. McGinn, C. (1983). *The Character of Mind*. New York: Oxford University Press.

7. Deutsch, David. (1997). *The Fabric of Reality*. London: Penguin Books, pp. 156–157.

8. Converse, Philip. (1964). "The Nature of Belief Systems in Mass Publics." In *Ideology and Discontent*, edited by David E. Apter. New York: Free Press.

9. Sniderman, Paul M., Richard A. Brody, and Philip E. Tetlock. (1991). *Reasoning and Choice: Explorations in Political Psychology*. Cambridge: Cambridge University Press.

10. Nisbett, R., and L. Ross. (1980). *Human Inference*. Englewood Cliffs, NJ: Prentice-Hall, pp. 175–179.

11. See: Averill, J. R. (1980). "A Constructivist View of Emotions." In *Emotions: Theory, Research and Experience*, edited by R. Plutchik and H. Kellerman. Vol. 1. New York: Academic Press, pp. 305–339.

12. See: Laird, J. D., and C. Bresler. (1992). "The Process of Emotional Experience: A Self-perception Theory." In *Review of Personality and Social Psychology: Emotion*, edited by M. S. Clark. Vol. 13. Lincoln: University of Nebraska Press, pp. 175–265.

13. Merabian, A., and J. A. Russell. (1974). *An Approach to Environmental Psychology*. Cambridge: MIT Press.

14. Foxall, Gordon R. (1997). "The Emotional Texture of Consumer Environment: A Systematic Approach to Atmospherics." *Journal of Economic Psychology*, 18: 505–523.

15. Averill, James R. (1994). "It's a Small World, but a Large Stage." In *The Nature of Emotion*, edited by Paul Ekman and Richard J. Davidson. New York: Oxford University Press, pp. 143–145.

16. Goldie, Peter. (2000). *The Emotions*. Oxford: Oxford University Press.

17. Damasio, Antonio. (1994). *Descartes' Error: Emotion, Reason, and the Human Brain*. New York: Putnam.

18. Smith, C. A., and P. C. Ellsworth. "Patterns of Cognitive Appraisal in Emotion." *Journal of Personality and Social Psychology*, 48: 813–838.

19. O'Shaughnessy, John. (1987). *Why People Buy*. New York: Oxford University Press.

20. Ross, Lee, and Richard Nisbett. (1980). *Human Inference: Strategies and Shortcomings of Social Judgment.* Englewood Cliffs, NJ: Prentice-Hall.

21. Sniderman, Paul M., Richard A. Brody, and Philip E. Tetlock. (1991). *Reasoning and Choice: Explorations in Political Psychology.* Cambridge: Cambridge University Press.

22. Ullmann-Margalit, E., and S. Morgenbesser. (1977). "Picking and Choosing." *Social Research,* 44 (winter): 757–785.

23. Velleman, David J. (2000). *The Possibility of Practical Reason.* New York: Clarendon Press.

24. See Schauer, Frederick. (1991). *Playing by the Rules.* Oxford: Clarendon Press.

25. Englefield, F. R. H. (1985). *The Mind at Work and Play.* Buffalo, NY: Prometheus.

26. Gronow, Jukka. (1997). *The Sociology of Taste.* London: Routledge.

27. Klein, Gary. (1998). *Sources of Power: How People Make Decisions.* Cambridge: MIT Press.

28. See: Damasio, Antonio R. (1994). *Descartes' Error: Emotion, Reason and the Human Brain.* New York: Putnam.

29. Simon, H. A. (1957). *Administrative Behavior.* New York: Macmillan.

30. Evans, Philip, and Thomas S. Wurster. (1999). "Getting Real about Virtual Commerce." *Harvard Business Review* (Nov.–Dec.): 9.

31. Scriven, Michael. (1992). "Evaluation and Critical Thinking: Logic's Last Frontier." In *Critical Reasoning in Contemporary Culture,* edited by Richard A. Talaska. Albany: State University of New York.

32. Deutsch, David. (1997). *The Fabric of Reality.* London: Penguin Books.

33. Underhill, Paco. (1999). *Why We Buy: The Science of Shopping.* London: Orion Business Books.

34. Hare, R. M. (1979). Contrasting Methods of Environmental Planning. In *Ethics and Problems of the Twenty-First Century,* edited by K. E. Goodpaster and K. M. Sayre. Notre Dame, IN: University of Notre Dame Press, pp. 63–78.

35. See Green, Paul E., Abba M. Krieger, Manoj K. Agarwal, and Richard M. Johnson. (1991). "Adaptive Conjoint Analysis: Some Caveats and Suggestions: Comment." *Journal of Marketing Research,* 28 (May): 215–225.

36. Lash, S. (1994). "Reflexivity and Its Doubles." In *Reflexive Modernization,* edited by U. Beck, A. Giddens, and S. Lash. Cambridge: Polity Press.

37. Marder, Eric. (1997). *The Laws of Choice.* New York: Free Press.

38. Lewis, David, and Darren Bridges. (2001). *The Soul of the New Consumer.* London: Nicholas Brearley.

39. Elster, Jon. (1999). *Alchemies of the Mind: Rationality and the Emotions.* Cambridge: Cambridge University Press.

40. Velleman, J. David. (1989). *Practical Reflection.* Princeton, NJ: Princeton University Press.

41. Damasio, Antonio R. (1994). *Descartes' Error: Emotion, Reason and the Human Brain.* New York: Putnam.

42. Douglas, Mary, and Baron Isherwood. (1979). *The World of Goods.* New York: Basic Books.

43. Luce, Mary Frances, James R. Bettman, and John W. Payne. (2001). *Emotional Decisions: Tradeoff Difficulty and Coping in Consumer Choice.* Chicago: University of Chicago Press.

44. Thagard, Paul. (2000). *Coherence in Thought and Action.* Cambridge: MIT Press.

45. Festinger, Leon. (1957). *A Theory of Cognitive Dissonance.* Palo Alto, CA: Stanford University Press.

46. Ehrlich, D., I. Guttman, P. Schonback, and J. Mills. (1957). "Post-Decision Exposure to Relevant Information." *Journal of Abnormal Psychology,* 54: 38–56.

47. Bell, David E. (1982). "Regret in Decision Making under Uncertainty." *Operations Research,* vol. 30, no. 5 (Sept.–Oct.): 961–981; Bell, David E. (1985). "Disappointment in Decision Making under Uncertainty." *Operations Research,* vol. 33, no. 1 (Jan.–Feb.): 2–27.

48. Mayhew, Leon H. (1997). *The New Public.* Cambridge: Cambridge University Press.

CHAPTER 5

1. Barlow, Janelle, and Dianna Maul. (2000). *Emotional Value.* San Francisco: Berrett-Koehler.

2. Kahneman, D., and A. Tversky. (1982). "The Simulation Heuristic." In *Judgment and Uncertainty,* edited by D. Kahneman, P. Slovic, and A. Tversky. Cambridge: Cambridge University Press.

3. Underhill, Paco. (1999). *Why We Buy: The Science of Shopping.* London: Orion Business Books, p. 170.

4. Bower, Gordon H. (1994). "Some Relations between Emotions and Memory." In *The Nature of Emotion,* edited by Paul Ekman and Richard J. Davidson. New York: Oxford University Press, pp. 303–306.

5. Cole, Jonathan. (1998). *About Face.* Cambridge: MIT Press.

6. Dennett, D. (1987). *The Intentional Stance.* Cambridge: MIT Press.

7. Velleman, David J. (2000). *The Possibility of Practical Reason.* New York: Clarendon Press.

8. Cherniak, Christopher. (1986). *Minimal Rationality.* Cambridge: MIT Press.

9. Fodor, J. (1987). *Psychosemantics.* Cambridge: MIT Press; Churchland, P. M. (1991). "Folk Psychology and the Explanation of Human Behavior." *The Future of Folk Psychology: Intentionality and Cognitive Science,* edited by J. D. Greenwood. Cambridge: Cambridge University Press.

10. Heal, Jane. (1995). "Replication and Functionalism." In *Folk Psychology,* edited by Martin Davies and Tony Stone. Oxford: Blackwell, pp. 45–59.

11. Winch, P. G. (1958). *The Idea of a Social Science.* Boston: Routledge and Kegan Paul, p. 91.

12. Searle, John. (1999). *Mind, Language and Society.* London: Weidenfeld and Nicolson.

13. Goldman, Alvin I. (1995). "Interpretation Psychologized." In *Folk Psychology,* edited by Martin Davies and Tony Stone. Oxford: Blackwell, pp. 74–99.

14. Dube´, L., B. H. Schmitt, and F. Leclerc. (1991). "Consumers' Affective Responses to Delays at Different Phases of a Service Delivery." *Journal of Applied Social Psychology,* vol. 21, no. 10: 810–820.

15. Luce, Mary Frances, James R. Bettman, and John W. Payne. (2001). *Emotional Decisions: Tradeoff Difficulty and Coping in Consumer Choice.* Chicago: University of Chicago Press.

16. Taylor, Charles. (1964). *The Explanation of Behavior.* New York: Humanities Press. Quine, W. V. (1953). "Two Dogmas of Empiricism." In *From a Logical Point of View.* Cambridge: Harvard University Press, pp. 20–46.

17. Gordon, Robert M. (1995). "Folk Psychology as Simulation." In *Folk Psychology,* edited by Martin Davies and Tony Stone. Oxford: Blackwell, pp. 60–73.

18. May, Ernest. (2000). *Strange Victory: Hitler's Conquest of France.* New York: Hill and Wang.

19. Gopnik, Alison, and Henry M. Wellman. (1995). "Why the Child's Theory of Mind Really Is a Theory." In *Folk Psychology* edited by Martin Davies and Tony Stone. Oxford Blackwell, pp. 232–258; Perner, Josef, and Deborrah Howes. (1995). "He Thinks He Knows": And More Development Evidence against the Simulation (Role Playing) Theory. In *Folk Psychology,* edited by Martin Davies and Tony Stone. Oxford: Blackwell, pp. 159–173.

20. Harris, Paul. (1995). "From Simulation to Folk Psychology: The Case for Development." In *Folk Psychology,* edited by Martin Davies and Tony Stone. Oxford: Blackwell, pp. 207–231.

21. Gordon, R. M. (1987). *The Structure of Emotions.* Cambridge, England: Cambridge University Press.

22. Hempel, C. G. (1965). *Aspects of Scientific Explanation.* New York: Free Press.

23. Nozick, Robert. (1989). *The Examined Life.* New York: Simon and Schuster.

24. Hochschild, A. R. (1983). *The Managed Heart: Commercialization of Human Feelings.* Berkeley: University of California Press.

25. Parkinson, Brian. (1995). *Ideas and Realities of Emotion.* London: Routledge.

26. Klein, Gary. (1998). *Sources of Power: How People Make Decisions.* Cambridge: MIT Press.

27. Hatfield, E., J. T. Cacioppo, and R. Rapson. (1992). "Primitive Emotional Contagion." In *Review of Personality and Social Psychology: Emotion and Social Behavior,* edited by M. S. Clark. Vol. 14. Lincoln: University of Nebraska Press, pp. 151–177.

28. Gottman, J. M. (1979). *Marital Interaction: Experimental Investigations.* New York: Academic Press.

29. Tye, Larry. (1998). *The Father of Spin: Edward L. Bernays.* New York: Crown.

30. De Sousa, Ronald. (1990). *The Rationality of Emotion.* Cambridge: Cambridge University Press.

31. Goldman, Robert, and Stephen Papson. (1996). *Sign Wars: The Cluttered Landscape of Advertising.* New York: Guilford Press.

32. Pratkanis, A. R., and A. Aronson. (1991). *The Age of Propaganda.* New York: Freeman.

33. Tajfel, H. (1981). *Human Groups and Social Categories.* Cambridge: Cambridge University Press.

CHAPTER 6

1. Putnam, Hilary. (1991). *Representation and Reality.* Cambridge: MIT Press.
2. Barlow, Janelle, and Dianna Maul. (2000). *Emotional Value.* San Francisco: Berrett-Koehler.
3. Kosslyn, Stephen Michael. (1980). *Image and Mind.* Cambridge: Harvard University Press.
4. Tait, Nikki. (1999). *Financial Times,* July 8; Deloitte Consulting and Deloitte & Touche. (1999). *Making Customer Loyalty Real: A Global Manufacturing Study.*
5. "On the Brandwagon." (1990). *Economist,* January 20, pp. 17–18.
6. Tomkins, Richard. (1999). "What a Good Name Adds up To. *Financial Times,* June 22.
7. Gerber, G. et al. (1986). "Living with Television: The Dynamics of the Cultivation Process." In *Perspectives on Media Effects,* edited by J. Bryant and D. Zillman. Hillsdale, NJ: Erlbaum.
8. Douglas, Mary. (1996). *Thought Styles.* London: Sage.
9. Twitchell, James B. (1999). *Lead Us into Temptation: The Triumph of American Materialism.* New York: Columbia University Press.
10. Campbell, Colin. (1987). *The Romantic Ethic and the Spirit of Modern Consumerism.* Oxford: Blackwell, p. 48.
11. Marder, Eric. (1997). *The Laws of Choice.* New York: Free Press, pp. 85, 84.
12. Larson, C. U. (1995). *Persuasion: Reception and Responsibility.* New York: Wadsworth.
13. Gregory, James R. (1996). *Marketing Corporate Image: The Company as Your Number One Product.* New York: NTC Business Books.
14. Calkins, Earnest Elmo. (1928). *Business the Civilizer.* Boston: Little, Brown.
15. Marchand, Roland. (1998). *Creating the Corporate Soul.* Berkeley: University of California Press.
16. Gregory, James R. (with G. Wiechmann). (1996). *Marketing Corporate Image: The Company as Your Number One Product.* New York: NTC Business Books.
17. Hollinger, Peggy. (1999). "Tasteful Campaign to Counter a Stale Image." *Financial Times,* June 29.
18. Klein, Naomi. (2000). *No Logo: Taking Aim at the Brand Bullies.* New York: Picador.
19. Burton, John. (1999). "Selling Buy Korea." *Financial Times,* September 8.
20. McCracken, Grant. (1988). *Culture and Consumption.* Bloomington: Indiana University Press.
21. Lay, Luc Le. (1999). "The value of the 'Made in France' label." M.B.A. thesis, Judge Institute of Management Studies, Cambridge University, Cambridge.
22. Jarvis, Robert. (1989). *The Logic of Images in International Relations.* New York: Columbia University Press.
23. Schwartz, Tony. (1973). *The Responsive Chord.* Garden City, NY: Doubleday.
24. Shaw, R., and J. Bransford. (1977). *Perceiving, Acting and Knowing.* Hillsdale, NJ: Erlbaum.
25. O'Shaughnessy, John. (1994). *Competitive Marketing.* New York: Routledge, p. 420.

26. Thurow, Lester C. (1999). *Building Wealth: The New Rules for Individuals, Companies, and Nations in a Knowledge-based Economy.* New York: HarperCollins.

27. Underhill, Paco. (1999). *Why We Buy: The Science of Shopping.* London: Orion Business Books.

28. See "Back in the Real World." (1999). *Economist,* August 21.

30. Brown, John Seely, and Paul Duguid. (1999). *The Social Life of Information.* Cambridge: Harvard Business School Press.

31. Bank, David. (1998). "Buying Power." *Wall Street Journal,* December 7.

32. Evans, Philip, and Thomas S. Wurster. (1999). "Getting Real about Virtual Commerce." *Harvard Business Review* (Nov.–Dec.).

33. Gregory, W. L., R. B. Cialdini, and K. M. Carpenter. (1982). "Self-relevant Scenarios as Mediators of Likelihood Estimates and Compliance: Does Imagining Make It So?" *Journal of Personality and Social Psychology,* 43: 89–99.

34. Lewin, K. (1947). "Group decision and social change." In *Readings in Social Psychology,* edited by T. M. Newcomb and E. L. Hartley. New York: Holt, pp. 5–41.

CHAPTER 7

1. Aaker, David A. (1991). *Managing Brand Equity.* New York: Free Press.

2. Marder, Eric. (1997). *The Laws of Choice.* New York: Free Press.

3. Hine, Thomas. (1995). *The Total Package.* New York: Little, Brown.

4. (1992). *New York Times,* September 16.

5. Hine, Thomas. (1995). *The Total Package.* New York: Little, Brown.

6. Marder, Eric. (1997). *The Laws of Choice.* New York: Free Press.

7. (1999). *New York Times.* February 28.

8. Kidd, Colin. (1999). *British Identities before Nationalism.* Cambridge: Cambridge University Press.

9. Porter, Michael E. (1985). *Competitive Advantage.* New York: Free Press.

10. Robinette, Scott, and Claire Brand, with Vicki Lenz. (2001). *Emotion Marketing: The Hallmark Way of Winning Customers for Life.* New York: McGraw-Hill.

11. Schlosser, Eric. (2001). *Fast Food Nation.* New York: Allen Lane.

12. Smith, Adam. (1776 [1937]). *The Wealth of Nations.* New York: Modern Library, p. 741.

13. Finke, Roger. (1997). "The Consequences of Religious Competition: Supply-side Explanations for Religious Change." In *Rational Choice Theory and Religion,* edited by Lawrence A. Young. New York: Routledge, pp. 45–64.

14. Lauro, Patricia Winters. (2001). "Advertising." *New York Times,* May 8, p. C2.

15. Kanner, Bernice. (1999). *The 100 Best TV Commercials—and Why They Worked.* New York: Times Business.

16. Mayhew, Leon H. (1997). *The New Public.* Cambridge: Cambridge University Press.

17. Ibid.

18. Rothenberg, Randall. (1994). *Where the Suckers Moon: An Advertising Story.* New York: Knopf.

19. Dawkins, Richard. (1989). *The Selfish Gene*. Rev. Ed. Oxford: Oxford University Press.

20. Koehn, Nancy. F. (2001). *Brand New: How Entrepreneurs Earned Consumers' Trust from Wedgwood to Dell*. Cambridge: Harvard University Press.

21. Blumer, Jay. (1979). "The Role of Theory in Uses and Gratification Studies." *Communication Research*, 6: 9–34.

22. Zajonc, R. B. (1968). "The Attitudinal Effects of Mere Exposure." *Journal of Personality and Social Psychology*, 9, monograph supplement: 1–27.

23. Schumann, D. W., R. E. Petty, and D. S. Clemons. (1990). "Predicting the Effectiveness of Different Strategies of Advertising Variation: A Test of the Repetition-variation Hypothesis." *Journal of Consumer Research*, 17: 192–202.

24. Brown, S. (1995). *Postmodern Marketing*. London: Routledge.

25. Goldman, Robert, and Stephen Papson. (1996). *Sign Wars*. New York: Guilford Press.

26. Mantle, Jonathan. (1999). *Benetton: The Family, the Business and the Brand*. New York: Little, Brown.

27. Bailey, F. G. (1983). *The Tactical Uses of Passion*. Ithaca, NY: Cornell University Press.

28. Jamieson, Kathleen Hall. (1988). *Eloquence in an Electronic Age*. New York: Oxford University Press.

29. Cialdini, R. B. (1984). *Influence*. New York: Morrow.

30. Brehm, Jack. (1966). *A Theory of Psychological Reactance*. New York: Academic Press.

31. Etcoff, Nancy. (1999). *Survival of the Prettiest*. Boston: Little, Brown.

32. Person, Ethel S. (1996). *The Force of Fantasy*. New York: HarperCollins.

33. Mollard, Angela. (1998). "Delia Power." *Daily Mail*, November 19.

34. Gladwell, Malcolm. (2000). *The Tipping Point*. New York: Little, Brown.

35. Godin, Seth. (2000). *Unleashing the Ideavirus*. New York: Do You Zoom.

Index